The Strategy of Social
Inquiry

The Strategy of Social Inquiry

A new programme in methods and measurement for the student of sociology

John Wakeford

Lecturer in Sociology
Brunel University

MACMILLAN
London · Melbourne · Toronto
1968

Published by
MACMILLAN & CO LTD
Little Essex Street London W C2
and also at Bombay Calcutta and Madras
Macmillan South Africa (Publishers) Pty Ltd Johannesburg
The Macmillan Company of Australia Pty Ltd Melbourne
The Macmillan Company of Canada Ltd Toronto

Printed in Great Britain by
ROBERT MACLEHOSE AND CO. LTD
The University Press, Glasgow

Contents

Foreword

Professor W. J. H. Sprott

Sociology is an amorphous subject, and it is becoming increasingly popular. It is amorphous in the sense that the areas studied do not fit tidily together. In most courses in the subject you will find three topics discussed: theory, comparative social institutions, and Modern England. The theoretical part is concerned with the most convenient model to use when discussing societies, which, after all, are figments of the imagination and therefore you need models to cope with the empirical material. Should you think in terms of an organism, or a network of positions with appropriate roles, or a more complicated system of interaction which will give due weight to conflict? From this necessary discussion you will not find any clue as to the structure of any given society. You may decide that there are certain requirements to be satisfied – some method of socialisation, some economic system, some political organisation and so on, but what form the institutions which deal with these requirements will take cannot be derived from theory alone.

The study of comparative institutions brings one nearer to reality, and you may come to the conclusion that certain combinations are highly improbable, such as an extended kinship system and industrialisation. This will throw some light on the study of Modern England, but you cannot infer much about the structure of Modern England from your study of comparative institutions. The sequence is perfectly sensible; you have to decide in what terms you are going to order the empirical material, you have to note that societies solve their problems variously, and one of the objects of the exercise is, presumably, to produce a more sophisticated approach to the society in which the student lives. And yet the three topics I have selected do not tie in neatly together, and the student is often confused during his first year – if not longer.

And yet the subject is more and more popular. The sociology of sociology has yet to be written, but I think at least one reason for the increasing popularity of sociology is an increasing and more widespread concern about social problems. This is encouraged by the press, by television and by sound broadcasting. The word 'sociology' is frequently used in this connection, and students contemplating a university course think that somehow they will learn from sociology something that will help them to be of service to the community. Of course they have not a clue as to what they are letting themselves in for, but when they are asked why they want to study sociology and say: 'Because I am so interested in people' we know that they are not speaking the truth – they are not interested in people, they want to alter them – nevertheless they are, I believe, expressing their concern about the society in which they live. Of course a few candidates for places in sociology courses have taken the trouble to read a book on the subject; a few may opt for sociology in the hope that it will be a soft option. But the great majority choose sociology because they want to do good.

What value is a three-year course in sociology to them? A few will find the subject so attractive and intellectually satisfying that they will want to pursue their studies further, to carry out research projects, and to join the academic sociological world. The majority will hope to get a job, perhaps, though by no means necessarily, in the social services, in which their study of sociology will be of use. What kind of 'use'? In general I suppose it would be admitted that sociology, with its wide range of topics, has obvious educational advantages; theoretical discussions may help to sharpen the wits, the study of comparative institutions is interesting and informative, and the study of Modern England will bring to their notice features of their society of which they were unaware. This educative aspect of the subject, however, is not all that useful.

There are, as I see it, two further acquisitions which are more directly useful to them in their future careers. The first is what might be called the 'sociological point of view'. By this is meant a detached attitude to social phenomena, a recognition that our society is only one of a vast set of possible societies, and the habit of thinking about any social phenomenon in the social context in which it is found. This will at most lead to a more sophisticated understanding of society, and at least serve to undermine prejudice and insularity. Such detachment and such a relativistic approach is clearly of use in any job which involves 'dealing with people' either face to face or in a wider context of administration.

The second useful acquisition that should be derived from a course in sociology is some skill in handling data. This is where Mr Wakeford's textbook comes in. By 'handling data' is meant two things: (1) the assessment of evidence from official statistics to reports of sociological research, and (2) methods of collecting data and processing it.

The student will doubtless be taught something about scientific method; he may be induced to read up a few social psychological experiments, and he will be invited to read and discuss a few social surveys, but all too often he has no direct experience of doing any survey work himself, or carrying out any experiments, or practising the assessment of evidence provided by official documents or collected by himself.

Mr Wakeford's laboratory course is just what is needed, and it gives me great pleasure to have been invited to write a preface to it. It contains thirty-six projects, which range from handling official material, carrying out surveys, opinion polling, and sociometric assessment, to the use of simple sorting apparatus and digital computers.

Each project contains a clear statement of its purpose and precise instructions for carrying it out. The student is introduced to a number of simple statistical methods of processing the material he has collected, and it is reasonable to suppose that since he is processing his own data this may well be a less painful method of acquiring statistical skills than attending a formal course on statistics. We all know that some students find statistics a grave difficulty; Mr Wakeford's method may be a way of making these calculations less formidable.

Many students find sociology a somewhat remote subject, interesting, no doubt, but not particularly practical. I am convinced that by following Mr Wakeford's course they will feel that they are actually doing the kinds of things they read about, and that what they get out of their three years' study of sociology will be the more useful to them in the years to come.

List of Projects arranged by their principal Methodological Content

[1] Vacation projects.

Projects Arranged by Sociological Content

Acknowledgments

The prospect of employing laboratory techniques, similar to those used in the teaching of psychology, in the teaching of sociology arose in discussion with a psychologist at University College, Cardiff, John Liggett. Together we worked on this idea, producing outlines for some individual projects and developing the basis for a complete laboratory course combining the teaching of method with the teaching of sociology. We read a paper on the subject in 1964 to an informal group of the Teachers' Section of the British Sociological Association. Our co-operative efforts at this early stage provided the base from which at a later date this manual developed.

My move to Exeter provided me with the opportunity to develop this approach and produce a systematic scheme of study. The individual projects were tested and used with all the second-year sociology degree students in the Department there. During this period a number of colleagues and students suggested improvements in several projects, and several organisations, in particular National Opinion Polls Ltd and Gallup Polls Ltd, gave helpful information. Also Brian Housley of the University computer staff wrote and tested the computer programme used in Project 36, and John Mack kindly gave permission for his article to be reprinted for Project 34.

Finally I am indebted to Professor W. J. H. Sprott for contributing his foreword and for many useful suggestions, and to my wife, Frances, who at each stage provided not only additions and amendments but also a number of deletions from which the final work has clearly benefited.

The work of typing and retyping the initial manuscript was at different stages carried out by Arlene Liggett, Pam Ffooks and Sue Jones, to whom I am also grateful.

Introduction

Note: a special *Tutor's Manual* is available which includes an introduction to the method of teaching used in this book and suggestions on the organisation of each project. A *Data Pack* has also been prepared comprising magnetic tapes, punched cards and computer programs used in the projects.

Hanan Selvin published in 1965 what amounted to an indictment of sociology departments in Britain; he criticised both the overall neglect of methodology and in particular the absence of training facilities in social research techniques.[1] In contrast to the United States, where he claims every sociology department requires its students to complete courses in methodology and statistics, Professor Selvin commented on a 'backwardness' in Britain all the more surprising in view of its long tradition of empirical social research, and 'pre-eminent' place in the development of modern statistics.

In 1967 the situation Selvin described has undoubtedly changed – especially since the Heyworth Committee, and the subsequent creation of the Social Science Research Council; many sociology departments now run courses in research techniques at graduate and undergraduate level. However, in some departments Selvin's criticisms are as valid now as when he wrote them. In such departments, sociology is still taught, particularly at the undergraduate level, without resort to the basic methodological and analytical processes involved in providing the subject-matter. As long as this is the case, these departments will continue to produce inadequate first-degree sociologists, especially since the majority of students

---

[1] *Training for Social Research: The Recent American Experience* (the full reference, as for all works referred to by author or short title, will be found in the Bibliography on page 253 ff.

studying sociology do not register for a higher degree but go into industry, education or social work.

In many sociology departments today the introduction of field-work or single 'project' component into existing sociology courses has certainly stressed a more active and potentially creative approach generally, whilst stimulating interest, encouraging reading and providing experience in specific techniques. But experience shows that both the knowledge and the skills acquired in the course of such a single 'project' are small in relation to the time and energy consumed, especially on data collection. Moreover, the single fieldwork assignment can make only a very limited contribution to the student's appreciation of the wide range of methodological strategies available, and does little to increase his statistical sophistication. The fieldwork assignment (in common with courses in social statistics) still tends to be segregated in the student's mind from the sociology taught in his other courses; he fails to appreciate the active role of the research process in 'initiating, reformulating, deflecting and clarifying theory'.[1]

Instruction in sociological research should not only give the student practical experience of using specific techniques. It should also teach him to review critically the range of available research methods – often borrowed from other fields of study – and their underlying assumptions, and instruct him in the selection and adaptation of such methods as are appropriate to his conceptual scheme and his sociological research objectives. Thus the student is socialised into the role of empirical sociologist at an early stage in his instruction.

This book is an attempt to reformulate the fieldwork method and develop and integrated and comprehensive approach to the teaching of methodology in the context of sociological analysis and elementary statistics.[2] Each project is focused on a single representative sociological topic and uses an appropriate methodological and statistical approach of different degrees of sophistication, based as far as possible on elements of designs which are readily available in the literature, scaled down as necessary for completion by a class in a few hours.

[1] Merton's essay, 'Social Theory and Social Research', in Merton, R. K., *Social Theory*.

[2] Liggett, J., and Wakeford, J., 'Sociology as a Laboratory Subject', *Sociological Review*, vol. 12, no. 2, 1964.

The book is not a text and is intended to be used in conjunction with the suggested literature; each project includes certain recommended major references – preferably to be read before the class meets. A suggested list of further reading, including critical commentaries, indicates further lines of enquiry, and usually a possible theoretical orientation for use at the discretion of the tutor and student. The topics suggested are intended for class discussion or for consideration when the student is writing up the project.[1]

The projects included here have been greatly revised on the basis of experience at Exeter, and certainly it is anticipated that further modifications and developments will result from the experience of staff and students using it in other courses and other institutions. May I make an open invitation to all who use it to send me their comments and criticisms on the projects, to enable revisions to be made in the future?

JOHN WAKEFORD

School of Social Sciences,
Brunel University

[1] Each student should collect a 'laboratory file' of completed project reports for periodic discussion, and assessment by the tutor.

General Reading List

Welford, A. T. *et al.* (eds.) *Society: Problems and Methods of Study*
Hammond, P. E. (ed.) *Sociologists at Work*
Thomlinson, R. *Sociological Concepts and Research*
Selltiz, C. *et al. Research Methods in Social Relations*
Moser, C. A. *Survey Methods in Social Investigation*
Madge, J. *The Tools of Social Science*
Madge, J. *The Origins of Scientific Sociology*
Wootton, B. *Testament for Social Science* (chaps. 1-4)
Gould, J. (ed.) *Penguin Survey of the Social Sciences*. See especially article by H. C. Selvin: 'Training for Social Research'.
Young, P. V. and Schmid, C. F. *Scientific Social Surveys and Research*
Festinger, L. and Katz, D. *Research Methods in the Behavioral Sciences*
Phillips, B. S. *Social Research*
Goode, W. J. and Hatt, P. K. *Methods in Social Research*
Durkheim, E. *The Rules of Sociological Method*
Duverger, M. *Introduction to the Social Sciences*
Sorokin, P. A. *Fads and Foibles in Modern Sociology* (esp. chaps. 7, 8, 9, 10, 11)
Beveridge, W. I. B. *The Art of Scientific Investigation*
Stephan, F. J. and McCarthy, P. J. *Sampling Opinions*

For special consideration of various aspects of methodology and analysis

Coleman, J. S. *Introduction to Mathematical Sociology*
Cicourel, A. V. *Method and Measurement in Sociology*
Cochran, W. G. and Cox, G. M. *Experimental Designs*

Greenwood, E. *Experimental Sociology*. (The possibilities of experiment in sociology.)
Riley, M. W. *Sociological Research*, vol. 1, 'A Case Approach'
Bruyn, S. T. *The Human Perspective in Sociology*
Merton, R. K. *Continuities in Social Research*
Lazarsfeld, P. F. and Rosenberg, M. *The Language of Social Research*
Hyman, H. H. *Survey Design and Analysis*
Mueller, J. H. and Schuessler, L. F. *Statistical Reasoning in Sociology*

Scientific Method in Sociology

Rex, J. *Key Problems of Sociological Theory* (chap. 1)
Argyle, M. *The Scientific Study of Social Behaviour* (chaps. 2, 3)
Gibson, Q. *The Logic of Social Enquiry*

Values and Sociological Research

Myrdal, G. *Value in Social Theory* (chap. 7)
Rex, J. *Key Problems of Sociological Theory*
Spencer, J. *Stress and Release in Urban Estate* (N.B. 'Action Research')
Simey, T. S. 'What is Truth in Sociology?'
Rose, A. M. 'Sociology and the Study of Values'
Weber, M. *On the Methodology of the Social Sciences*. See also Madge, 1963 (chap. 8)

Research and Sociological Theory

Merton, R. K. *Social Theory and Social Structure*
Zetterberg, H. L. *On Theory and Verification in Sociology*

Project 1 **The Social Background of University Graduates and the Pool of Ability** The interpretation of statistical tables

OBJECTIVE

Interpretation of research findings.

REFERENCE

Tables taken from *Higher Education* (The Robbins Report), appendix I (pp. 54, 60, 86, 87).

INTRODUCTION

The system of higher education provides an important avenue for social mobility in modern industrial society. In British society the Robbins Report represents the first systematic account of the British system of higher education.

The Report's recommendations included the proposal that higher education should be expanded to allow many more students to enter university. The Committee maintained that many (especially working-class) children of high ability were excluded from the existing universities. Such a proposition has been criticised on the grounds that experience of past expansion has led to a dilution of the student population as a result of the near exhaustion of the 'pool of ability' from which students were drawn.

In this project the class will consider these and related issues in the light of some of the evidence presented in the Report.

METHOD

Consider the following four tables from the Report and, by answering the questions following them, write two or three paragraphs drawing your own conclusions from the data.

TABLE 1

Age of completing full-time education: by father's age of completing full-time education

Percentage of children born in Britain in 1940–1

Age at which father completed full-time education	Age at which child completed full-time education			
	18 and over	16 or 17	Under 16	All children
18 or over	50	47	3	100
16 or 17	23	45	32	100
Under 16	4	20	76	100

1. What proportion of the children whose fathers left school before they were 16 continued their education after 17?
2. Does this table show high or low intergenerational mobility?

TABLE 2

Percentage of boys aged 18 in 1928–47 and 1960 entering university: by social class

Social class	Boys aged 18	
	in 1928–47	in 1960
A. Non-manual	8·9	16·8
B. Manual	1·4	2·6
C. All boys	3·7	5·8
A divided by B	6·4	6·5

3. To what extent has the total proportion of boys entering university increased?
4. Which social class has benefited more from that increase?

TABLE 3

Percentage of British undergraduates who left without success: by year of entry

Year of entry	Percentage leaving without success
1952	16·7
1955	13·9
1957	14·3

TABLE 4

Percentage of British university graduates obtaining various classes of degrees

Year of graduation	1st	1sts or Upper 2nds	1sts or 2nds
1953	8·0	27·2	55·3
1954	7·9	27·8	56·9
1958	7·3	28·2	59·0
1959	7·3	28·4	59·6
1960	7·1	28·9	60·5

5. Do these tables give any evidence for or against the proposition that 'the standard of those admitted to university has been deteriorating'? Explain.

6. Is there anything in these figures to suggest that a further expansion in university places would lead to a lowering of entrance standards?

DISCUSSION

Put your answers into a sociological framework and write a concluding paragraph on the implications of these figures for educationalists.

Further Reading

Higher Education (Robbins Report) (chaps. 6 and 13)
Fifteen to Eighteen (Crowther Report) (vol. 2, chap. 1)
Floud, J. E. *et al.*; Jackson, B. and Marsden, D.; Little, J. and Westergaard, J. H.; Kelsall, R. K.; Abbott, J.; Musgrove, F. (recent discussion of the relationship between the family and the educational system)

Project 2 **The Causes of Suicide**
The use of official sources of statistics for planning a research project; introduction to secondary analysis

OBJECTIVE

A consideration of the General Register Office statistics of suicides in England and Wales, and the setting up of theoretically significant and empirically testable hypotheses to explain suicide.

REFERENCES

Tables taken from the *Registrar-General's Statistical Review of England and Wales, 1961*, part 3.
Madge, J. *The Origins of Scientific Sociology*, chap. 2.

INTRODUCTION

In the early stages of a research project it is generally necessary to consider material which has already been documented, such as official censuses or records, newspaper reports, personal communications, etc. The investigator's own initiative is required in searching for material which might provide insight for his research: Lloyd Warner, for instance, utilised cemetery records in research on mobility.

Students should note the limitations of such data, especially since it has probably been collected for some other purpose than the research project for which it is being considered, and there may well be no check on the reliability of such data.

Durkheim's *Suicide* is still a model of social research. One of the reasons Durkheim chose the phenomenon of suicide was that there were many statistics available on the subject, both in Europe and in the United States, which, as Madge points out, provided not only data on the number of suicides but also various related statistics. In fact, Durkheim based almost all his analysis on material that had already been published. (See J. Madge's (1964) chapter on Durkheim's *Suicide*.)

METHOD

Consider the following extracts from (selected) tables noting down any lines of further enquiry they suggest to you.

TABLE 1

Deaths from suicide, at all ages, by sex, 1901 to 1961, England and Wales (Table cxxiii)

	Males	Females		Males	Females
1901	2,318	803	1931	3,624	1,523
1906	2,655	797	1936	3,441	1,638
1911	2,655	933	1941	2,318	1,339
1916	2,063	792	1946	2,673	1,639
1921	2,763	996	1951	2,831	1,638
1926	3,099	1,350	1956	3,198	2,084
			1961	3,025	2,175

(Table cxxiv of the *Statistical Review* gives 'Crude rate/million living', a similar picture.)

TABLE 2

Suicides: death rates per million living by sex and age 1901 to 1961 England and Wales (Table cxxv)

	Males					Females				
	15–24	25–34	35–44	45–64	65+	15–24	25–34	35–44	45–64	65+
1901–5	63	157	250	446	492	42	57	80	107	81
1911–15	65	147	226	372	418	40	52	76	108	72
1921–5	48	100	199	378	471	31	48	78	122	82
1931–5	68	140	210	452	520	37	77	108	159	119
1941–5	53	105	127	223	357	16	52	77	117	103
1946–50	50	82	129	262	426	19	47	80	146	144
1955	40	97	130	257	435	13	45	75	167	174
1960	57	115	139	247	347	26	56	86	162	160
1961	51	108	147	238	349	23	55	93	174	168

TABLE 3

Percentage distribution of suicides by month of occurrence, 10-year period 1951–60 (Table cxxvi)

	Jan	Feb	Mar	Apr	May	Jun	Jul	Aug	Sep	Oct	Nov	Dec
Percentage distribution	8·3	8·3	8·7	9·6	9·0	8·8	8·0	7·8	7·5	8·0	7·9	8·1

TABLE 4

Suicide and all causes: Standardised mortality ratios, males and married women aged 20–64 according to social class for periods 1921–3, 1930–2 and 1950, England and Wales (Table cxxvii)

Persons	Cause	Period	I	II	III	IV	V
(a) Occupied and retired males	Suicide	1921–3	116	128	91	89	98
		1930–2	120	137	95	87	87
		1950	134	110	89	99	119
	All causes	1921–3	82	94	95	101	125
		1930–2	90	94	97	102	111
		1950	97	86	102	94	118
(b) Married Women	Suicide	1930–2	128	109	101	82	92
		1950	150	97	103	91	88
	All causes	1930–2	81	89	99	103	113
		1950	96	84	101	104	117

TABLE 5

Suicide death rates per million living, by sex . . . aged 15 years and over, in conurbations and urban and rural aggregates 1960–1, England and Wales (Table cxxviii)

	Males	Females
Conurbations	202	128
Other urban areas with populations over 100,000	181	118
Other urban areas with populations over 50,000 and under 100,000	198	126
Other urban areas with populations under 50,000	173	107
Rural Areas	145	83

Tables cxxix and cxxx (*Statistical Review*) give suicide rates for standard regions of England and Wales and for individual metropolitan and county boroughs in 1950 and 1960. The following places appeared among the 'top 20' in both years: Chelsea, Hampstead,

Holborn, Kensington, Paddington, St Marylebone and Westminster (metropolitan boroughs); Burnley, Halifax and Oldham (industrial towns); and Bournemouth, Eastbourne and Southport (resort towns). The seven metropolitan boroughs show high proportions of one-person households (*Statistical Review*, pp. 260–2).

Table cxxii gives suicide rates by method, by sex, at two-yearly intervals 1912–60.

Main changes indicated are

(1) Increasing use of domestic gas
(2) Decreasing use of 'Hanging and Strangulation', 'Drowning', 'Firearms and Explosives', and 'Cutting and Piercing Instruments'.

TABLE 6

The percentage of effective suicides as measured by the ratio Verdicts/(Verdicts and cases attempted) 1954 to 1960, England and Wales (Table cxxiii)

Males

	1954	1955	1956	1957	1958	1959	1960
8 and under 14	25	38	100	22	—	22	—
14 and under 17	30	24	24	23	14	22	23
17 and under 21	19	19	16	16	21	18	18
21 and under 30	26	27	27	25	26	28	28
30 and under 40	40	37	37	38	41	40	43
40 and under 50	59	56	57	55	57	55	56
50 and under 60	70	67	67	65	69	71	69
60 and over	72	70	72	71	74	74	76

Females

	1954	1955	1956	1957	1958	1959	1960
8 and under 14	—	17	—	—	—	8	5
14 and under 17	4	1	5	7	5	3	8
17 and under 21	7	5	5	8	6	10	6
21 and under 30	19	13	14	14	17	16	18
30 and under 40	29	27	26	27	29	31	30
40 and under 50	42	42	44	44	44	46	47
50 and under 60	61	57	59	62	63	62	63
60 and over	67	67	68	71	73	73	73

DISCUSSION

1. Note in particular what these figures *really* indicate. For instance, note the main sources of error. Could these errors differ between different groups and over time?

2. Draw up
    i. A list of limitations of secondary data as research data
    ii. The main hypotheses immediately suggested to you by the figures

3. By referring to any of the following, or to any other work you feel is relevant, outline in one paragraph the suggested aim and method of a research project to investigate one (or perhaps two) of these hypotheses, and specify the information you feel should be collected.

4. What further categories of information would have improved the *R.-G.S.R.* tables?

5. What are the main disadvantages of using sources of this sort as 'indirect clues' to significant sociological hypotheses?

Further Reading

Registrar-General's Statistical Review 1961, part iii (pp. 240–66)
Sainsbury, P.; Durkheim, E. (1952); Wolfgang, M. E. *et al.* (chap. 7); Welford, A. T. *et al.* (chap. 2); Stengel, E. (1963); Stengel, E. (1965); Giddens, A. (this article also gives a large number of detailed references); Stengel, E. and Cook, N. G.; Henry, A. F. and Short, J.; Lazarsfeld, P. F. and Rosenberg, M. (section 2D, 'The Testing and Verification of Hypotheses'); Benjamin, B.; Dublin, L. I.; Gibbs, J. P. (1961/3) (see further bibliography in this); Clinard, M. B. (1963) (chap. 14; see further bibliography in this); Clinard, M. B. (1964) (appendix: 'Inventory of Empirical and Theoretical Studies of Anomie'); Gibbs, J. P. and Martin, W. T.; Coleman (1964a) (chap. 15, 'The Method of Residues').

Project 3 [Vacation Project] Occupational Roles A case study

OBJECTIVE

To examine, within a sociological framework, the occupational role of an individual.

REFERENCES

Caplow, T. *The Sociology of Work*.

Hughes, E. C. 'Institutional Office and the Person', *American Journal of Sociology*.

Hughes, E. C. 'The Sociological Study of Work: An Editorial Foreword', *American Journal of Sociology*.

Hughes, E. C. *Men and Their Work*.

INTRODUCTION

This project is concerned especially with the social roles appropriate to an occupation; a man's occupational position being the classification of that man by the work which he does. The student should bear in mind E. C. Hughes's note that each occupation 'tends to have its peculiar realm of sacred and secular objects. The sacred objects are its interests and prerogatives. Its secular objects are within the realm of its technique.'

The case-study method – the intensive study of one instance, or a very small number of instances, of a phenomenon – has the advantage of being an integrated and flexible approach which is amenable to reformulation and redirection as new information is obtained. Such a method therefore has utility particularly in the early stages of research in relatively unformulated areas. Students must note, however, the inherent limitations of such an approach.

METHOD

The student should select an occupation to study from a sociological point of view. It should preferably be one pursued by a friend or relative. However, alternatives would be the occupation the student hopes to enter himself, one he finds in his favourite literature or one already studied and written up by sociologists.

This is also an exercise in the use of the case study method. So it is suggested that the student selects an individual with whom he can conduct one or two informal interviews. However, beyond this, the methods used are left to the choice of the student.

The final account should concentrate on any one aspect of the role which is found to be particularly important. The following aspects should be considered at the outset:

1. The evolution of the occupation
2. The technical activities involved
3. Its rank in the social hierarchy
4. Its context – the institutional complex, the ownership of its tools, rewards, relationship with other occupations, the dominant relationship (e.g. professional–client etc.), and entry
5. The fellow-worker group: how is this organised? Who is admitted and who excluded? Who are the dominant central members of the occupation? Who the peripheral or subordinate groups? What are the obligations assumed by members of the occupation? Who controls the behaviour of members (colleagues, clients, members of other professions, etc.)
6. The career: how visible is the occupation? What career expectations is the entrant likely to hold? What career pattern is involved in the occupation? Who controls the career progression of the individual?
7. Do members regard the occupation as a profession? Does the group seek professional status? What relationship does the occupational group have with the outside world?

TREATMENT OF RESULTS

The account, giving details of methods used, should be written up as a research report with conclusions and, if appropriate, suggestions for further research. The best of these reports may be copied and retained for the laboratory reference library.

DISCUSSION

Include in the account a critical appraisal of the case study method. For instance, how does it differ from biography? What are the advantages and the limitations of this approach?

Further Reading

Apart from that appropriate to the subject chosen

METHODOLOGY

Madge, J. (1953) (chap. 4, for introduction to interviewing procedure)

Young, P. V. (chap. 12, discussion of the case study method)

Selltiz, C. *et al.* (chap. 3, descriptive studies)

Riesman, D. and Glazer, N. (1952, 1965) (example of the use of case studies)

Conwell, C.

OCCUPATIONAL STUDIES

Studies have been made of clerks, agricultural occupations, mining occupations, steel workers, car workers, bus and lorry drivers, cowboys, morticians, gangsters, fishermen, advertising executives, doctors, nurses, scientists in industry and universities, librarians, managers and engineers.

For instance:

Tunstall, J. (1962); Lockwood, D.

Project 4 **Social Norms** Tabulation of research data based on observation

OBJECTIVE

To investigate the nature of a social norm by a simple field experiment and graphical analysis of data.

MATERIALS

2–3 sheets of graph paper.

REFERENCES

Davis, K. *Human Society* (chap. 3) *or*
Sprott, W. J. H. *Science and Social Action* (chap. 1).

INTRODUCTION

Social norms are group-developed and group-held standards for the behaviour of members of the group. The empirical study of norms is hampered by the complexity of the concrete behaviour of members of any society. Therefore there are three main approaches generally used when considering the subject. The investigator can (1) get some members of the society or group to estimate the frequency of certain behaviour and give their opinion of it. Alternatively (2) he can observe its frequency and regularity or (3) observe the approval or disapproval of others towards it. Although frequently the sociologist chooses the first course of action (protecting himself against biased reporting by using a number of informants and checking some of their statements), in this experiment we shall use the second method.

METHOD

Since the normative order acts as one determinant of the factual order, systematic observation of repeated events can throw light on the social norm.

Students, working in pairs, should select a simple human activity which can be observed in public. Some topics are suggested below, but the students should not be restricted by this list. The essential points are that:

1. The single 'activities' are repeated, so that a number of observations can be made (between 30 and 50 will be sufficient).

2. These activities can be divided into five to ten categories for investigation.

3. These categories must form a continuous series.

It will probably be found that *timing* certain activities is one of the most appropriate subjects, e.g.:

1. Parking times of vehicles in a restricted zone.

2. Length of time people spend at a bookstall, in a café, coffee bar, etc.

3. Speed of traffic on a stretch of road (time vehicles along a measured section of about 200 yards).

4. Numbers of people arriving at different times for a meeting, etc.

5. Time mothers arrive at infants school to collect their child.

6. Length of time taken to drink a first glass of beer.

However, there are other possibilities which, if carefully selected, are suitable, e.g.:

1. Drivers' reaction to a 'stop' sign (categories can range from 'ignored', 'barely slowed', to 'slowed to one or two m.p.h.', or 'dead stop').

2. Number of books being carried by individual students.

Students can have considerable latitude in choosing their subject; however, they should decide on the activity and discuss it with their tutor before starting their observations.

It is suggested that the basis of the experiment should be *observations*. A possible alternative is to ask a number of people a single question (for instance about frequency of an activity or ownership of books, etc.).

Categories should be decided on the spot when the activity has been observed for a few minutes. Attempt to get a good distribution between categories. Use the form suggested in Appendix 2 for recording observations.

Treatment of Results

1. *Histogram.* Construct a histogram by plotting frequency (vertical plane) against category of action, using vertical lines at the limits of the class intervals to form a series of contiguous rectangles:

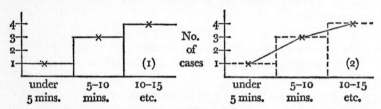

2. *Frequency polygon.* Using the same scale, repeat, but this time joining the midpoints of the intervals (see above).

3. *Smoothed frequency curve.*[1] Since many frequency distributions are based on relatively small samples, it is sometimes desirable to portray the data by a smoothed curve. This can often be done by eye, but a more accurate method is as follows:

    i. Re-draw the frequency polygon using light or broken line.

    ii. Join *all* alternate points on the graph.

    iii. Draw a vertical line through each of the original points (*AB* in diagram).

    iv. Find by inspection the midpoints of these lines (*A–B*), and join with a smooth curve.

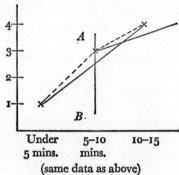

(same data as above)

[1] Valid only for continuous data.

4. Calculate:
   i. *The arithmetical mean* from your results (for each category multiply the mid-value by the number of cases; then total and divide by the total number of cases).
   ii. *The median value* (the middle value – the one with the same number of values below as above).
   iii. *The mode* (the value which occurs most often).

DISCUSSION

1. Describe in one paragraph the methods you used in your observation, noting likely errors, etc.

2. Is there a difference between your values for mean, median and mode? Which if any of these would indicate the *social norm* in this case?

3. Draw what conclusions you can from the shape of your graphs. For instance what are the reasons for any distortions?

4. What are the social sanctions for illegitimate conduct? What light do your observations throw on their efficacy?

5. Would it be accurate to call the extreme cases on your graph 'deviants'? How would you divide the 'normal' from the 'deviant'?

6. What are the advantages and disadvantages of this method of investigation, compared with 'armchair generalisations'?

Further Reading

METHODOLOGY

Duverger, M. (part 2, chap. 2, section 2, graphical presentation of frequency distribution)

Young, P. V. (chap. 13 – graphical presentation of frequency distribution)

Loveday, R. (chap. 3, elementary approach to averages and how to calculate them)

Huff, D. (chap. 2, light-hearted comment on the use and misuse of mean, median and mode)

Moroney, M. J. (chap. 4, explanation of averages and commentary on their uses)

Wallis, W. A. and Roberts, H. V. (chap. 7, full discussion of averages)

Yule, G. U. and Kendall, M. G. (chap. 5, full discussion of averages).

SOCIAL NORMS

Sumner, W. G. (classic work on social norms and their classification); Morris, R. T.; Fearing, F. and Krise, E. M.; Sellin, T.

Project 5 **Culture and Sub-culture in Child-rearing Practices** The comparative method in anthropology and sociology

OBJECTIVE

The use of anthropological and survey findings in making comparisons between different cultures.

REFERENCES

Young, K. 'Culture and Personality' in *Handbook of Social Psychology*.
Klein, J. *Samples from English Cultures*, vols. 1 and 2.

INTRODUCTION

It is maintained that comparative sociological studies should contribute to the development of concepts and generalisations at a level between 'pure theory' and descriptive area studies.

By taking a single issue that is to be found in many (possibly all) societies, comparative sociological studies seek to illuminate it by showing how different societies have dealt with the same issue.

In particular S. F. Nadel (1958) has strongly advocated the use of the comparative method in social anthropology. Nadel emphasises the need to examine social facts 'in the artificial isolation entailed in any comparison and increasing with its range' and contends that 'the anthropologist (or any scientist) whose motto is "never depart from contexts" ignores that we possess intellectual means for isolating elements from their setting without disastrous loss of meaning.' (Quoted in Gould and Kolb (eds.), *A Dictionary of Social Sciences*.)

METHOD

Select two accounts of child-rearing practices in different societies,
preferably one 'primitive', and one 'contemporary'. It will be best if
the two methods of investigation are also different. (There is a list of
suggested sources below, but do not be limited by this in your
choice.)

You should then produce a table using three columns, one for the
Arapesh and one for each of the two societies you have selected. It
should not be necessary to read the accounts exhaustively; use the
authors' sub-headings, list of contents, index, etc. Give a comparison
of the authors' principal methods of investigation, noting length of
period of fieldwork, etc.

SOURCES

Primitive Societies
Whiting, B. B. (ed.), *Six Cultures: Studies of Child-rearing*
Kardiner, A. *The Psychological Frontiers of Society*
Mead, M. *Sex and Temperament in Three Primitive Societies*
Mead, M. *Male and Female: A Study of the Sexes in a Changing World*
Or any monograph on child-rearing in a specific culture.

Contemporary Western Societies and Subcultures
Newson, J. and Newson, E. *Infant Care in an Urban Community*
Kerr, M. *The People of Ship Street*
Lynd, R. S. and Lynd, H. M. *Middletown*
Robb, J. H. *Working-Class Anti-Semite*
Miller, D. R. and Swanson, G. E. *The Changing American Parent*
Spinley, B. M. *The Deprived and The Privileged*
Gorer, G. *Exploring English Character*
Klein, J. *Samples from English Cultures*, vol. 2, Child-rearing Practices

Summary of Principal Features of Child-Rearing Practices in three societies
Questions to be answered in a table showing the principal features of
child-rearing practices in the three societies. (Selected answers for
Arapesh are in italics.)

1. Cultural definition of conception.

Fortunate? Biological knowledge? Attitudes and practices with regard to contraception, abortion, etc.

2. Childbirth.

Traditions, treatment of child and mother.

3. Early socialisation in the first few months.

Indulgence/strictness. Regularity. Agency of socialisation. *Little or no rigid training. Rather indulgent towards child. Any nursing mother may indulge child. Father-son affection strong.*

4. Practices in detail.

    i. Weaning. Gradual? When? *Late, in 3rd or 4th year.*

    ii. Eating and nursing. Feed on demand? *Irregular. Breast to pacify.*

    iii. Toilet training. *Slight training. Mild punishment for soiling. Use of example and imitation.*

    iv. Infantile sexuality.

    v. Other. Sleep, walking, etc. *Gradual training in walking.*

5. Development of conscience in child.

Rewards or punishment: shame, threats, ridicule? *Few threats of punishment. Co-operation with relatives and friends taught early. Sense of guilt; anxiety over loss of affection, loss of health, lack of co-operation from others. Shielded from adult problems, and not hurried towards adulthood.*

6. Rituals in child's first year.

Rite de passage? Ritual gifts, bathing, meals. Ceremonial.

DISCUSSION

1. List the main methodological shortcomings of the three studies in brief.

2. Compare the methods used. To what extent are they appropriate to the subject matter? For instance, should survey techniques have been the same in all three studies?

3. How far could these findings provide a basis for the development of hypotheses and theory?

4. How far can we generalise about the 'English', 'American' or 'Arapesh' family?

Further Reading

Bronfenbrenner, M.; Havighurst, R. J. and Davis, A.; Sprott, W. J. H. *et al.*

METHODOLOGY

Banton, M.; Radcliffe-Brown, A. R.; Spencer, R. F.; Naroll, R.; Udy, S. H.; Whiting, J. W. M.

Project 6 **Problem Solution and Group Size** Simple comparison in the laboratory

OBJECTIVE

To consider efficiency in problem-solving as a function of size of group.

REFERENCES

Taylor, D. W. and Faust, 'Twenty Questions: efficiency in problem-solving as a function of size of group' in *Small Groups*, ed. Hare, A. P. *et al.*

Argyle, M. 'Experimental Studies of Small Social Groups' in Welford, A. T. *et al.* (ed.), *Society*.

MATERIALS

List of objects.

INTRODUCTION

Where the situational conditions and stimulus are amenable to the control of the investigator in a situation set up by him for the purposes of his investigation, the approach is variously called the 'laboratory', 'controlled' or 'artificial' experiment. Typically a laboratory experiment includes the following features:

1. The observation of a dependent variable.
2. The manipulation of an independent variable.
3. The control of all other relevant factors.

However, the student should bear in mind that in many sociological investigations, designated by some sociologists as 'natural experiments', neither the situational conditions nor the manipulation of the stimulus is imposed by the investigator.

The investigator conducts laboratory experiments on small groups on the assumption that he has created valid replicas of the concepts under investigation (note Cicourel's comments on this assumption) and that there are benefits – such as precision, economy and speed – to be gained from such set-ups. However, the limitations of this approach are well documented in the literature and should not be neglected. The student should consider these criticisms in the light of Lazarsfeld's emphasis on the controlled experiment in *or* outside the laboratory as *the basic frame of reference* in considering problems of social causation.

METHOD

The class should be assigned by chance to work alone, in pairs or in groups of four, and an experimenter (E) or question master assigned to each group.

The rules of 'Twenty Questions' as a parlour game should, in cases of doubt, be discussed. To start the game E tells the group only whether the object they are to attempt to identify is animal, vegetable or mineral. In searching for the object which is the solution to the problem, they ask a series of questions, each of which can be answered 'Yes' or 'No'. (The only other responses to be allowed are 'Partly', 'Sometimes' and 'Not in the visual sense of the word'.)

Each E should be given a list of twenty objects from the Tutor's Manual, Appendix 1 and told to take his group to a separate room for about one hour. The object is for the members of the group working together to guess the twenty objects in the minimum number of questions. In each case the results should be recorded by all members of the group on a table that shows the number of questions taken to guess each object, or the failure to do so after forty questions. The total amount of failures and questions and the average number of failures and questions must also be shown. The participants should then work out the number of 'failures' (i.e. not guessing object in twenty questions) and the average number of questions necessary to succeed (scoring unsolved objects as forty).

TREATMENT OF RESULTS (with tutor using black-board as necessary)

Tutor. Put results of all groups on black-board as groups return.[1]

[1] *Note to tutor*: if some groups have not completed task, it may be necessary to work out mean number of questions per object right through the experiment.

Problem Solution and Group Size

1. Compare mean number of failures per group on a table using on the horizontal axis three sizes of group: Working Alone; In Pairs; In Fours; and on the vertical axis: Total Number of Failures (x); Number of Groups (y); Arithmetic Mean (x/y).

2. Students should calculate mean number of questions per group in the three sizes of group, labelling table appropriately.

Rate of Learning and Group Size

1. Compare mean number of failures in first ten and second ten objects on a table, using on the horizontal axis three sizes of group: Working Alone; Working in Pairs; Working in Fours; and on the vertical axis: Total Number of Failures; Total Number of Groups; Arithmetic Mean. On the vertical axis each of these headings should be broken down: First Ten; Second Ten.

2. Prepare simple graph to represent the differences (if any). Plot mean number of failures against first or second group of objects.

3. Repeat for mean number of questions per group.

DISCUSSION

1. What hypotheses would you put forward, on the basis of these results, relating problem, solution and group size?

2. Consider the practical implications of this. For instance, is there an ideal size for a committee? How would the kind of problem presented affect the result?

3. List (*a*) the advantages, and (*b*) the disadvantages, of the laboratory situation for making controlled comparisons.

4. How far was the method of dividing the class satisfactory for the purposes of these comparisons?

Further Reading

METHODOLOGY

Welford, A. T. *et al.* (chap. 9 by Welford); Madge, J. (1963) (chap. 12); Cicourel, A. V. (chap. 7); Swanson, G. E.; Edwards, A. L. (1954); Selltiz, C. *et al.*

SMALL GROUP RESEARCH

Hare, A. P. (1962)

Project 7 **A Group's Treatment of a Deviate** Observation of an experimental group

OBJECTIVE

To examine a discussion group's behaviour towards a deviant member.

MATERIALS

Closed circuit TV and 5 volunteers.

REFERENCES

Schachter, S. 'Deviation, Rejection and Communication', *Journal of Abnormal and Social Psychology*, reprinted in Cartwright, D. and Zander (ed.), *Group Dynamics*.

Madge, J. *The Tools of Social Science* (chap. 5) (or Selltiz, C. *et al. Research Methods in Social Relations*).

INTRODUCTION

A simplified version of Schachter's experiment on deviation is adopted in this project.

METHOD

1. Five volunteers (perhaps from other departments) chosen independently, and preferably strangers to each other, should be invited by the tutor to attend for a discussion of about one hour. They are told that as part of a study of problems of young people and delinquent behaviour they will be given two or three case histories

of local delinquents to discuss and that they will be asked to consider their possible treatment. One of the five should be asked to arrive 15 minutes early and ask to see the class tutor.

2. This person will be given instructions to take an independent line during the discussion of the *second* case only. Without changing his or her behaviour in any other way this student should take a firm or authoritarian line compared with the perceived group norm, justifying stricter discipline or more positive treatment as appropriate.

3. At the beginning of the laboratory period the discussion group should meet, be given numbers and sit where they are all clearly observed by the class via the closed circuit TV system. No other contact between the groups should be allowed.

The class tutor will then give out the three brief case histories (Appendix 3) and explain that the group should read them and then try to agree on the treatment they would recommend. After about twenty minutes on each, they should write down their group decision, whether or not they have managed to agree. They are then left for the hour.

4. At the end of the hour a sociometric test should be administered. The tutor should give each person a card and tell them that if a further meeting becomes necessary he would require smaller groups next time. They are requested to put down the numbers of any particular preferences they would have for other members of this group for a further meeting on the same subject. These cards will be collected by the tutor. The group should then be thanked and released.

5. The class should observe the whole procedure and attempt to analyse the communication patterns in the group during the experiment. They should do this by indicating each 'communication' during the hour by '1' in a table laid out as follows; if the communication lasts for more than thirty seconds, this should be indicated by ringing, i.e. ①.

TABLE 1

Communications in discussion group,
during discussion of Cases 1, 2 and 3

			Speaker			Totals	
Recipient	1	2	3	4	5	Long	Short
1							
2							
3							
4							
5							
Whole group or nor clear							
TOTALS long short							

TREATMENT OF RESULTS

1. The tutor will now inform the group (if it has not already become apparent) who was his 'stooge', and the results of the sociometric test, from which Table 2 can be completed on a matrix as laid out below:

TABLE 2

Matrix for sociogram of discussion group

Object of choice		Subject of choice			
	1	2	3	4	5
1					
2					
3					
4					
5					
Object totals					

2. Students should then make their own analysis of the communication patterns and in particular compare
   i. the number of communications to the deviate with the average for other members;
   ii. the number of communications to the deviate in different stages in the experiment.

Using these, the sociometric choices (converted into a sociogram as in Project Twenty-two) and any other analysis of his data the student should give his conclusions on the results.

DISCUSSION

1. Comment on this approach to the study of deviant behaviour.

2. How can the results of this project be reconciled with generalisations made by sociologists about society's treatment of the deviate? Give an example.

3. This was an artificial group. What effect did this seem to be having on members' behaviour? Could this effect have been lessened in any way by the design of the experiment?

4. What are the advantages and disadvantages of this kind of observation in practice?

5. Suggest a design for a 'natural' experiment to investigate this issue further, giving an outline of the exact hypothesis you would suggest be considered.

Further Reading

SOCIAL REACTION TO DEVIANT BEHAVIOUR

Sutherland, E. H. and Cressey, D. R. (part 1)
Sprott, W. J. H. (1954) (chap. 6)
Clinard, M. B. (1963) (chap. 1)
Wootton, B. (1959) (chaps. 1 and 2 in particular)
Durkheim, E. (1958/50) (chap. 3, classic view of functions of deviant behaviour for society)
Durkheim, E. (1947) (esp. pp. 424 ff.: moral facts, their recognition and functions of punishment)
Becker, H. S.

OBSERVATION AND EXPERIMENTS IN SOCIOLOGY

Selltiz, C. *et al.* (chap. 4, studies testing causal hypotheses)
Thomlinson, R. (chap. 4 includes brief introduction to experiments)
Duverger, M. (part 2, chap. 1, section 2, elementary introduction to notion of experiment in sociology)

Greenwood, E. (esp. chap. 5 which describes types of experiment in sociology)

Cicourel, A. V. (chap. 7, comment on experimental designs in sociology)

Hyman, H. H. (1958/55) (chap. 6, thorough discussion of experiment and control in experiments)

Swanson, G. E.

McGinnis, R. in Gould, J. E. and Kolb

Madge, J. (1963) (chaps. 6 and 13, use of experiment in Hawthorne research and small communities)

Project 8 **Group Influences on the Formation of Norms** Group influence in an experimental situation

REFERENCE

Wallach, M.A., Kogan, N. and Bem, D. 'Group influence on individual risk-taking', *Journal of Abnormal and Social Psychology*.

INTRODUCTION

In all societies there exist rules or norms that lay down appropriate and inappropriate behaviour which are normally based on the values of the wider culture; their formation can normally only be studied over a considerable period of time. However, small changes in some norms can be created in an experimental situation. One instance of this is in an experimental group discussion of hypothetical decisions. The relationship between individual decisions and group consensus in this artificial situation will illustrate some aspects of the process of norm formation.

METHOD

Stage 1

There follows a series of situations that might well occur in everyday life. The central person in each situation is faced with a choice between two alternative courses of action, which we might call X and Y. Alternative X is more desirable and attractive than alternative Y, but the probability of attaining or achieving X is less than that of attaining or achieving Y.

For each situation on the following pages, indicate on the first decision form (Appendix 4) the minimum odds of success you would demand before recommending that the more attractive or desirable alternative, *X*, be chosen.

For each situation, your answer must be chosen from the following ten possible answers:

		Score
As *minimum* odds of success, I require 1 chance in 10		1
2	10	2
3	10	3
4	10	4
5	10	5
6	10	6
7	10	7
8	10	8
9	10	9

The more attractive alternative should not be   10
attempted, no matter what the probabilities.

Read each situation carefully before giving your judgment. Try to place yourself in the position of the central person in each of the situations. There are six situations in all. Please do not omit any of them.

Note: The more risky alternative is always assumed to be more desirable than the safer course, if the former should prove successful.

Situation 1

Mr *A*, an electrical engineer, who is married and has one child, has been working for a large electronics firm since graduating from university five years ago. He is assured of a lifetime job with a modest, though adequate, salary, and liberal pension benefits upon retirement. On the other hand, it is very unlikely that his salary will increase much before he retires. While attending a conference, Mr *A* is offered a job with a small, newly founded company which has a highly uncertain future. The new job would pay more to start and would offer the possibility of a share in the ownership if the company survived the competition of the larger firms.

Imagine that you are Mr *A*. You are thinking about the chances of the new company proving financially sound.

What are the *lowest* odds of success that you would consider

acceptable to make it worth while for Mr *A* to take the new job?
Put your answer on the decision form.

Situation 2

Mr *B*, a 45-year-old accountant, has recently been informed by his
doctor that he has developed a severe heart ailment. The disease
would be sufficiently serious to force Mr *B* to change many of his
strongest life habits – reducing the amount of work he can do,
drastically changing his diet, giving up favourite leisure time
pursuits. The doctor suggests that a delicate medical operation could
be attempted which, if successful, would completely relieve the heart
condition. But its success could not be assured, and in fact that
operation might prove fatal.

Imagine that you are Mr *B*. You are thinking about the chances
that the operation will prove successful.

What are the *lowest* odds of success that you would consider
acceptable for the operation to be performed?

Situation 3

Mr *G*, a competent chess player, is participating in a national chess
tournament. In an early match he draws the top-ranked player in
the tournament as his opponent. Mr *G* has been given a relatively
low ranking in view of his performance in previous tournaments.
During the course of his play with the top-ranked man, Mr *G* notes
the possibility of a deceptive though risky manœuvre which might
bring him a quick victory. At the same time, if the attempted
manœuvre should fail, Mr *G* would be left in an exposed position
and defeat would almost certainly follow.

Imagine that you are Mr *G*. You are thinking about the chances
that Mr *G*'s deceptive play would succeed.

What are the *lowest* odds of success that you would consider
acceptable for the risky play in question to be attempted?

Situation 4

Mr *J*, who is British, is captured by the enemy in World War II and
placed in a prisoner-of-war camp. Conditions in the camp are quite

bad, with long hours of hard physical labour and a barely sufficient diet. After spending several months in this camp, Mr *J* notes the possibility of escape by concealing himself in a supply lorry that shuttles in and out of the camp. Of course, there is no guarantee that the escape would prove successful. Recapture by the enemy could well mean execution.

Imagine that you are Mr *J*. You are thinking about the chances of a successful escape from the prisoner-of-war camp.

What are the *lowest* odds of success that you would consider acceptable for an escape to be attempted?

Situation 5

Mr *L*, a married 30-year-old research physicist, has been given a five-year research appointment by a major university laboratory. As he contemplates the next five years, he realises that he might work on a difficult long-term problem which, if a solution could be found, would resolve basic scientific issues in the field and bring high scientific honours. If no solution were found, however, Mr *L* would have little to show for his five years in the laboratory, and this would make it hard for him to get a good job afterwards. On the other hand, he could, as most of his professional associates are doing, work on a series of short-term problems where solutions would be easier to find, but where the problems are of lesser scientific importance.

Imagine that you are Mr *L*. You are thinking about the chances that a solution would be found to the difficult long-term problem that you have in mind.

What are the *lowest* odds of success that you would consider acceptable to make it worth while for you to work on the more difficult long-term problem?

Situation 6

Mr *D* is the captain of University *X*'s rugby team. University *X* is playing its traditional rival, University *Y*, in the final game of the season. The game is in its last minute, and Mr *D*'s team, University *X*, is behind in the score. University *X* is attacking strongly. Mr *D*, the captain, must decide whether it would be best to settle for a draw by going for a dropped goal, which would be almost certain to work; or, on the other hand, he could attempt the much riskier play of going for a try and conversion which would bring victory if it succeeded, but defeat if not.

Imagine that you are Mr *D*. You are thinking about the chances that the riskier play will work.

What are the *lowest* odds of success that you would consider acceptable for the riskier play to be attempted?

When the class have completed this task (which should not take more than 15 minutes), students should mark the Stage 1 forms with their names, and hand them in to their tutor.

Stage 2

The class should then be divided by some random method into groups of five, who are to discuss each situation in turn and arrive at a unanimous decision on each. In Stage 2 the group must not return to an earlier situation, but must discuss each one until the group decision is reached before going on to the next. If a deadlock occurs, those who disagree should restate their reasons and the situation should be re-read carefully. If decision is still not unanimous, a compromise or majority decision must be taken as final. Each student should then mark the second decision form with his name and group decision, returning it to the tutor if the project is to proceed to Stages 3 and 4.

OPTIONAL EXTENSIONS OF THE PROJECT

Stage 3 and Stage 4

One or two further sessions of individual decision can take place on reassembling, and 2–6 weeks later, for participants to reconsider the situations (*not*, remember, decisions made previously). If this is done, results should be treated in exactly the same way as those of Stages 1 and 2.

Control Groups

For a strictly controlled situation, the tutor may decide that some groups should omit Stage 2. In this way any shifts in decisions taking place over time in the absence of the discussion process can be considered.

Comparison

If the number of students and distribution between the sexes in the class allow, this is a suitable experiment for a comparison between (*a*) all male, (*b*) all female, and (*c*) mixed groups. Results can be treated in the same way.

TREATMENT OF RESULTS

1. Each individual student's total score at each stage should now be written on the board and recorded on a table.

2. *Using the same scale and axes*, draw frequency polygons (cf. Project 4) of these totals, superimposed, but using a different style or colour of line for each. Note the main difference(s), if any, between shapes of graphs, and consider what they indicate. (Use intervals of 3 for score totals.)

3. Calculate and compare arithmetical mean class scores for each stage. What do any differences between these indicate?

4. Look at the 'dispersion' (the scatter or spread) of the scores. This may be very different even where means are similar. There are several measures of dispersion. One is to consider merely the 'range' of the scores. What are the ranges over different stages? What are the disadvantages of using this measure of dispersion?

5. Interquartile range. Another measure of dispersion can be calculated in the following way:

   i. Find the *median* value of the scores at one stage.

   ii. Set the scores in order of size and divide them into four equal groups. (The two extreme groups are called the 'upper' and 'lower quartiles'.) Then 50 per cent of the scores are seen to be between these quartiles, and this is the 'interquartile range'.

What is its chief advantage over the simple range? Compare results for different stages.

DISCUSSION

1. Comment on the implications of any differences that emerge between the results at different stages in the experiment. In particular, note the effect of group discussions on an individual's willingness to take risks.

2. One optional feature is the use of a 'control group' in the experiment. What would be the point of this suggestion?

3. How far do individual differences in readiness to change affect the results? Are they allowed for in the design of this project?

4. To what extent does the structure of the group affect changes in norms? For instance, are there any situations, in general, where *all* norms are amenable to change?

5. In the situations dealt with here, three main types of risk are involved. How should the design of the experiment be altered, so that norms in different spheres could be investigated?

6. Give a short summary of the general implications of the results for the theories of the relative rigidity of norms.

Further Reading

METHODOLOGY

Moroney, M. J. (chap. 5, elementary discussion of dispersion)

Loveday, R. (1958) (chap. 4, basic statistical procedures in measuring dispersion)

Milgram, S. (an example of a simple experimental control procedure)

Himmelweit, H. T. *et al.* (a more sophisticated example of experimentation, both with control groups and over time)

Schofield, M. (note his whole methodology including the use of paired comparisons)

Cicourel, A. V. (chap. 7, advanced and critical discussion of experimental designs in sociology)

Greenwood, E. (the use of experiments in sociology)

NORM FORMATION AND CHANGE

Sumner, W. G. (or extracts in various Readers, or see Broom, L. and Selznick, P. (chap. 3, section 3)

Myrdal, G. (chaps. 5 and 7, critique of Sumner and re-evaluation of concept of norms)

Sherif, M. (description of early experiments and orientation of social psychologists)

Sprott, W. J. H. (1965) (chap. i, this is a particularly clear description of the emergence of norms)

Or other introductory text.

Klein, J. (1963) (the social psychology of discussion and decision)

Project 9 **The Group Leader and Patterns of Influence** The controlled experiment, rank correlation, and interpretation of correlations

OBJECTIVE

To compare two kinds of leadership (participatory and supervisory) and their effect on changing the preferences of group members.

REFERENCES

Preston, M. G. and Heintz, R. K. 'Effects of Participatory versus Supervisory Leadership on Group Judgement' in Cartwright, D. and Zander, A. *Group Dynamics*.

Selltiz, C. *et al. Research Methods in Social Relations* (chap. 4).

INTRODUCTION

Basically, in an experimental design, an 'experimental' group is exposed to the independent variable (the hypothetical cause) while a control group is not, the groups being then compared in terms of the dependent variable (the assumed effect).

The stages at which the dependent variable is measured provide the basis for the distinction between the two main types of design – 'after-only' and 'before-after'. The use of control groups can also differ within these two types.

Selltiz distinguishes six main types of experiment on this basis. Table 1 gives a simplified version of the schematic representation given in *Research Methods in Social Relations*:

1. *After-only.* Experimental and control groups are observed with respect to the dependent variable only after exposure of the experimental group to the hypothetical cause.

2. *Before-after, with a single group.* The experimental group is

assessed on some criterion/criteria before and after exposure to the hypothetical cause. Here the 'before' measurement acts as control.

3. *Before-after, with interchangeable groups.* The 'before' measurement is taken on one group of subjects and the 'after' measurement on another similar (i.e. factor-equated) group.

4. *Before-after with one control group.* This is the standard experimental design, where before and after measurements are of *both* experimental and control groups.

5. *Before-after with two control groups.* This design provides for the possible influence of the initial measurement. It enables any such influence to be measured and allowed for in the results. The second control group is not measured at the outset but only after exposure to the hypothetical cause.

6. *Before-after with three control groups.* This is a further elaboration to enable the influence of other changes not associated with the experiment to be measured. A third control group is incorporated in the design, which is neither initially measured nor exposed to the hypothetical cause. In effect this amounts to conducting the experiment twice, once using type 1 and once using type 4.

METHOD

This experiment is based on that reported by Preston and Heintz and is concerned with the 'extent to which the character of the leadership is a condition affecting the degree to which the individual will shift his preferences in the direction of the preferences of the (experimental) group of which he is a member'.

1. There follows a list of ten 'characteristics'. Working alone, each student should rank these by the extent to which he considers each is *socially restrictive* in this country. Students should produce an order in which the most socially restrictive characteristic is ranked 1, and the least is ranked 10, without consultation with other members of the class, and write on the first form provided (Appendix 5).

The first ranking will be collected by the tutor. The class should keep no record of their decisions.

2. The class will be divided into groups of four students and each instructed to elect a leader, each of whom will be given written instructions for producing group rankings of the characteristics in half an hour. A second form will be used for this. Each student should

TABLE I

Six types of experimental design

		Before measurement	Exposure	After measurement	Change due to hypothetical cause
1. After only	Experimental group		✓	x	$x - x'$
	Control group			x'	
2. Before-after with single group	Experimental group	x_1	✓	x_2	$x_2 - x_1$
3. Before-after with interchangeable groups	Experimental group		✓	x_2	$x_2 - x_1$
	Control group	x_1'	(possibly)	x_2	
4. Before-after with one control group	Experimental group	x_1	✓	x_2'	$x_2 - x_1 - (x_2' - x_1')$
	Control group	x_1'		x_2'	
5. Before-after with two control groups	Experimental group	x_1	✓	x_2'	$x_2 - x_1 - (x_2' - x_1' + x_2'' - x_1'')$
	Control group 1	x_1'		x_2'	
	Control group 2	$\dfrac{x_1 + x_1'}{2} = x_1''$		x_2''	
6. Before-after with three control groups	Experimental group	x_1	✓	x_2'	$x_2 - x_1 - [x_2' - x_1' + x_2'' - x_1'' - (x_2''' - x_1''')]$
	Control group 1	x_1'		x_2'	
	Control group 2	$\dfrac{x_1 + x_1'}{2} = x_1''$		x_2''	
	Control group 3	$\dfrac{x_1 + x_1'}{2} = x_1'''$		x_2'''	

write down his or her group's final agreed rank order and hand it in to the tutor. Again, no record should be kept by the student.

3. (Preferably after a break, or discussion on previous week's project.)

Working alone, each student should rank the ten characteristics for a third time on a third form. When this has been completed the tutor will return to each student his initial and group rankings and provide him with a copy of both types of leaders' instructions. Three rankings should be transcribed on to Table 2, as follows:

TABLE 2

Individual and group rankings

Character-istics ($n = 10$)	*Your first ranking order* $= R_1$	*Your second ranking order* R_2	*Your third ranking order* R_3	*Rank diff-erence* $R_1 - R_2$ $= D_1$		*Rank differ-ence* $R_2 - R_3$ $= D_2$		*Rank differ-ence* $R_1 - R_3$ $= D_3$	
					$D_2{}^2$		$D_2{}^2$		$D_3{}^2$
Blind									
Deaf-mute									
Feeble-minded									
Half-caste									
Heir apparent									
Illegitimate									
Jew									
Midget									
Orphan									
Trans-vestite									
Total ($= \epsilon$)									

TREATMENT OF RESULTS

1. Each student should calculate the value of Spearman's *Coefficient of Rank Correlation* for each rank difference: $R_1 - R_2$, $R_2 - R_3$ and $R_1 - R_3$. Use the formula:

$$R_{ho} = 1 - \frac{6\sum D^2}{n(n^2 - 1)}$$

to complete Table 3.

The denominator can be taken as 1000 rather than 990 for the purposes of this experiment.

$$\text{TABLE } 3$$

Student's individual values for the coefficient
of rank correlation

(correct to 2 places of decimals)

R_{ho}: $R1 - R2 =$......　　$R2 - R3 =$......　　$R1 - R3 =$......

(*Note.* Where $R_{ho} = 0$ there is no correlation, and the nearer the value approaches 1 or -1, the higher the correlation. You can check this in the formula.)

2. *Class Results*

Using the results from the experiment the tutor will collect details for Table 4, which the students should complete, for each type of leader and follower.

$$\text{TABLE } 4$$

Class values for coefficient of rank correlation

Number of students	R_{ho} $R1 - R2$	Mean R_{ho} $R1 - 2$	R_{ho} $R2 - R3$	Mean R_{ho} $R2 - R3$	R_{ho} $R1 - R3$	Mean R_{ho} $R1 - R3$
Type A leaders						
Type B leaders						
Type A followers						
Type B followers						

3. Write down the conclusions you draw from these results:
   i. Effect of individual upon group, due to type of leadership (compare values for mean R_{ho} 1–2).
   ii. Effect of group on individual (R_{ho} 2–3).
   iii. Extent to which rankings are unaltered by the intervening group experience (R_{ho} 1–3).
   iv. Do the results enable you to conclude anything about the effects due to the role of the individual in the group?
   v. Calculate the difference between R_{ho} $R1 - R3$ and R_{ho} $R2 - R3$ for each type of leader and follower.
Comment on the relative effect of the initial ranking and the group experience upon final rankings.

DISCUSSION

1. How far would (*a*) the kind of characteristics provided, (*b*) the type of person in the experiment, affect the results?

2. In the original experiment Type *A* leaders were called 'participatory' leaders, and Type *B* 'supervisory'. How far can you generalise from these results to the effect of the type of leadership on changing opinions? (See conclusions of original article.)

3. Describe the method of selection of members for different groups. Was this satisfactory for the purposes of the experiment? Suggest an alternative method.

4. Discuss the attitudes of your group towards the type of leadership imposed.

5. How far are the results of this kind of laboratory experiment relevant for the political sociologist when he considers the problem of decision-making?

Further Reading

METHODOLOGY

Loveday, R. (1958) (vol. 1, chap. 7, simple explanation of correlation by ranks; also in most other texts on statistics. See also vol. 2, chap. 12)

Madge, J. (1963) (chap. 5, section 4)

Festinger, L. & Katz, D. (chap. 4, laboratory experiments)

GROUP DYNAMICS AND THE SOCIOLOGY OF LEADERSHIP

Sprott, W. J. H. (1958) (chap. 9, general discussion on leadership in experimental groups)

Young, Kimball (1957) (chap. 10, discussion by social psychologist of dominance and leadership)

Hare, A. P. (1955) (repeat of original experiment on boy scouts)

Lewin, K. (1959) (definitive article by leading proponent of group dynamics)

Lippitt, R. O. and White, R. K. (another classic experiment using similar approach to compare autocracy and democracy)

Whyte, W. F. (study of actual leadership patterns in Italian slum gang in Chicago)

Weber, M. (1947/57) (pp. 324 ff., discussion of types of authority in sociological framework)

Barnard, C. I. (pp. 161 ff., discussion of the source of authority in organisations)

Project 10 **Moral Norms and the Legal Code** Comparison using statistical data and an elementary scaling technique

OBJECTIVE

To compare the non-institutionalised ('conduct') norms of a student with institutionalised norms as represented by the sanctions of the legal code.

REFERENCE

Sutherland, E. H. and Cressey, D. R. *Principles of Criminology* (chap. i).
 Or any similar discussion of relationship of law and morality.

INTRODUCTION

Much of modern law incorporates customs and moral norms that have come down from the past. Law does not, like custom and morality, ask what a man *should* do, but informs him what he *must* do, provided he can be made to comply. Such law must take an ever larger part in total social control as custom becomes more various and confused, and as interests diverge. When a particular moral standard is enacted into law in modern society it is not accomplished by universal affirmation but by a special interest with sufficient power to get that law passed. Particular moral standards are rarely enacted into law; more often, they are compromised by the law. (For notes on scaling techniques, see Project 12.)

METHOD

Students should work in pairs.
 1. *Scaling moral and legal evaluation of eighteen activities*
   i. Consider the list of activities on pages 63–64. Most of them are

minor breaches of the law and many might be considered to a greater or lesser extent morally wrong. After reading the whole list, working by yourself, allocate each activity a place in column 1 in the table on page 64 on the basis of how wrong you consider each act is. Do not take too long over this, but attempt to get a reasonably even distribution along the scale. (This is a simple exercise in '*direct classification*' on a graphic rating scale.)

ii. Repeat the process for column 2 without reference to your first list. But this time use the method of '*binary comparison*'. Working with your partner, present him with the series of activities in pairs asking him which he considers the more morally wrong. Perhaps the quickest method is to use eighteen slips of paper each with one action written on it. Take one and compare with the rest of the list until the extreme case is found. Then repeat. The final order of preference is established automatically according to the relative place given to each in the whole series. Each individual comparison should take less than five seconds on average. When one partner has completed column 2, reverse notes. This section will take about thirty minutes.

Note: Further details on this method and an alternative ranking procedure are described in Project 11.

List of Activities

Advertising adoption arrangements
Advertisement relating to abortion
Affixing indecent advertisements
Being client of a known prostitute
Being found drunk on highway
Common assault
Cruelty to animals
Cruelty to children
Defacing coin
Driving while disqualified
Exceeding speed limit
Infidelity to spouse
Keeping a brothel
Keeping dog without licence
Making a disturbance in church
Publicly offering obscene book for sale

Selling tobacco to young person under sixteen
Simple larceny (dealt with summarily)

iii. Most of these activities would normally be dealt with by a
magistrates' court and the most likely penalty would be a fine (in
1962, 98 per cent of offenders found guilty of non-indictable offences
were fined). Now list the actions by the amount of the maximum
fine applicable for first offence. Use the five-point scale again:

Most deviant 1 = maximum fine about £100
          2 =   ,,   ,,   ,,   £50
          3 =   ,,   ,,   ,,   £25
          4 =   ,,   ,,   ,,   £5
Least deviant 5 = £2, less, or none.

Your tutor will give you the figures from the *Tutor's Manual*. (Taken
from *Oke's Magisterial Formulist* by Wilson, J. P., Butterworth, 1963,
Supplement 1964; published annually, which is a text used by
magistrates' courts for this purpose.)
Lay out the table in this form:

Scaling moral and legal evaluation of activities

| | Your moral evaluation | | |
Five-point scale	Direct classification	Binary comparison	Legal evaluation (maximum fine)
	1	2	3
1 (most deviant)			
2			
3			
4			
5 (least deviant)			

2. *Four Actual Cases* (1965)
A number of factors normally affect both the legal punishment
inflicted and the moral view of an offence. Consider the following
press reports of actual cases[1] which resulted in a fine, and then put
down the fine you feel appropriate in each case. Then compare your
order of seriousness with that of the magistrates. (Assume first
offence.)
Case A. A fine of £x was imposed by Newbridge magistrates on

[1] Names and places have been altered.

Friday on *AB* of Charles Road, Newbridge, who admitted by letter wilfully damaging an electric light bulb to the extent of ninepence.

Police-Constable David Roberts said he saw the smashed bulb on the ground outside a telephone kiosk and after making inquiries he saw *B*, who admitted he had broken it.

B was also ordered to pay the cost of the bulb.

Max. fine £5. Your fine: £   Actual fine: £

Case B. SS, aged 31, a professor and lecturer at *P* University, Spain, of Newton Gardens, London, was fined £*x* with £5 5*s*. costs at Marlborough Street Magistrates' Court yesterday when he admitted stealing twenty-five textbooks worth £19 from a Charing Cross Road bookshop.

The court was told that the accused was seen to put twenty-two books into a holdall in an hour. Three more were found hidden on him later.

Max. fine (dealt with summarily): £100

Your fine: £   Actual fine: £

Case C. A 20-year-old hospital porter, *DNM* of Barford Avenue, Eastwick, was fined £*x* by Eastwick magistrates yesterday for insulting behaviour likely to cause a breach of the peace.

Superintendent S. Catts told the court that *M* was one of a large number of youths behaving in a manner hostile to the police in Floss Street, Eastwick, last Sunday evening.

He had attempted to incite the crowd to try to release another youth from a police van.

Max. fine: £100. Your fine: £   Actual fine: £

Case D. A fine of £*x* was imposed by Newbridge magistrates on Friday on *LD* of Avenue Road, Newbridge, who admitted making a false representation in order to obtain National Assistance.

Mr James Edwards, prosecuting, said that on May 6, *D*, who was in receipt of National Assistance, signed a declaration that only herself and two children were the members of her household.

She also declared that she had not received any other income than that provided by the Assistance Board.

Mr Edwards said *D* was given further assistance but it was subsequently found that a man named *W* was living at the same address.

After investigation, it was revealed that *D* had received an excess payment of £166 1*s*. 6*d*. from the board.

D told the court that from January of this year until her money was stopped, she had received odd amounts of money from *W*.

c

D, who said her present income was eight shillings a week family allowance, was given twenty-eight days in which to pay the fine.

Max. fine: £100. Your fine: £   Actual fine: £

3. *Four Serious Crimes*

Read the following press reports of cases.[1]

With the widow of the detective he had brutally murdered present in court, Desmond Harold *W*, 19, grinned broadly as Mr Justice Glyn-Jones donned the black cap and sentenced him to death at Stanport Assizes yesterday.

It was the last flamboyant gesture of the boastful killer who took a girl to the pictures to watch a film called 'Never Mention Murder', two hours after stabbing Detective-Sergeant George Stevens to death in the doorway of a Worslade wine shop on Aug. 20.

W, of Roberts Road, Worslade, had pleaded not guilty to capital murder.

Det.-Sgt. Stevens knew the risk he was running when he tackled *W*, a Borstal absconder. In 1961 *W* had stabbed another detective five times, and when he was convicted psychiatrists reported that he had a 'mania for knives'.

After the stabbing of his police colleague, Det.-Sgt. Stevens told a friend: 'If ever anyone comes for me with a knife, on police pay, I shall be off at 90 m.p.h.' But when the test came Stevens did not run.

He closed with the youth he knew always carried a knife, and was stabbed through the heart. Before he died he whispered the name of his killer.

W, it was said during the trial, boasted of the killing and showed friends his bloodstained knife. Seven hours after the murder he was trapped in the stalls of a Worslade cinema.

W's defence, led by Mr Martin Dawson, Q.C., did not attempt to dispute the facts of the killing. They relied on medical evidence of diminished responsibility and asked for a manslaughter verdict.

Summing-up, Mr Justice Glyn-Jones said the murder was 'cold and brutal'. He told the jury, 'We don't have trial by doctors. We have trial by judge and jury.'

The jury, which included three women, found *W* guilty of capital murder.

[1] Names and places have been altered.

Mrs Helen Stevens said after the trial: 'I felt I had to come to hear the verdict. My husband would have wanted it.'

Sentence of life imprisonment was passed by Mr Justice Melford Stevenson at Singleton Assizes yesterday on Derek *F*, aged 18, lighting engineer, of Ayres Road, Danbury, near Brayton, after he had been found guilty of murder.

He had pleaded Not Guilty to murdering Pauline *P*, aged 18, a factory worker, of Mossford, at Shelhurst, near Brayton.

Mr Donald Franklin, Q.C., for the prosecution, said that *F* picked up the girl in a car. They indulged in some petting and when she refused to allow him to go farther he strangled her.

F had said in a statement to the police that he panicked after realising the girl was dead. He rode around until he found a good place to dump the body. He added: 'I would not have done it if I had not had so much beer.' He said in evidence that he put his hand on the girl's throat but had no intention of killing her.

Dr Peter *S*, aged 41, of Langton, was found Guilty at Langton Assizes yesterday on the charge of using an instrument or other unknown means to procure the miscarriage of a schoolgirl, aged 18, on February 16. He was sentenced to twelve months' imprisonment.

He was found Not Guilty on other charges relating to a woman, aged 23, and the girl.

Asked if he had anything to say before sentence was passed, *S* said: 'I am not guilty of the crime with which I am charged.'

Mr Justice Stephenson said to him: 'I take into account the disgrace you have brought upon yourself and the profession, but this case illustrates the terrible dangers of even a professional man doing what you chose to do for, I suppose, money, in somebody else's house without all the proper accompaniments.'

A devoted father who killed his son aged 12 as he lay dying from incurable cancer was told by Mr Justice Streatfield at Shotwood Assizes yesterday: 'Without exception this is the most tragic case which has come before me.'

Andrew *G*, aged 44, assistant foreman of Ashchurch, pleaded Not Guilty to murdering his only child John on July 11, but Guilty to manslaughter on grounds of diminished responsibility. His pleas were accepted.

Placing *G* on probation for two years the Judge said to him: 'I am the last person in the world to think of punishing you for this offence, dreadful though it was.

'Your circumstances were quite intolerable and although it may be wrong ethically to take life, I can quite understand your motives in this case in that you felt positively driven to do it.

'I can quite understand, too, that you felt you did the right thing. I am perfectly certain there is not a single person in this court or outside it who will feel you are in any sense a criminal, and I feel equally certain there is forgiveness hereafter for you, just as there will be on earth.'

The Judge said a condition of the probation order was that *G* should attend a hospital for psychiatric treatment for a period not exceeding twelve months.

Mr Keith Jackson, Q.C., for the prosecution, said the boy, bed-ridden, was in constant pain and even the pressure of the bedclothes on him caused him agony. He was also partly paralysed.

G, determined to put an end to the boy's suffering, gave him sleeping-tablets and gassed him when he was asleep.

DISCUSSION

1. Discuss the factors which you considered when scaling the original activities. How consistent were your standards? Compare your scale with your partner's.

2. How far does the scale indicate your actual morality? (Refer here to your answer to Q. 26 in the Student's Personal Inventory if you have completed it.)

3. Look at *Method*, Section 2, and compare your decisions with those of the magistrates. Where is the greatest disparity? Why?

4. Do age, social class, sex of the offender, affect moral or legal evaluations?

5. In Section 3 there are some clear disparities between the legal code and moral norms. What happens when the law and morality are out of step? What is the effect of making an action, not considered wrong by an individual, illegal?

6. Could penalties be related to public attitudes to an offence? Explain.

7. What light does this throw on our definition of a person as a 'criminal' and criminal statistics in general.

Further Reading

SCALING METHOD

Selltiz, C. *et al.* (chap. 10); Young, P. V. (chap. 14); Duverger, M. (chap. 3, section 2); Edwards, A. L. (1957)

LAW AND MORALITY

Quinney, R.; Walker, N. and Argyle, M.; Home Office; Sellin, T. and Wolfgang, M. E.; Sprott, W. J. H. (1965) (chap. 6); Willett, T. C.; Walker, N.; Thornton, A. *et al.*; Levens, G. E.; Wootton, B. (1963*a*); Wootton, B. (1959); Wootton, B. (1963*b*); Wootton, B. (1965); Wakeford, J.; Wilkins, L. T. (1963); Allen, F. A.; Radzinowicz, L. and Turner, J. W. C. (part 1)

Note: Some students may be interested in visiting a court in action. Details of times and places of local sittings can be obtained from the local police station.

Project 11 **Language and Social Class** Elementary rating scales

O B J E C T I V E

To compare language patterns in the interview responses of five schoolchildren using a graphic voting scale.

M A T E R I A L S

Tape recording of five extracts from interviews with boys, arranged in pairs.

R E F E R E N C E S

Method
Selltiz, C. *et al. Research Methods in Social Relations* (chap. 10).

Sociology of language
Bernstein, B. 'Social structure, language and learning', *Educational Research* (or see other articles by Bernstein under Further Reading).

I N T R O D U C T I O N

Much of the work of Bernstein has been concerned with the distinct forms of spoken language associated with different social groups: 'linguistic differences, other than dialect, occur in the normal social environment and status groups may be distinguished by their forms of speech.' In particular, Bernstein contrasts the mode of speech of the middle class with that of the lower working class, and much of his research has been concerned with comparing the language codes of social groups at opposite extremes of the social hierarchy (see, for instance, Bernstein, 1960, under Further Reading).

First, the middle-class child shows an 'awareness of the importance of means and long term ends', and 'a discipline to orient behaviour to certain values, but with a premium on individual differentiation within them'. He is curious, oriented towards the future rather than the present, and presents a range of implicit values which are fundamental in his relationships within the educational system. On the other hand there is a pattern of difficulties for the lower working-class child. He is particularly activity-dominated, and therefore slow in learning to read and write. His verbal comprehension is too frequently limited from the start, so grammar and syntax pass him by, limiting his later grasp of new concepts and relationships. He thinks in a short time-span and has difficulty in generalising to wider contexts. He is uninterested in detail. He prefers clear-cut, concrete situations to ambiguous and formalised ones. Thus his whole social environment conditions his language and learning.

Second, his regional accent (not stressed by Bernstein) will produce difficulties in the structure of formal education. His teacher's pronunciation, his use of volume and tone, will sound stranger to him than to the middle-class child.

Third, the lower working-class child has a 'restricted' code of language, which limits him, for instance, to descriptive rather than abstract concepts. He uses an unsubtle arrangement of words, which Bernstein describes as 'public' (as distinct from 'formal') language. By this he means that the lower working-class child communicates in short phrases and unfinished sentences; his grammar is poor where middle-class 'formal' language is accurate. Conjunctions are repetitive rather than complex. Adjectives are rigid and limited rather than selected with discrimination. He formulates his statements in the form of questions ('Wouldn't it?', 'It's only natural, isn't it?') which set up a 'sympathetic circularity', where the middle-class child uses language comparatively rich in qualification. In this public language 'the personal qualification is left out of the structure of the sentence, therefore it is a language of implicit meaning'.

Thus the lower working-class child has not only to learn *what* is to be learned, but also *how* to learn, *and* a new language for the purpose. For the child brought up using formal language, education merely represents a development. For the child used to public language education involves a linguistic *change*.

In a later article Bernstein also contrasts 'elaborated' and 're-stricted' codes of language, and suggests that while the middle-class child has developed both the elaborated code (for his communication with adults) and the restricted code (for his communication with his friends), 'some sections of the working-class strata, particularly the lower working class, can be expected to be limited to a restricted code'.

In this project these hypotheses are considered against a scale of occupational status, and the material considered for other differences in content.

METHOD

1. Students should listen in silence to the extracts of interviews with *A*, *B*, *C*, *D* and *E*, who are all 12- or 13-year-old schoolboys. They will be played in pairs in the following order with short intervals when notes are to be taken:

$$AB, AC, AD, AE, BC, BD, BE, CD, CE, DE$$

Each extract is about 1 minute in length. Students should note any aspects of the material which seem relevant to Bernstein's hypothesis, giving phrases, words, construction, etc., as necessary and as far as time allows. For instance, the length and construction of sentences used, or the degree of abstraction and generalisation could be noted. Since every extract is repeated in conjunction with each other extract, this allows considerable scope for notes. These should later be used for completing Table 2.

After each pair of extracts denote the one which you consider to be from the higher occupational stratum by giving it one mark on a table as follows. (The tutor may stop the recorder after two or three pairs have been considered to check that students are recording observations correctly.)

TABLE I

Marks for judged relative status

	Marks	Total
A		
B etc.		

Make notes on language (etc.) of each interview (Table 2) as you go along.

TREATMENT OF RESULTS

1. Construct and complete Table 3.

TABLE 3

Judged[1] *ranking order*	*Registrar-General's ranking of father*	*Rank Difference (col. 1 – col. 2) = D*	*D²*
A			
B etc.			

Calculate the value of Spearman's *Coefficient of Rank Correlation* (R_{ho}) using the formula:

$$R_{ho} = 1 - \frac{6\sum D^2}{n(n^2-1)} \text{ where } n = \text{number of classes } (=5)$$

2. The tutor will put class values for R_{ho} on board. Calculate class mean value for R_{ho}.

3. (optional) *Coefficient of Consistency*

Although the nature of many rating scales and ranking methods do not make this apparent, it is possible that the judge may be inconsistent (or circular) in his judgments. (For instance he may prefer A to B, B to C, and C to A.) However, the nature of this project enables the student to check on his own consistency in ranking.

i. Record your earlier marks in this form:

TABLE 4

	(1) A	(2) B	(3) C	(4) D	(5) E	*Total of row = t*	$[t - \frac{1}{2}(n-1)]^2$
(1) A	—						
(2) B		—					
Rows (3) C			—				
(4) D				—			
(5) E					—		
Total						10	= T

[1] If two or more values are the same, give them the same ranking (e.g. 1, 2 =, 2 =, 4, 5). Providing you always made a choice during the recordings, this will have arisen because of your inconsistency in judgment. See para. 3, Coefficient of Consistency.

If the result of the comparison of A with B was that A was chosen as higher class, denote this by 1 in row (1), column (2), and 0 in row (2), column (1). However, if B were chosen, denote this by 0 in row (1), column (2), and 1 in row (2), column (1). Therefore in the completed table row (1) will represent the number of times A was chosen as higher class to B, C, D and E.

ii. Calculate totals in each row (Grand Total should be 10), and write them in the table.

iii. If $n =$ number of rows in the table, complete the next column, and calculate total $(= T)$.

iv. The maximum value of T $(= T_{max}) = (n^3 - n)/12$. In this case $T_{max} = (5^3 - 5)/12 = \frac{120}{12} = 10$.

v. The number of inconsistent judgments (d) is given by:

$$d = \frac{T_{max} - T}{2} = \frac{10 - T}{2}$$

$$\therefore \ d = \quad \text{(this should be a whole number)}.$$

vi. The Coefficient of Consistency (K) is given by:

$K = 1 - [24d/(n^3 - n)] \quad$ for n an odd number

$(Note: K = 1 - [24d/(n^3 - 4n)] \quad$ for n an even number$)$

$$\therefore K = 1 - \frac{24}{120}d$$

$$= 1 - \frac{1}{5}d$$

$$=$$

If there are *no* inconsistent judgments, $K = 1$.
If there is the *maximum* number of inconsistent judgments, $K = 0$.

DISCUSSION

1. Scales are techniques for registering differences in degree; what errors could be expected to appear in actual use? How could they be overcome?

2. On the basis of this project devise a scale which you suggest might be used for distinguishing between children of different social classes on the basis of recordings of their language.

3. When the same group of children are tested using verbal *and* non-verbal tests, how would you expect the results to differ?

4. What are the implications of the results (of this project and/or Bernstein's research) for (*a*) the sociologist concerned with social mobility, and (*b*) the educationalist.

Further Reading

METHODOLOGY

Moser, C. A. (chap. 12, part 6, general introduction to scaling methods)

Moroney, M. J. (chap. 18, discussion of the statistical basis of scaling and ranking, in particular testing consistency in ranking, pp. 342 ff.)

Young, P. V. and Schmid, C. F. (chap. 14 by Schmid on 'Scaling Techniques in Sociological Research')

Madge, J. (1963) (chap. 11, examination of scales used by Bales in his systematic observation of small group behaviour)

Veness, T. (uses of paired comparisons in investigation of work choice)

LANGUAGE AND SOCIAL CLASS

Bernstein, B. (1958)
Bernstein, B. (1960*a*)
Bernstein, B. (1965)
Opie, I. and P. (see also Bernstein's (1960*b*) review of this)

Project 12 **Urban Classification and Urban Phenomena** Hierarchical scaling methods and operational definitions

OBJECTIVE

To examine the use of an ordinal scale for urban classification and correlation with the incidence of some other suggested urban phenomena.

MATERIALS

Municipal Year Book, London (pub. annually).

REFERENCES

Rural–urban classification
Davis, K. *Human Society* (chap. 12).

Scaling methods
Moser, C. A., *Survey Methods in Social Investigation* (chap. 12).

INTRODUCTION

There is some difficulty in producing an adequate definition of 'urban'. Clearly it is usually associated with large populations living and working together in a place with a high density of population. However, there are places – such as some of the agricultural villages of India, which have high density, and others where a large population lives – which have one of these attributes but yet are not generally described as 'urban' by sociologists.

The way of life normally associated with an urbanised society, the *social* as distinct from the physical condition, is called 'urbanism'. However, urbanism is not restricted to cities, and the extent to which the urban way of life is extended to those outside the urban centres has been the subject of several sociological studies. The modern city has an influence on the way of life of the surrounding population that is probably as great as the influence it has on its own inhabitants.

The growth of cities in the modern world has been a remarkable phenomenon, and to some sociologists the city is one of man's greatest achievements. A city requires considerable technical knowledge, social organisation and considerable consensus among its inhabitants. It is a highly sophisticated kind of society which has led to both its achievements and failures, and a nostalgia for a less urbanised society has perhaps resulted in emphasis of the latter rather than the former of these.

In his classic essay, *Urbanism as a Way of Life*, Wirth was perhaps a little influenced by this nostalgia, but his thesis remains important. Cities, he suggests, are characterised by large heterogeneous populations, living at high density. This gives rise to a way of life where ideas are 'segmental'; '(a person's) dependence on others is confined to a highly fractionised aspect of the other's round of activity'. There is considerable scope for differentiation and the typical social relation is a secondary contact rather than a primary relationship. Wirth then describes the results of urban life: 'loss of a sense of participation', 'representation', 'depersonalisation', 'spectatorism', etc. Life tends to be organised around formal social controls, bureaucratised means of communication and competition. As a result the individual may feel isolated without his sentimental ties, impotent as an individual to change his way of life, and his intimate relations may suffer. The city may as a result lead to social breakdown. However, as Davis and Reissman point out, the achievements of the city are at least as great as its apparent costs.

The Registrar-General includes some figures for urban-rural analysis in the census reports published every ten years. The 1951 reports include figures based on a revised definition, where any ward or parish of which part was 'built-up land' (i.e. a density of more than ten people to the acre) was categorised as 'urban', and the population living on so-defined urbanised land as 'urbanised population'. As can be seen, about three-quarters of the population of England and Wales falls into this category.

From *General Report*, Census 1951 : From Census 1961.

Size of 'urban cluster' (population)	Total no. of population (England and Wales) (thousands)	
	1951	*1961*[1]
over 500,000	16,214	
100,000–499,999	7,791	
25,000– 99,999	4,928	
10,000– 24,999	2,172	
5,000– 9,999	383	
2,000– 4,999	32	
Non-urban cluster	12,238	
TOTAL (000's)	43,758	

Operational or 'Working' Definitions
Once a formal definition of any concept has been decided on, a way must be found of translating it into 'observables' so that research is possible. It is not possible to study 'urban' populations or 'urbanism' as such, since these constructions have no direct counterpart in observable characteristics. We must devise some operations which will produce data we can accept as *indicators* of each concept, and here considerable ingenuity may be required. Frequently an investigator may have to be content with data which constitute only a very limited reflection of the concept he has in mind, but in the early stages he may not be able to devise a more satisfactory one, and it must be remembered that, although findings may be reported in terms of abstract concepts, the relationships found are between two sets of data that are intended to represent the concepts involved.

Hierarchical scaling methods
There are four main types of scale in current use in sociology:
    i. *Ranking scales* (Moser: simple 'ordinal' scale) (see Projects 10 and 11 for examples). Each individual (or item) is ranked in order by being classified into one of a number of hierarchically arranged groups. This classification can be by direct inspection or by binary comparisons. No implication of distance between different scale positions is implied.
    ii. *Thurstone Scales* (as used for attitude measurement). A series of propositions are submitted to a subject who merely indicates whether

[1] The student should look up and compare the figures for 1961.

or not he agrees with them. The propositions are drawn up so that agreement with the first indicates the most favourable reaction, agreement with the last as the most unfavourable. (This is done by submitting a large number of propositions to a hundred or so expert judges who assess their 'favourability' by individually allotting them to one of eleven piles, and rejecting the propositions about which there is greatest disagreement, also those which are unclear or ambiguous.) The subject singles out those propositions with which he agrees and his attitude is assessed according to the median of the values on the scale of the propositions to which he has agreed. This method (sometimes called the method of 'equal-appearing intervals') has been criticised because it may not be independent of the attitudes of the judges themselves.

iii. *Lickert Scales* (as used for attitude measurement). The two main differences from the Thurstone scale introduced by Lickert are that (*a*) the initial judgments are carried out by people considered representative of the population to be studied, and (*b*) responses at both stages are in terms of one of five categories, ranging from 'strongly approve' to 'strongly disapprove'. This is used to gauge the intensity of opinion. However, the Lickert scale is clearly more relative than the previous one, being less concerned with an objective order.

iv. *Scalogram analysis* (Guttman's method), a 'hierarchical scale'. The intention here is to construct a strictly hierarchical scale – i.e. one in which *agreement with a proposition at a particular level implies agreement with propositions at an inferior level*. For instance, for a (hypothetical) scale of height the following three propositions are hierarchical: (*a*) Are you over 6 ft. tall? (*b*) Are you over 5 ft. 6 in. tall? (*c*) Are you over 5 ft. tall? The reply 'yes' to question (*a*) implies 'yes' to the other two, etc.

In practice the scalogram rarely achieves a perfect hierarchy and is usually considered valid if its reproduction coefficient is 90 per cent or more. This project attempts to apply the Guttman technique to urban phenomena.

METHOD

(For this project use any agreed definition of 'home town', but it should be a town where the student is living or has lived for some time recently.)

1. Look up the *population* of your home town (most towns are given in A.A. and R.A.C. handbooks. Alternatively, look in Census County Reports or the *Municipal Year Book*.)[1]

If you live outside a town, take the nearest city, borough, or urban district (*not* rural district) for this purpose.

Pop.:............

2. Look up the *area* of the town (city, borough or urban district). This will be found in the *Municipal Year Book*.

Area:............

3. Calculate the density of population/acre:

Density:............/acre

4. Indicate with a cross which of the following apply to your home town:

A. Own corporation bus service
B. Railway station (with passenger service)
C. A *General* Post Office (not combined with shop)
D. Branches of all five principal banks (Barclays, Midland, Lloyds, Westminster and National Provincial)
E. Symphony orchestra
F. Commercial theatre
G. Cathedral (either denomination)
H. Civil aerodrome within ten miles
I. Publishes (morning or evening) daily newspaper
J. Department store (*not* general clothing, supermarket, etc.)
K. Sports stadium (accommodating 500 or more seated spectators)
L. Public museum or art gallery
   Total Number of Items = ... (out of 12)

TREATMENT OF RESULTS

1. Complete a table of class replies for the class, putting a cross where each student has done so above and including the density of population per acre and the total of items crossed.

2. Each student (working on rough paper) should then attempt to see if it is possible to classify the items in a hierarchical order, rejecting up to seven of them if necessary, so that the final table,

---

[1] For London Boroughs answer for London as a whole.

after recording students and items is as near the following shape as possible (in this case for ten students and five items):

```
X X X X X (all items)
  X X X X
  X X X X
  X X X X
    X X X
    X X X
    X X X
      X X
        X
          (no item)
```

To some extent the process is trial and error, but it may help at the outset to collect together questions and students according to the frequency of positive response.

3. Construct your completed scalogram: 'Scalogram of Urban Phenomena'.

4. Give the items used in order of 'urbanness'.

5. Calculate the *Coefficient of Reproduction* (R) for the final scalogram where $R = 1 - E/(Q \times S)$ in which $E =$ total number of errors,[1] Q is the number of items used, and S is the number of students.

$$R = 1 - \ldots \ldots, \therefore R = \ldots \ldots$$

6. (optional). Using any technique you like, attempt to relate the scaled items to population size and density of home town for the class.

DISCUSSION

1. How could any one or any combination of several of the items used above be used as an operational definition in an investigation of the distribution of urban phenomena in Great Britain? How would this relate to the concept of urbanism as described by Wirth?

2. Take any *one* theoretical concept in this field used by Wirth or Davis and suggest a possible operational definition of it, giving the indices which might be used.

[1] Seen as gaps or extraneous crosses on the final scalogram.

3. What are your comments on the place of the scalogram in sociological research? Comment on the Coefficient of Reproduction obtained ($R = 1$ means items completely scaleable).

4. Suggest alterations to improve the list of items used. Give reasons for your suggestions.

5. Discuss the concept of an urban-rural dichotomy. Where should the line between 'urban' and 'rural' be drawn, and why?

Further Reading

SCALING METHODS (for more detailed treatment see Moser (1958) bibliography)

Duverger, M. (chap. 3, section 2, clear introduction to use of Lickert, Thurstone and Guttman scales – alternative to Moser, C. A.

Festinger, L. and Katz, D. (see in particular article by Stouffer)

Goode, W. J. and Hatt, P. K.

Selltiz, C. *et al.* (see chap. 10, placing individuals on scales)

Young, P. V. and Schmid, C. F. (see article by Schmid on scaling techniques)

Madge, J. (1963) (see chap. 9 for the use of Guttman scales by Stouffer *et al.*, and chap. 11 for the use of Lickert's scale)

OPERATIONAL DEFINITIONS

Selltiz, C. *et al.* (chap. 2, establishing working definitions)

Madge, J. (1953) (esp. chap. 3)

Young, P. V. and Schmid, C. F. (chap. 5)

URBAN CLASSIFICATION AND URBANISM

Reissman, L. (1964) (see in particular chap. 4 where the rationale of urban classification is discussed)

Wirth, L.

Milner, H.

Moser, C. A. and Scott, W. (an attempt to classify British towns – with useful appendix giving complete data – and official sources –

on all 157 towns in England and Wales with a population of 50,000 or more. Particularly relevant figures given are proportions of one-person households, of population employed in primary industries, and proportion voting at elections, and also illegitimate birth rate)

Census (1951, 1961 and following), *General Report*

Gibbs, J. P. (1961) (reader on all aspects of methods in this field. See in particular the foreword by K. Davis, and part 6, 'Rural–Urban Differences')

Schnore, L. F.; Hauser, P. M. and Schnore, L. F.; Mann, P. H. (uses some British material); Keyes, F.; Reissman, L. (1965).

Project 13 [Vacation Project] **The Structure of Social Groups** Systematic observation

OBJECTIVE

To make a qualitative comparison of two small social groups in action by passive observation.

MATERIALS

Portable tape recorder (optional) *or* closed circuit TV equipment if available.

REFERENCES

Method

Madge, J. *The Origins of Scientific Sociology* (chap. 6, full discussion of observational techniques used in *Management and the Worker, the 'Hawthorne Experiment'*; see also discussion of observational techniques used by the Lynds in *Middletown*, chap. 5).

Types of Small Groups

MacIver, R. M. and Page, C. H. *Society* (chap. 10).

INTRODUCTION

The two principal problems which concern small group sociologists are (i) the function of the primary group in formal organisations, and (ii) the internal dynamics of the primary group. The studies concerned with both these problems deal with such issues as the conditions of the development of solidarity among the members, the emergence of certain types of relations with leaders, the formation of subgroups and of cleavage within groups, the conditions of the effective incorporation of new members, and the consequences of the techniques of leadership among the rank and file (see, for instance, Project 9).

An important distinction is frequently made between the 'formal' and 'informal' *levels* of organisation. The formal organisation of an association consists of the formally recognised and established statuses of the members in accordance with the rank of the offices and other positions they occupy, together with the rules and regulations that set out the obligations, privileges and responsibilities of these positions. These statuses have differential prestige independent of their occupants. However, this independence is difficult to maintain in the dynamics of associational life. So an 'informal' organisation arises to exist alongside the formal one. This consists of roles rather than statuses, and of the patterns of dominance and submission, affection, hostility or indifference that form among the members in accordance with their personal evaluations of one another or implicit societal norms. Thus the role patterns may or may not coincide with the hierarchy of the formal organisation.

A wide variety of theoretical frameworks have been used in the study of groups. References to some of the best known works on the subject are listed below (page 88).

METHOD

1. *Preparation.* Each student should select a relevant issue and one theoretical framework within which he intends to study one aspect of the behaviour in the two social groups, for instance an aspect of leadership, informal and formal organisation, interpersonal influence, communication networks, decision-making, etc. He should then take notes on the analytic framework and methodological approach used and extract in an abbreviated form the chief characteristics of the approach.

2. *Selection of groups.* Two groups should then be selected for study in this project. Both should be small, preferably unconnected with the university or college, and hold meetings, one of which the student might be allowed to attend during the appropriate vacation. It is suggested that *one* be relatively formal in character – for instance,

suitable groups might be: parish council, club committee, local party committee, townswomen's guild, union local branch committee, boy scouts, rotary or consumer group committee, etc. The other should be *less* formal in constitution – for instance, discussion groups, coffee parties, musical group, or groups in public houses, recreational clubs, factories, old people's day centres, youth clubs, etc.

The two groups chosen should preferably be small, say 5–20 members, although in some cases much larger groups might (at the tutor's discretion) be compared, e.g. a crowd at a sports stadium with a church congregation. Also the two groups should be as far as possible similar except for the presumed level of formality of the proceedings. However, there is no need for standardisation amongst the class as a whole.

3. *Research procedure.* Each student should obtain permission to attend one meeting of each group he has selected, including permission to take notes or to record part of the proceedings. He should then take along the tape recorder or make relevant notes of all or of a section of the proceedings as required by the approach selected. The record of the proceedings can then be analysed and a report drawn up as suggested below.

Optional extension or alternative (if closed-circuit television is available)
This project can be extended by using a CCTV installation so that the class can together observe two groups for their analysis. The two meetings can either be videotaped and edited for use in the laboratory, or two groups can be invited to hold their meetings in the laboratory at suitable times for observation.

TREATMENT OF RESULTS

1. *Class discussion.* If time allows, the tutor may select several of the taped excerpts and use them to introduce a discussion of the structure of social groups and comparisons of different theoretical approaches.

2. Each student should write a short report in four parts:
   i. Theoretical framework used.
   ii. Types of groups observed (general description).
   iii. Method of observation used (including any shortcoming of this approach).
   iv. Results and conclusions.

Discussion

1. What place has systematic observation in sociological research? (Note in particular industrial sociology and anthropology.)

2. Suggest a few of the main rules for observers for the successful study of small groups at work.

3. In your case comment on the suggestion that your observation may have modified the situations being observed.

4. '. . . Observation, if it is to be at all scientific, must be guided by a working hypothesis which enables the observer to make active discriminations in the complex interplay of factors before him. Without such guidance he is likely to miss much of significance and become lost in a welter of irrelevancies.' Beveridge, quoted by Madge (see Further Reading). Comment in the light of your experience.

5. How could the values of the observer affect the results of this kind of research?

Further Reading

OBSERVATION (see also references in Project 14)

Moser, C. A. *et al.* (1958) (chap. 9 includes an introduction to the use of observation)

Festinger, L. and Katz, D. (chap. 6, discussion of the problems of objective observation)

Young, P. V. and Schmid, C. F. (chap. 9, introduction to various types of observational technique)

Madge, J. (1953) (introduction and chaps. 1 and 3, discussions of (i) objectivity, (ii) distinguishing observation from inference, and (iii) the importance, applications and difficulties of observation)

Hammond, P. E. (chap. 2, hazards of observation in practice; Blau records the research process for his study of bureaucracy)

Warner, W. L. *et al.* (the authors produced a number of studies based mainly on systematic observation of the social life of a large town)

THE ANALYSIS OF SMALL SOCIAL GROUPS

(*a*) *Introductory*

Bierstedt, R. (chaps. 8 and 9); Shils, E. in Coser, L. A. and Rosenberg, B. M.; Broom, L. and Selznick, P. (chap. 7); Sprott, W. J. H. (1958); Greer, S. A. (chap. 3); Olmstead, M. S.

(b) Some principal theoretical frameworks

Homans, G. C.; Lewin, K. (1952); Cartwright, D. and Zander, A.;
   Bales, R. F. (1950); Bavelas, A., in Cartwright, D. and Zander;
   Klein, J. (1956).

Project 14 [Vacation Project] **Total Institutions** Participant observation

OBJECTIVE

To design and carry out a small but complete research project by using participant observation to study the central features of a 'total institution', and compare them with those described by Goffman.

REFERENCES

Method

Madge, J. *Origins of Scientific Sociology* (or Whyte, W. F. *Street Corner Society*).

Wilson, B. 'Analytical Studies of Social Institutions' in Welford, A. T. (ed.), *Society: Problems and Methods of Study*.

Total Institutions

Goffman, E. *Asylums*.

INTRODUCTION

Goffman defines a total institution as a place of residence and work where a large number of like-situated individuals, cut off from the wider society for an appreciable period of time, together lead an enclosed, formally administered round of life. According to Goffman, prisons, boarding-schools, mental hospitals, convents, monasteries, ships' companies, are all examples of total institutions.

Although not all individual elements described by Goffman are exhibited by such institutions to the same degree, he suggests that some common features can be established 'with the hope of high-lighting significant differences later'. In contrast to the basic social arrangement of the rest of society in the total institution, (i) 'all aspects of life are conducted in the same place and under the same single authority'; (ii) 'each phase of the member's daily activity is carried on in the immediate company of a large batch of others, all of whom are treated alike and required to do the same thing together'; (iii) 'all phases of the day's activities are tightly scheduled, with one activity leading at a pre-arranged time into the next, the whole sequence of activities being imposed from above by a system of explicit formal rulings and a body of officials'; and (iv) 'the various enforced activities are brought together into a single rational plan purportedly to fulfil the official aims of the institution' (see *Asylums*, pp. 5–6).

These features give rise to a way of life which has 'certain similarities from one institution to another, independent of their manifest purpose'.
from one institution to another, independent of their manifest purpose'.

The type of field research technique which should be used for this study, participant observation, involves the observer being present in the social situation and becoming part of the context being observed for the purpose of the investigation. He plays a role so that his understanding of the situation can be deepened. A good description of the process is given by Whyte, Malinowski and others, and it can be seen that the approach, although invaluable for many purposes, involves a number of practical and especially methodological hazards (see Cicourel, A. V.)

METHOD

Each student should select an institution which he feels approaches Goffman's description, with a view to arranging at least a month's work as a temporarily residential member of staff or, if suitable, as an inmate. The choice of institutions is wide, but some of the following may prove particularly suitable:

Prison, borstal, detention centre

Boarding-school – independent, 'public', 'preparatory', 'approved', etc.

Mental hospital, hostel for mentally retarded, sanatorium, some hospital wards

Abbey, convent, monastery, children's home, old people's home (private or local authority)

Ship's company, army barracks, isolated large mansion's servants' quarters, holiday-camp staff.

The range of such institutions is large and the student may select any which, after consultation with his tutor, might seem to allow a student to work or participate in it for the period of the research. It should be made clear when arranging the project that the student intends to be *a full residential member* and take a full part in all the work of the institution. It will often be found, for instance, that a holiday relief is welcomed by some institutions, or that after the summer examinations in July a student can be given useful tasks in a boarding-school.

Much of the value of the project will be lost if each student does not

i. read some background material on the purpose and organisation of the type of institution and, if possible, the particular institution selected,

and, even more important,

ii. *thoroughly prepare himself as a participant observer*. The references given here should be some guide, but it is not sufficient to start reading them when he arrives on the first day. It will also be found useful to take *Asylums* (or his notes on it) and a guide to participant observation to the institution.

It will often be helpful to prepare, well in advance, a note of the main features and issues that the student expects to investigate so that, right from the start, his interpretations of his experiences are relevant.

Preliminary Notes on Procedure

1. Since the social life may be polarised between 'staff' and 'inmates', it will be extremely difficult not to become partisan.

2. The outsider may be expected to play a particular role (see Madge and Whyte), for instance expert, confidant, etc. This may be used to advantage in many cases, but care must be taken so that participation changes the situation being studied as little as possible.

3. The student may be pressed for a definition of his purpose in residing in the institution for a period. It will often be found most acceptable to attribute this to the tutor or university, etc. For example, 'We have to work at a place like this as part of the course.'

Reasons given should not be too sophisticated, and the student need not necessarily be very precise about them.

4. One of the greatest dangers of this project is 'going native' – taking over the group's way of perceiving and interpreting the environment to the detriment of the scientific objective, and thus becoming blinded to many points of sociological importance. The solution frequently used by researchers is the device of 'leaving the field' for periodic reviews of what has happened.

5. Right through the fieldwork the student should keep an accurate record in note form of as much of his observations as possible.

Quite apart from keeping a diary, day by day, he should keep small cards available for noting down key 'overheards' or situations that arise (Whyte and others have often used frequent visits to the lavatory for this purpose). One of the greatest problems to overcome is often that of the time interval between observation and recording (see Cicourel, A. V., p. 46). In some institutions, with uninhibited inmates it is sometimes possible to make use of a tape recorder, but in most cases this will prove more of a hindrance than a help *in data collection*; however, it can sometimes be used for recording the observer's description of key events.

TREATMENT OF RESULTS

A full account of the method of the research should be prepared. This should be followed by an analysis of the institution using the concepts suggested by Goffman. (A mere description of the month is to be avoided.) These concepts and generalisations should be examined in the light of the research, and the account should conclude with suggested modifications to his approach and one or two hypotheses for further research.

DISCUSSION

As far as possible the various accounts should be circulated or stored in the laboratory, and class discussion might consider the use of participant observation as a research technique, and a detailed criticism of Goffman's approach and concepts, and the scientific status of his conclusions.

Further Reading

METHODOLOGY

Whyte, W. F. (pioneering research, clearly described, on gang life in an Italian slum in U.S.A. in 1930s. Appendix gives outline of his problems as participant observer)

Schwartz, M. S. and Schwartz, C. G.

Hammond, P. E. (see in particular contributions by Dalton and by Greer)

Festinger, L. and Katz, D. (chap. 2 gives general introduction to field studies)

Malinowski, B. (pp. 1–23, discussion of participant observation in anthropological research)

Kluckhorn, F. R.

Young, P. V. and Schmid, C. F. (see chapters on methods in field investigation and studies of social institutions)

MASS OBSERVATION

War Factory: a report, or

The Pub and the People: a Work-town study (see criticism of method by Firth, R. (1939))

Cicourel, A. V. (chap. 2, evaluation of participant observation as a research technique)

Frankenberg, R. (elementary description of the technique)

Phillips, M. (discussion of participant observation in use in comparative research)

SOME STUDIES OF TOTAL INSTITUTIONS

Sykes, G. M.; Cressey, D. R.; Clemmer, D.; Mathiesen, T.; Morris, T. and Morris, P.; Dunlop, A. B. and McCabe, S.; Giallombardo, R.; Spiro, M. E. (marginal Total Institution)

There are a large number of books on public schools, convents, monasteries, borstals, etc., but few utilise a sociological perspective.

Project 15 **Investigation of Class and Kinship Patterns** The interview and interview schedule

Objective

To consider an interview schedule in use (designed as a pilot for a large-scale survey) and draw up principles for questionnaire design and interview procedure.

Materials

Two tape recordings of schedule in use.

References

Moser, C. A. *Survey Methods in Social Investigation* (chap. 11) *or*
Madge, J. *The Tools of Social Science* (chap. 4) *or*
Festinger, L. and Katz, D. *Research Methods in the Behavioral Sciences* (chap. 8).
Payne, S. L. *The Art of Asking Questions.*

Introduction

The interview, as a frequently used method of collecting data, is a particularly useful tool with which to investigate beliefs, feelings, past experiences and future intentions. The reliability and validity of the data collected depend on the design of the interview schedule (or questionnaire) and the manner of its administration.

The schedule has a dual purpose. While it is designed as a tool to collect information, it must also assist the interviewer in establishing rapport and in motivating the interviewee to respond, and so maximising the amount and quality of data collected. One of the major problems of this approach is the inability, or unwillingness, of the respondent to communicate information.

The adequacy of a research technique should be judged in terms of its *reliability* – repeated measurements should yield results which are identical, or fall within narrow and predictable limits of variability – and *validity* – measurement should be meaningfully related to specified research objectives. On these criteria the interview falls short of a really adequate research technique.

Interview techniques range from the unstructured (or 'informal') interview, where the questions asked, rather than being predetermined, evolve from the flow of conversation with the interviewee, to the highly structured questionnaire where the questions are systematically read out in order by the interviewer.[1] The form of interview employed depends on the topic of the research. Each has its own advantages and disadvantages which the student should consider. A basic contradiction probably underlies the whole procedure since the respondent generally is less concerned with the scientific interest of the data he provides than its normative significance, and his personal involvement in it.

The interview itself is a process of social interaction, and elements of systematic bias are introduced as the result of both interviewer's and interviewee's expectations and their perceptions of each other. Students should consider the methods that have been used in attempts to eliminate bias and to measure its effects.

METHOD

1. The class should examine the following interview schedule which has been designed as a pilot questionnaire in an investigation relating kinship patterns to class position and class consciousness. It contains a variety of techniques of differing quality used in a number of ways. (Students note their comments in Column 1 on the questions as they stand.)

Interview Schedule

Question to householder	Column 1 Comments on the question	Column 2 Comments on interviewer 1	Column 3 Comments on interviewer 2
1. Can you tell me who lives in this household?			
2. How long have you been here?			
3. Where were you brought up?			

[1] See Projects 16–19 for examples of different interview techniques.

4. Are your parents still alive?
5. Are you for or against living with your parents?
6. How far away do your parents live? under 5 miles; 5 to 50 miles; over 50 miles.
7. How much did you spend on presents to your relatives last Christmas?
8. To how many do you send a birthday card? (give list).
9. Is there any one of your relations whom you think has done particularly well for himself?
10. Why do you regard him as having done well for himself?
11. People often talk about there being different classes, what do you think? [Note to interviewer: follow up as necessary to discover (a) class names and boundaries; (b) distinguishing criteria; (c) own class situation; (d) differences of people above/below respondent.]
12. Is there much class distinction around here?
13. Do you agree that class should be abolished?
14. Which church do you go to?
15. Did you know that fewer and fewer people visit their relations nowadays?
16. What do you feel about people who neglect their elderly parents?
17. How much does your family earn?
18. When were you last in the local pub?
19. How much did you spend there on that occasion?
20. Who were you with on that occasion?

2. The class should listen to two examples of the schedule in use, recording or noting down comments on the interviewers' techniques in the columns provided (if necessary each interview can be played back twice).

3. Note what appear to be the main sources of bias in these interviews.

4. From your notes and the references work out the principles of good questionnaire design and check these against those listed in any books on survey methods. Summarise into not more than ten principles. (The first principle might be, for instance, 'leading questions should be avoided'.) Give the question numbers where examples of these occur in the schedule used above. Also suggest ten rules for interviewers (giving instances of good and bad technique in the interviews presented).

DISCUSSION

1. What are the major drawbacks in using the questionnaire-based interview in collecting research data?
2. Questions can range from the fully structured to the un-

structured; what are the advantages of the two extreme types of questions? In what circumstances would they be useful?

3. Under what circumstances would you allow the interviewer to prompt the interviewee? (For instance, on what subjects? Would these have to be special conditions?)

4. Suggest an alternative methodological approach for an investigation of kinship and social class.

5. Accepting that an interview of this type has to be used in this case, produce your alternative schedule using a similar number of questions and working on the principles you have arrived at above.

Further Reading

Maccoby, E. E. and Maccoby, N.

Richardson, S. A. *et al.*

Selltiz, C. *et al.* (chap. 7 and appendix C, discussion of questionnaires and interviewing procedures)

Hyman, H. H. *et al.*

Bottomore, T. B. and Rubel, M. (chap. 6, full questionnaire used by Karl Marx)

Cicourel, A. V. (chap. 3, critical examination of interview situation)

Project 16 **The Structural Isolation of the Elderly** The informal interview

OBJECTIVE

To investigate by informal interviews the kinship ties of the elderly.

MATERIALS

Portable tape-recorder (optional).

REFERENCES

Firth, R. 'Family and Kinship in Industrial Society', *Sociological Review*.

Townsend, P. *The Last Refuge*.

Townsend, P. *Family Life of Old People* (esp. chaps. 13 and 14).

INTRODUCTION

Parsons (1954*a*) suggests that in the United States with advancing age comes a structural isolation from kinship, occupational and community ties which is a greater problem than financial hardship. In fact it could be suggested that the high incidence of social pathology and disabilities of the old might be in part attributed to this structural situation.

Support, reassurance, recipient of confidences, cathartic for hostility and aggression are aspects of the code of behaviour of kin; and normally every individual has one or more kin whom he treats with particular consideration as an object of emotional interest, depending on his own needs. Firth suggests (see References) that these are the most significant roles of extra-familial kin, which he describes as the 'expressive sphere'.

Goode (1963) suggests that in modern Western society relatives are now assimilated to the status of 'ascriptive friends'; one has an obligation to be friendly to them, but they, in turn, have an obligation to reciprocate, and they may not intrude merely because they are relatives (p. 76).

In this project we shall be considering the role of the closest kinship link for the elderly person.

See Projects 15 and 17 for notes on the interview.

METHOD

1. Students, working in pairs, should arrange a visit to
   (i) a home for the aged, and
   (ii) an elderly person living at home (for instance one who visits a day centre or lives in local authority housing designed for the elderly).

It should be made clear at the outset that the purpose of the visit is an interview.

The method proposed is a guided but informal interview, which should be conducted by one of the students and recorded as far as possible by the other, using a recorder for the purpose if at all possible. A full description of this type of interview is given in most texts (e.g. Moser, Young, Madge, in Further Reading). However the basic principle is that preselected topics are covered in a systematic fashion, whilst allowing the respondent a good deal of freedom. Most of the questions are open ones, and prompting is necessary to encourage the respondent to talk freely around the topics under consideration.

In this instance it is suggested that the interview should start by attempting to draw up a genealogy (or 'family tree') for the respondent. He or she should be encouraged to participate in this as far as is practicable in the circumstances. As the interview progresses and the respondent becomes more at ease the interviewer should start to concentrate his questions on the respondent's most recent and most important kinship link. This may be someone not now alive, but should exclude his spouse. If the response at an early stage is 'I have no relatives', the interviewer should attempt to obtain details of the previous family history.

This principal kinship link is the concern of this project. Before setting out, the interviewers should consider what manifestations of the link they may attempt to investigate. Some indicators used by various research workers have been:

    obligations of all kinds
    face-to-face contacts
    wedding (etc.) invitations (sent or withheld) assistance in illness
    communications (cards, letters, telephone calls, radio requests)
    sharing holidays (day out, drive in the car)
    services (shopping, decorating, clothing)
    economic
    finding job, accommodation
    entertainment
    gifts (and other property)
    etc.

A provisional list of topics should be drawn up in advance, but the interviewer and assistant can vary this as necessary.

Also, where a recorder is used the operator should be thoroughly conversant with the controls.

2. The interview should then turn to the respondent's chief friendship, and this should be probed in the same way.

TREATMENT OF RESULTS

1. From the records of the two interviews should be abstracted the principal points made about the kinship and non-kinship links of the two respondents. These should be briefly summarised and comparisons made (i) between the two kinds of link and (ii) between the two respondents. If appropriate, this may allow you to suggest one or two hypotheses for further study.

2. (if recorded) Play back the tapes taking notes and then make a criticism of your own interviewing technique.

DISCUSSION

1. How do your findings support Parsons', Firth's and Goode's generalisations?

2. How far do *either* Firth's *or* Bott's classificatory systems seem appropriate and useful in the consideration of your respondents' extended family? (See Firth and Bott under Further Reading, and Project 33 for a summary.)

3. In the light of your experience (and that of other members of the class) on this project, suggest what research is necessary as a basis for a policy for the accommodation of the elderly.

4. What are the chief advantages of this method of interviewing *in practice*?

5. What are its chief disadvantages?

6. If a full-scale comparative survey were carried out on the lines of this project, what reservations would you have when interpreting the results?

Further Reading

METHODOLOGY

Moser, C. A. (introduction to informal interviewing technique, chap. 11, esp. para. 5)

Madge, J. (chap. 4*b* comments on informal interviews, advantages, uses and disadvantages)

Festinger, L. and Katz, D. (chap. 8, the collection of data by interviewing)

Young, P. V. and Schmid, C. F. (chap. 11, the interview, introduction to various kinds)

Hyman, H. H. *et al.*

Merton, R. K. *et al.* (development of the informal interview in depth to a more rigorous research procedure)

Madge, J. (1963) (chap. 10, analysis of Kinsey's methods, in particular non-directive interviewing and group sampling. See also chap. 6, non-directive interviewing technique in *Management and the Worker*)

Zweig, F. (any of his publications are examples of research using the informal interview, including the most recent, Zweig, F. (1965). See also reviews of his work, in particular Wilson, B. (1965)

Marriott, R.

KINSHIP AND OLD AGE

Parsons, T. (1961); Parsons, T. (1964a); Marris, P.; Sheldon, J. H.;
Tibbitts, C. and Donahue, W.; Williams, W. M.; Bott, E.;
Firth, R. (1956); Goode, W. J. (1963); Bell, N. W. and Vogel,
E. F. (see in particular Radcliffe-Brown, and Michel); Woodside,
M.; Tunstall, J. (1966).

Project 17 The Concept of Poverty
The focused interview – designing and testing a schedule

OBJECTIVE

To design and test a schedule as the basis for a focused interview intended to develop an empirically testable definition of poverty.

REFERENCES

Method
Merton, R. K. *et al. The Focused Interview* (or summaries in Madge, J. 1953 and 1963, and Selltiz, C. *et al.*).

The Concept of Poverty
Townsend, P. 'The meaning of poverty', *British Journal of Sociology*.

INTRODUCTION

Much of the earliest empirical research of a sociological nature in Britain was concerned with social conditions, and in particular poverty. In their early surveys Booth and Rowntree attempted to assess the extent of poverty in Britain, and since then there have been a variety of investigations of various kinds into this issue. One of the first aims of public policy in the late 1940s was to eliminate poverty. However, the basis for all estimates of poverty is the standard or concept of poverty used. In the early surveys the 'poverty line' was often determined by the estimated minimum weekly cost of maintenance for each size of family, in some cases (e.g. Rowntree's second survey of York) based on medical estimates of the minimum expenditure on food essential to maintain health and working capacity. (See Caradog Jones for review of early poverty surveys).

Townsend (*BJS*, 1954 below) has suggested that these standards
were too arbitrary, and that the 'necessaries' must be more liberally
defined than the mere immediate needs for food and clothing.
Poverty is a sociological as much as an economic issue. 'The main
fault in the standards used has been their lack of relation to the
budgets and customs of life of working people. . . . How those on the
borderline of poverty ought to spend their money is a very different
thing from how they do spend their money. It would be unrealistic
to expect them . . . to be skilled dieticians with marked tendencies
towards puritanism.'

More recently there has developed a common belief that poverty
has been virtually eliminated in Britain, and (though not in the
U.S.A.) it has become a less fashionable topic for social research.
However, there is some evidence (Abel-Smith and Townsend
below) that poverty may be both widespread and increasing. This
means that the concept of poverty is an important one to clarify and
define.

Townsend has in his more recent article (above) suggested that
'subsistence' and 'poverty' are relative concepts and 'can only be
defined in relation to the material and emotional resources available
at a particular time to the members either of a particular society or
different societies'. There is no list of universal absolute necessities
for life without reference to the social structure and culture of the
population under investigation. His suggestions for a new approach
are:

1. An investigation of the actual number of families which secure
a defined level of nutrition (which may or may not be 'adequate' by
the standards of the investigation).

2. Study of what budget items are in fact considered most
necessary by investigating the behaviour of households whose
income is drastically reduced by illness, or the death of the bread-
winner.

3. Following Galbraith ('People are poverty-stricken when their
income, even if adequate for survival, falls markedly behind that of
the community'), Townsend suggests that, having measured total
disposable income per head, the number of households having an
income less than 50 per cent or 66 per cent of the average might be
defined as being in poverty.

4. Also a study could be conducted of the distribution of non-
monetary resources among individuals and families – such as

educational, medical and welfare resources. For instance, staffing ratios, amenities and standards of comfort in schools and hospitals differ in different districts and areas of the country.

5. A comparative approach is necessary. The poverty line in one society would be comparative affluence in another.

Thus Townsend suggests that investigations of poverty should consider a group's *relative* deprivation of its share of the resources that are available to all.

In this project it is suggested that the interview procedure should be based on the 'focused' interview technique developed by Merton. Although this was originally invented to analyse the effects of mass communication, it can be applied to a wide range of subjects in sociological research. The approach is an attempt to make use of some of the advantages of the completely unstructured interview without some of its disadvantages. The flexibility of unstructured interviews frequently results in a lack of comparability of one interview with another. Their analysis is also more difficult and time-consuming; although the data are frequently fascinating and revealing, they often provide no sure basis for generalisation. Unstructured interviews also require highly skilled interviewers, who are able to adopt temporarily the beliefs and attitudes of the informants so as to secure the most uninhibited responses.

One innovation of the Hawthorne studies was to steer the informant on to particular topics (but not if possible away from others), so influencing the selection of areas for discussion without affecting the content of the responses. The focused interview was a further development of this approach. It has the following characteristics:

1. It takes place with people who share a particular *concrete situation*.

2. It refers to *situations which have been analysed* before the interview takes place.

3. It proceeds on the basis of an *interview 'guide'* rather than a detailed schedule.

4. It is focused on *subjective experiences* – attitudes and emotional responses which are related to the concrete situations being studied.

This means that the interviewer can begin to distinguish objective facts of the case from the subjective definitions of the situation. He can follow up the interviewee's selective perception of the situation rather than merely record it at its face value.

METHOD

Each student should prepare a short interview guide for himself on the subject of 'relative deprivation' of resources as a possible criterion for measuring poverty. Since he is concerned with investigating the meaning of poverty, he should choose issues which may lead to answers relevant to his approach. For instance, it will probably *not* be sensible to start with direct questions about income, property, expenditure, family size, etc., but these pieces of information should be volunteered during the interview when discussions are manifestly concerned with housing conditions, schools, rent increases, prices, etc. The interview guide should be made up of issues *relevant* to the concept of poverty (as the student has chosen to define it), but not include direct questions to the respondent on the subject. For instance, in suitable circumstances it is better to use a leading question, 'You probably find most of the money goes on rent?' than 'What is the rent here?'.

If necessary after consultation with his tutor each student should conduct one interview on the basis of his interview guide, and from it suggest how the concept of poverty might be further refined. (The local authority will often give a guide to where the poorest sections of the population live, so that a suitable interviewee can be selected in this area. But each student should attempt to interview someone he expects to be living on low earnings.)

TREATMENT OF RESULTS

1. Find out the present scale of Supplementary Allowances and compare this with your interviewee's income (if not receiving these allowances). If he is receiving Supplementary Allowances, how much more would he have to earn to be independent? Would this be possible?

2. Use the latest *Abstract of Statistics* or the Ministry of Labour *Gazette* (usually the February number) to find out the average weekly earnings, including overtime and before deductions, of manual workers.

(Figures for 1966 from the Ministry of Labour *Gazette*, vol. 74, no. 2, give £19 11s. 9d. for October 1965 (men over twenty-one). This issue also gives results of the 1965 *Family Expenditure Survey*.)

Is your interviewee in the bottom 10 per cent? 20 per cent?

3. Write up a short report of the interview, with quotations.

4. Summarise your conclusions on the concept of poverty, giving quotations if appropriate.

DISCUSSION

1. How far is it useful to attempt to distinguish between 'primary' poverty – where total earnings are insufficient to obtain the minimum necessaries for physical efficiency – and 'secondary' poverty where total earnings are sufficient for this but used for alternative expenditure? Illustrate your answer from your interview.

2. In his first survey of York in 1899 Rowntree drew attention to the 'poverty cycle'. Three periods of shortage were the experience of everyone in the labouring class – at birth, when he has his first children and in old age when his children have left home. From your interview, is there any evidence of a 'stage' of this kind? How could it most appropriately be alleviated?

3. Summarise the purposes of a 'pretest' of an interview schedule or guide.

4. With reference to your own experience, describe some ways in which the interviewer affects the responses in this kind of interview.

5. Suggest ways in which the deficiencies of the 'focused' interview could be minimised in practice.

Further Reading

METHODOLOGY

Madge, J. (1953) (chap. 4*b*, description of interview techniques where informant has relative freedom)

Selltiz, C. *et al.* (chap. 7, description of various kinds of interview technique)

Young, P. V. and Schmid, C. F. (chap. 11, outline of interviewing procedures)

Duverger, M. (brief and elementary introduction to various types of interview)

Madge, J. (1963) (see in particular the description of the Hawthorne interviewing programme, pp. 189 ff.)

Kahn, R. L. and Cannell, C. F.

Hyman, H. H. *et al.*
Cicourel, A. V. (chap. 3, discussion of whether interviewing produces
  valid responses)

POVERTY

Townsend, P. (1954); Wedderburn, D. C.; Abel-Smith, B. and
  Townsend, P. (most recent investigation of the extent of poverty in
  Britain); Young, M.; Brown, R. G.; Seligmann, B. B. (poverty in
  U.S.A., see particularly 'The Dimensions of Poverty'); Jones, D.
  Caradog (description of early poverty surveys up to 1940s);
  Lapping, A.; Preston, M.

Project 18 **Marriage – Women's Expectations and Reality** Recording responses to questions in an interview schedule and a consideration of sampling frames

OBJECTIVE

To conduct an interview designed to investigate some differences between expectations and realities in marriage.

MATERIALS

Lists of names and addresses of (i) engaged and (ii) married women with addresses reasonably near the university or college. These lists can be compiled by a member of the class from recent issues of the local newspaper. Total number of names required for each list $= 2x$ number of students in class as a minimum.

REFERENCE

Hyman, H. H. *et al. Interviewing in Social Research.*

INTRODUCTION

The two main problems inherent in the design of samples are (i) the need to attempt to avoid bias in the selection procedure and (ii) the desire for maximum precision with the time and resources available. Bias can arise in the interview itself, through the wording of questions, the interpretations and emphasis of the interviewer, for instance. But it can also appear as a result of the selection procedure used for obtaining interviews. In particular, bias can arise:

(i) If the sampling 'frame' which serves as a basis for selection is inadequate, incomplete or inaccurate;

(ii) If the sample is drawn by some non-random method – i.e. if the selection is consciously or unconsciously influenced by human choice (see Project 27);

(iii) If some of the sample are not contacted or refuse to answer some or all of the questions (see Project 20).

These all lead to errors which will *not* be eliminated by increasing the sample size, even in (i) and (iii) if it is a complete coverage.

The characteristics desired for an ideal sampling frame are rarely all found in conjunction: that

i. It should *exactly* cover the whole population involved.

ii. It should not involve duplication or omissions.

iii. It should be accurate and up to date, and

iv. It should be conveniently available.

Moser (see Further Reading) gives an account of the national lists available to the social scientist, in particular the rating records (for a list of dwelling units) and the register of electors (for a list of adults). However, neither of these approaches the ideal.

Reliability of the results is also dependent on the interviewer. Apart from the actual questions on the schedule, the respondent will be influenced to a greater or less extent by every word or phrase used in the interview, every intonation and implication in the conversation, the speed at which it is conducted, for whom it is claimed the information is required, and the dress, age, sex, speech and manner of the interviewer. Thus it is vital to attempt as far as possible to minimise, standardise or measure the more important of these influences. There is a large variety of ways of attempting this, from giving the interviewer great freedom to probe and check himself, to a rigorously controlled situation, where as many factors are controlled as possible.

In this project we consider an area which is of some emotional concern to the interviewees; so some of these influences should be apparent. The questionnaire is *not* perfect, and questions of varying quality are included. However, it may be taken as a pilot questionnaire in an investigation of women's ideology of marriage in modern society.

METHOD

The students are provided with two lists of names and addresses. List 1 gives details of each woman whose engagement has recently been announced in the local press;[1] list 2 gives the same details for some recently married women (probably drawn from press reports of recent weddings). Students should be allocated three, or preferably four, interviewees who live in the same district (to minimise travelling time and time spent on re-calls).

The class should then have a preliminary discussion of:

1. *The sampling frame* and its limitations, with a report by the student(s) who drew the sample on the methods used (etc.). What kind of people will be under- or over-represented?

2. *The questionnaire* (Appendix 6). Minor changes may be suggested and made at this stage, but they must be made by the whole class.

3. *The approach and conduct of the interviewer.* (The interviewer may have to explain the basis of the sample and assure the interviewee that no names are recorded or used.)

During the next few days each student should attempt to contact and interview *two* from his list (note any bias resulting from this approach) using the appropriate schedule. The actual interview need not take more than ten minutes. If none of the women on the list is available for interview, the student should attempt to interview the fiancé or husband. If this fails, a substitute may be selected within the university or college.

After the interviews the interviewer should write out the answers on the schedule, which should be handed to one member of the class for analysis.

Before being filed in the laboratory library, their final report on the results should be circulated the following week and provide the basis for later class discussion and conclusions on the project.

TREATMENT OF RESULTS

1. The student(s) who are selected to write the report should do so on these lines (see Moser, chap. 15, for comments on presentation):

General Description of the Survey
   i. Purpose.
   ii. Sampling or selection method employed, noting omissions, etc.
   iii. Date and duration.
   iv. Number of interviewers and size of resulting sample (draw up a table relating successful interviews to whole sample).

---

[1] Or posted at the local register office.

General Outline of Results
The commentary should start with profiles of the two sets of interviewees, giving age distribution, social backgrounds, etc. (Are they significantly different?) It should then continue with a report of the results in a logical order (rather than the order in the questionnaire), noting in particular the largest differences that appear between the two groups. No *explanation* of individual results should be given at this stage.

The outline should end with a general comment on the frame, schedule and method of the survey, and suggest improvements.

2. When the report has been circulated, each student should comment on (*a*) methodological aspects of the project as a whole, and (*b*) its sociological implications (e.g. change in role expectations?).

DISCUSSION

1. Comment on the sample size, the sampling frame and the method of selecting those to be interviewed (see Moser, C. A., chaps. 7, 13).

2. What influence does the omission of those not contacted and those who refuse to be interviewed have on the final results?

3. Suggest some *Instructions for Interviewers* which would in this case have increased the reliability of the results.

4. List your criticisms of this approach to the research problem. Suggest an alternative approach. Would you consider a *panel* of engaged women re-interviewed after marriage a better method? What disadvantages would this have in practice?

5. Select two or three questions used, and make constructive criticisms of them, suggesting alternatives.

Further Reading

METHODOLOGY

Madge, J. (1953) (chap. 4, brief review of various types of interviewing procedures)

Moser, C. A. (chaps. 7 and 13, full discussion of sampling frames, non-response and response errors)

Cicourel, A. V. (chap. 3, discussion of the presuppositions and uses of various forms of interview and the reliability of different approaches)

Festinger, L. and Katz, D. (chap. 1, the sample survey)

MARRIAGE AND WOMEN'S ROLE

Friedan, Betty (popular exposition of the conflicts between women's roles in Western society)

Klein, V. (esp. chap. 1, general introduction to the topic of industrialisation and the changing role of women)

Myrdal, A. and Klein, V. (classic work on women and work outside the home)

Hubback, J. (study of over 1000 graduate women, using mail questionnaires)

Mayer, J. E.

Joseph, J.

Komarovsky, M. (1946)

Burgess, E. W. and Wallin, P. (study of 1000 engaged couples, followed up after marriage; an attempt to predict marital success)

Gouron, H.

Project 19 Long-term Departmental Research Project A sample survey (or alternatively a field study); experiment in time

OBJECTIVE
To participate in a full-scale research project.

REFERENCES
Campbell, A. A. and Katona, A. 'The Sample Survey', Katz, D. 'Field Studies', and French, J. R. P. 'Experiments in Field Settings', in Festinger, L. and Katz, D. *Research Methods in the Behavioral Sciences.*

Madge, J. *The Tools of Social Science* (chap. 5, part 4 – the experiment in time).

or as appropriate to the particular research chosen (see Further Reading).

INTRODUCTION
Three principal types of design are involved in the study of change. In the first, the *trend study*, the investigator follows up a small number of variables through time and interprets their relationships. In the second, *the panel study*, repeated interviews with the same respondents are used to reveal factors which make for observed changes. This approach increases the number of interrelations which can be investigated, but is limited by the mortality of the sample and possible changes induced by repeated interviews. The third type of design is the *prediction study*, where either the subject's own intentions or certain of his characteristics are used to test relevant hypotheses. (Examples of all these can be found in Lazarsfeld and Rosenberg, see Further Reading.)

Field studies in general can be distinguished from surveys by the fact that they are primarily concerned with depth rather than representativeness, and focus on the group or community rather than on a set or sample (which may only in the final outcome produce facts about interrelations in the structure). The field study either attempts observations of social interaction or reciprocal perceptions of people playing independent roles. However, the two approaches are not alternatives and much research attempts to include aspects of each.

If the research is to last over several years, there will probably be an initial 'pilot' or 'scouting' phase when the instruments are tested and the fieldworkers attempt to get a thorough understanding of the important aspects of the field. It is particularly important that a wide view is taken at this stage so that the focus chosen for the main investigation is significant and realistic.

The subject of the research programme will be selected by the tutor, but the class will participate in all aspects of the investigation, including the preparation of reports at each stage and a final analysis of the whole project.

METHOD

Each class of students will take part in one year of a long-term project. They will participate in the initial planning phase, testing of questionnaires, collection of data, analysis and writing the report. One or two possibly more experienced students may be appointed student directors of the project for the period and they will be responsible for co-ordination and the day-to-day organisation of the research. The subject will normally lie within the interests of the tutor and be compatible with the resources of the Department, but it is suggested that the dynamic aspect of sociological analysis be emphasised in the topic chosen. The following subjects could provide suitable areas for initial consideration:

1. The influence of changes in the educational system locally.
2. The influence of local housing, welfare, police (etc.) policy.
3. Changing *mores* of schoolchildren (students), mothers, etc.
4. The influence of any local social or economic change in the vicinity – a new road, bypass, industry, university, theatre, housing scheme, etc.
5. The changing nature of a neighbourhood – especially where rehousing, immigration, high crime rate, etc., are evident.

6. Adaptation to marriage, birth of first child, widowhood, divorce, retirement, etc.

7. Changing aspects of stratification, power structures, religious belief, etc.

Local authorities are generally helpful and will often co-operate closely with research of this type – especially where the 'applied' aspects are obvious.

TREATMENT OF RESULTS

At the conclusion of each stage the student directors should produce an interim report on the significant results at this point and an analysis of all results so far produced. They should include all methodological decisions made and make recommendations for the next stage. These reports and all data collected will be stored in the laboratory.

DISCUSSION

A full class discussion, led by the student directors, should be held at the conclusion of each stage to discuss fieldwork techniques and results.

Further Reading

SAMPLE SURVEYS, FIELD STUDIES AND EXPERIMENTS IN TIME

(More specific references should be used as relevant to the topic selected)

Lazarsfeld, P. F. and Rosenberg, M. (section 3, 'The Analysis of Change through Time')

Mannheim, H. and Wilkins, L. T. (see discussion of prediction studies in criminology)

Stephan, F. J. and McCarthy, P. J. (the design of *all* types of sample survey)

Moser, C. A.; Young, P. V. and Schmid, C. F.; Selltiz, C. *et al.*

Project 20 **Concepts and Indices**
The self-administered and mail questionnaire; precoded questions; response and non-response

OBJECTIVE

To complete a self-administered questionnaire and consider the objective indicators used in a mailed survey.

REFERENCES

Concepts and Indices
Lazarsfeld, P. F. and Rosenberg, M. *The Language of Social Research* (part 1).
(Operational Definition) Madge, J. *The Tools of Social Science* (chap. 1, section 3).

Design of Mail Questionnaires and precoded questions
Moser, C. A. *Survey Methods in Social Investigation* (chaps. 10 and 12).

INTRODUCTION

The theoretical concepts of sociology vary greatly in the precision with which they can be defined for the purpose of empirical investigation.

'A group remains a tenuous concept. A crowd, though recognisable, has indistinct edges. A society, when formal, can be defined as exactly, though as arbitrarily, as the city of Manchester. A household is definable, and a family less so. A married couple can be defined almost as rigidly as a man or a woman separately. . . .' (see Madge, in References).

The attributes and qualities of populations are not things-in-themselves; they come to life only in concrete instances. Thus the scales and categories used in an empirical investigation are only indicators of the properties under consideration, much as the thermometer *indicates* temperature. In this instance the fixed-choice questionnaire items are intended to indicate (or operate as 'operational definitions' of) sociological concepts. They do not replace them. (See also Projects 12 and 28.)

Fixed choice questions preclude the possibility of obtaining unanticipated definitions of the situation which might reveal a respondent's private thoughts and feelings. However, when the issues have been thoroughly analysed beforehand or where factual or merely classificatory data are required, they have considerable advantages – not least being that the characteristics of the population under consideration can be accurately compared with those of other groups, census returns, etc. (Note that 'factual' here refers to the type of information sought rather than the accuracy of the answers.)

METHOD

1. The Student's Personal Inventory (S.P.I. Appendix 7) should be completed by each student, if this has not already been done earlier in the year. (Some of the data in this are used in other projects.)

While completing it, each student should make comments on the form of the questions, criticise them and suggest alternatives as appropriate. It can be assumed at this stage that each question can be taken at its face value – no hidden inferences are intended.

2. Appendix 8 is the questionnaire – Improvements in the Social Services – used in 1966 in the City of Exeter in an experimental survey for the Sociological Laboratory Class at the University. After a pretest it was delivered by hand to a sample of 1,000 householders chosen by selecting at random dwellings in forty streets, which were themselves taken at random from the street directory. (Copies of some of the returns are included as Appendix 10.)

Each student should consider the original form and the returns and criticise the questions as with the S.P.I. (The items in Qs. 7 and 8 were selected with another project in mind (No. 25).)

3. (optional) Each student should select a research report which gives a full account of the survey methods and which used a self-administered or mail questionnaire, and write in note form a short critique of the questions used.

4. (optional) The class may revise and distribute the Social Services questionnaire, and use the returns for comparison in later projects – in particular Projects 28, 30 and 31, where 100 or more returns are needed. However, it is suggested that no revisions be made to Qs. 10 to 21 inclusive, as these are used in later projects. Further questions may be added.

Note: Students may collect and store a number of mailed questionnaires for this project or the laboratory library. Examples of research reports published which can be used are:

Gorer, G. *Exploring English Character.*
P.E.P. 'Graduate Wives', *Planning.*
New Society, 'What Sort of People', vol. 1, no. 25, March 1963. (Results, vol. 1, nos. 32 and 33, May 1963).
New Society, Survey of Readership, vol. 5, June 1964.
Research Services Ltd., *Britain Today, a study of the opinions of people listed in 'Who's Who'*, London: Research Services Ltd., 1963.
Greve, J., *People and their Houses*, J. S. Fry Ltd., Publication Dept., Bournville.
Report of the Committee on University Teaching Methods (Hale Committee).

TREATMENT OF RESULTS AND DISCUSSION
Each student should attempt to answer the following questions with reference to his comments above.
  1. *Mail Questionnaires*
      i. What are the merits of mail questionnaires?
     ii. What are their disadvantages? Why are they little used in sociology?
    iii. How can the drawbacks be minimised?
     iv. Describe what is meant by 'the problem of non-response' (e.g. in the Exeter Social Services Survey 12 per cent responded). What kind of people do you think will respond?
      v. How, in practice, can the response rate be increased?
  2. *Self-administered Questionnaire*
      i. Has this in practice an advantage over the mail question-naire? For what kinds of issues or respondents?
     ii. How can the results be validated?

3. *Precoded Questions*

By referring to the examples under consideration write a paragraph assessing the utility of precoded and fixed-choice questions. Give instances where these are suitable or unsuitable.

4. *a.* Select one of the concepts you feel is important in one of the questionnaires (e.g. class, educational experience, deviance, social mobility, etc.), and consider how effective is the index (or indices) which is used.

b. Suggest and justify an alternative, and in your view superior, index which could have been used.

Further Reading

CONCEPTS, INDICES AND THE OPERATIONAL DEFINITION

Selltiz, C. *et al.* (chap. 2, defining concepts and establishing working definitions as part of the formulation of the research problem)

FIXED CHOICE AND PRECODED QUESTIONS

Cicourel, A. V. (chap. 4, consideration of the role of fixed-choice questionnaires in sociological research)

Hyman, H. H.

THE SELF-ADMINISTERED MAIL QUESTIONNAIRE

Duverger, M. (chap. 2, section 2, brief introduction to the use of mail questionnaires)

Madge, J. (1963) (chap. 9, review of the methodology of *Studies in Social Psychology in World War II* (Stouffer *et al.*) in which the primary research tool was a self-administered questionnaire)

RESPONSE AND NON-RESPONSE

Madge, J. (1953) (chap. 4c, part 1, introduction to the problem of non-response in all types of survey)

Moser, C. A. (chap. 7, part 4, full account of the problem of non-response and suggested techniques for dealing with it)

Larson, R. F. and Catton, W. R. (see References)

Project 21 **Potential and Exercised Power** Power structure analysis

OBJECTIVE

To compare some alternative methods of identifying community or organisational power structures.

REFERENCES

Form, W. H. and Miller, D. C. *Industry, Labour and Community* (esp. pp. 517–33).
Presthus, R., *Men at the Top* (esp. chaps. 2 and 12).

INTRODUCTION

There have been three principal methods of measuring community or organisational power in sociological studies, and most discussions of power structures rely implicitly or explicity on the basic assumptions of at least one of them.

Firstly there have been attempts to identify individuals who have a *potential* for power because of their status or position in the formal structure (see for instance C. Wright Mills in *The Power Élite* or Lupton, T. and Wilson, B. R. *Manchester School, 1960*; also in Sampson, A. *Anatomy of Britain* (chap. 1)).

Next there is the approach which is mainly concerned with the individuals who have the *reputation* for having power and influence. In particular there is the influential study by Floyd Hunter of Atlanta, where a panel of heads of community organisations was asked to nominate leaders who then ranked each other. Using sociometric analysis Hunter showed that the top forty 'influentials' tended to interlock socially and culturally.

Finally, in the *decisional method* the roles played by different individuals and organisations in selected decisions can be used as the basis for identifying power (see Dahl, R. A. *Who governs? Democracy and Power in an American City*, or Banfield, C. *Political Influence*). Presthus in *Men at the Top* attempted to combine and compare the second and third methods.

In this project the student should use two, or if possible all three, of these methods in his analysis; however, there is no need to replicate the *exact* methodology here presented. The appraoch may be adapted to suit the circumstances.

METHOD

It is recommended that this project be undertaken within the university or college and that students work in pairs; however, in some cases it may be possible to consider a nearby community or an organisation such as trade union or local society. Each pair of students should select for analysis an organisation or interest group within the college. Probably the most suitable are hostels, halls, or other units of residence. But in many cases the students' union executive or one of its committees may provide suitable material (for instance Rag Committee, disciplinary committees, student newspaper staff, etc.). Otherwise any athletic or interest society will probably provide an appropriate subject. Considerable time and effort will be saved if the researchers are past participants or members of the group under investigation.

Potential Power

By considering the formal and informal structure of the group (or that part of it under investigation) a diagram should be drawn to show the distribution of power within it. Data can be obtained by a consideration of the constitution and precedents, and the formal and informal roles of the participants in this and other relevant organisations. For instance, one might have power within the group because of his status in another group.

Reputational Power

The 'reputational' question used by Hunter, Presthus and others was:
'Suppose a major project were before the community, one that required decision by a group of leaders whom nearly everyone

would accept. Which persons would you choose to make up this group – regardless of whether or not you know them personally ?'

A question should be devised on this basis to identify those reputed to be in positions of influence.

Exercised Power

To measure overt power the sociologist selects a number of important decisions and considers active participation in one or more of these as the basic criterion of individual power. Here the student should select *one* salient decision recently made by or on behalf of the group and record those who participated.

Notes: a. Criteria of importance could be the sum of money involved, the number of people affected or the nature of the issue; (for instance, a dramatic society's choice of play for performance, the disciplinary committee's decision on an incident, the changes in time of Hall dinner, etc.).

b. A decision is normally composed of a number of stages, some of which are more crucial than others. It will normally be best to take the *initiation* of the decision rather than the implementation.

c. If in doubt as to whether a person is an active participant in the decision, those more clearly participants should be asked for their opinion.

RESULTS

1. Give a clear title and description of your method of analysis, noting its strengths and deficiencies.

2. Indicate briefly your results and conclusions.

DISCUSSION

1. Compare the three methods of power structure analysis, and assess their utility in this kind of investigation.

2. How far are potential, reputational and exercised power associated in this instance?

3. Note the initial premises of the three approaches. For instance, what is the effect (in the reputational approach) of defining power as being structured?

4. Is there any evidence of a 'pressure group' or 'veto group' within the group studied? (See D. Riesman.)

5. Merton has distinguished between 'monomorphic influentials' (with power in a narrowly defined area) and 'polymorphic influentials' (who exert influence in several unrelated spheres). How far would you consider this a useful distinction in the group you have studied?

6. Compare the method you feel might be most appropriate for studying the power élite in a local community with that in mass society.

Further Reading

METHODOLOGY

Hunter, F.; Schulze, R. O. and Blumberg, L. U.; D'Antonio, W. V. and Erickson, E. C.

SOCIOLOGY AND POWER

Merton, R. K. (esp. chap. 10, 'Patterns of Influence')

Katz, E. and Lazarsfeld, P. F. (one of the most comprehensive studies of unitary and diverse influence)

Sampson, A. (esp. chap. 1, journalistic account of aristocracy's potential power in Britain)

Florence, P. S. (esp. chap. 5, power structure and ownership in joint-stock companies)

Lipset, S. M. *et al.* (note in particular theoretical orientation of this study)

Miller, D.; Hanson, R. C. *et al.*; Walton, J.; Riesman, D. *et al.* (chap. 10)

Project 22 **The Structure of Group Relationships** Sociometric techniques and the sociogram

OBJECTIVE

To examine some group relationships by using a simple version of the sociometric test.

REFERENCES

Lindzey, G. and Borgatta, E. F. 'Sociometric Measurement' in
   Lindzey, G. *Handbook of Social Psychology, or*
Proctor, C. H. and Loomis, C. P. 'Analysis of Sociometric Data', in
   Jahoda, M. *et al. Research Methods in Social Relations, or*
(rather brief) Selltiz, C. *et al. Research Methods in Social Relations.*

INTRODUCTION

Sociometry is the method of detailed and objective analysis of social groupings, was originated by J. L. Moreno and is concerned with the social interactions or lack of interactions among any group of people. The interaction that is investigated may be behavioural, or it may be desired or anticipated or fantasied. The content or type of such interaction may involve any one of a variety of activities – sitting next to, eating with, lending to, sharing with, having as a friend, etc. The methods of recording the interactions are equally varied – observation, records or questionnaires, for instance. Essentially sociometry is more a focus on a distinct type of subject matter, and a particular systematic method of analysis, than a data collection procedure.

Sociometric questionnaires are relatively easy to administer and are adaptable to a variety of situations. The simplicity of the method and the graphic qualities of the sociogram have led to its wide popularity as a research technique. Sociometric studies have been made of entire communities, fraternities, schools, camps and factories. They have been concerned with diverse issues such as leadership, morale, social adjustment, race relations, political cleavages and political opinion polling.

Moreno first applied his methods to groupings in an American 'public' school, and later in a (now classic) study of the Hudson State Training School for Girls. This institution is a closed residential institution of 500 girls living in 16 'cottages'. Each girl was asked to list the five girls she would most like to have as a housemate, work companion and table mate, and the five girls she would least like to have in these relationships.

Sociometric studies indicate that in most situations certain individuals are chosen for all activities and others only for specific activities. In the Hudson study Moreno distinguished five types of sociological nuclei:

1. Mutual first choice of two or more individuals among themselves, e.g. the 'mutual pair'.

2. Patterns represented by chains of a non-mutual character (A chooses B, B chooses C, etc.).

3. A clustering of a large number of choices around a single individual, the 'star'.

4. The powerful as distinct from the popular individual. For instance, Moreno cites one case, herself chosen by only four individuals, all of whose attraction she reciprocates. But these four are in turn chosen by nearly one hundred individuals.

5. The isolated individual chosen by nobody, although she may choose some other persons.

Moreno found that his analysis enabled him to explain events which occurred such as runaways, and reorganised the groups to relieve tensions.

Symbols:

Individual chosen	Individual rejected
o◄———————	o◄ — — — — — —
Individual choosing	Individual rejecting
o————————►	o — — — — — ►
Mutual Choice	Mutual rejection
o———|———o	o — — —|— — —o

METHOD

1. *Class Sociogram*

Each student is given a blank piece of paper on which he indicates his sociometric choice (positive and negative) as follows:

You are asked to decide on a partner for a research project in the coming vacation. Give the name of the person you would *most* like and the one you would *least* like to be your partner on this occasion.

The tutor will allocate a number to each student, collect the choices and put the results on the black-board in the form of an elementary matrix, which should be copied on to a table, using Subject of Choice as the horizontal axis and Object of Choice as the vertical axis and maintaining each student's anonymity.

Each student should then draw a sociogram of the class on the basis of this criterion.

2. (optional) After discussion of possible alternative criteria, the class may conduct further experiments and draw further sociograms using different criteria.

3. (optional) Each student should then conduct his own trial sociometric test on some group in the college. Although a variety of groups could be studied, it is suggested that the most rewarding would be a study of part of a hostel, hall of residence or other residential unit. The group chosen should preferably consist of between five and twenty individuals – for instance a 'wing' or 'stair-case' in a hall of residence. However, in suitable cases a study can be made of a work group or interest group in a factory, etc. The tutor should be consulted before the final choice is made.

Each student should decide on his own criterion – asking for past behaviour, present feelings or future intentions, etc.

TREATMENT OF RESULTS

A sociogram should be drawn to indicate the structure of relationships in the group chosen.

DISCUSSION

1. Give your conclusions on the results of the Class Sociograms, giving your criticisms of the criteria used.

2. It has been suggested that in residential institutions isolates are necessarily 'maladjusted'; comment on this.

3. Comment on the use of hypothetical questions in sociometry. How could they be avoided in this case?

4. What are the main limitations of sociograms in sociological research?

5. Suggest how a research project might be designed for *one* specific purpose in your college – for instance in room allocation or work groups, seminars, tutorials, etc.

Further Reading

Moreno, J. L. (1953) (the classic introduction to sociometry by its originator. See pp. 92 ff. in particular.)

Moreno, J. L. (1951) (collection of Moreno's further articles on sociometry)

Fleming, C. M. (ed.) (see description of sociometry in use and history of the development of this approach in the U.S.A.)

Any of the following works will give a good indication of how sociometric methods may be used in education:

Jennings, H. H. (1948) *or*

Northway, M. L. and Lindsay, Weld *or*

Smith, W. D. *or*

Horace Mann-Lincoln Institute of School Experimentation

The large variety of studies using sociometric tests is evident from the journal *Sociometry* in which the student will find reports of a large number of research projects. Some of the best known studies using the sociometric technique are the following:

Lundberg, G. A. and Lawsing, M.; Goodacre, D. M.; Taba, H. and Elkins, D. (school); Jennings, H. H. (1950) (leadership, training school, etc.); Festinger, L. *et al.* (1950) (college housing scheme); Criswell, J. H. (1937) and (1939) (formation of racial groups)

Young, P. V. and Schmid, C. F. (chap. 14, this and most other introductory texts give general description of sociometry)

Sorokin, P. A. (this is one of several critiques of sociometry)

Project 23 **Political Commitment**
The use of indirect techniques; introduction to tests of significance

OBJECTIVE

To investigate political attitudes using indirect testing methods.

MATERIALS

Tape-recording of by-election result; slide rule.

REFERENCES

Method
Selltiz, C. *et al. Research Methods in Social Relations* (chap. 8 – 'Data Collection: Projective and other indirect methods')

Political Commitment (see Further Reading below).

INTRODUCTION

Methods of investigation which depend on the respondent's own report of his behaviour, feelings and beliefs presuppose that he is willing and qualified to give such information about himself. But people are often unwilling to discuss certain topics, especially where they have a significant evaluative content. And in any case they may not be *aware* of their real feelings or have made convenient rationalisations.

In an attempt to overcome these limitations, a wide variety of strategies and techniques are used that are expected to be independent (to a greater or lesser extent) of the subject's self-insight and of his willingness to express his views explicitly.

E   W.S.I.

Selltiz *et al.* distinguish between two broad classes of technique: the less structured or 'projective' techniques, and the more structured or 'disguised' methods.

Projective Methods

These use stimuli which are capable of arousing a wide variety of reaction. There are no 'correct' or 'incorrect' answers. The individual is therefore asked to describe the material, give meaning to it or organise and manipulate it. The ostensible subject matter is the ink blot, picture, etc., but the results of his interpretations are expected to reveal something of the individual's own experiences or feelings. The most frequently used techniques are the Rorschach (Ink Blot) Test and the Thematic Apperception (Picture) Test, but others involve word association, sentence completion, doll play and figure drawing. A verbal technique now used widely in market research is that of asking the respondent to describe the kind of person who would behave in a specified way – own or buy certain commodities, for instance.

One example of a pictorial technique was used by Fromme (see Further Reading) who presented subjects with political cartoons, each with a number of alternative captions, and requested the subjects to choose one that 'best' fitted the cartoon.

Structural Disguised Methods

Many of these projective methods are difficult to administer, tedious to score and (see Sorokin) provide results which are open to a number of interpretations. (Several structured disguised tests have been devised to minimise these difficulties.) The assumption of these tests is that a person's attitudes are likely to influence his perceptions, beliefs, judgments and memory. Early examples of attempts of this kind will be seen in the work of Bartlett and Newcomb. The basic rationale is similar to that of projective techniques: 'When there is no clear, objectively verifiable basis for choosing alternative responses to a situation, an individual's response tends to reflect his predispositions' (Selltiz, p. 301).

A wide range of techniques of this kind has been used, some based on differences in knowledge, reasoning or perception, memory and judgment. However, the great majority have dealt with racial or ethnic prejudice, and in this project the class will attempt to test an experimental technique for investigating political commitment.

METHOD

(If time allows, and students have not already done so, they should complete the Student's Personal Inventory – Appendix 7 – at the beginning of the period.)

At the beginning of the class period a recording will be played of a news item which gives the results of a by-election.[1] Students should listen to this in silence without taking notes. (If possible, this is ideally carried out in some arrangement of soundproof booths, as in a language laboratory, or in different rooms to avoid audience effects.)

After an interval all students will be asked to answer some questions read out by the tutor. The answers should be written down leaving a column on the right-hand side of the page for scoring.

The answers for Qs. 1–9 should then be corrected, and wholly correct answers marked with a tick in the right-hand column.

Q. 12 / Q. 13 (a) / Q. 13 (b) / Q. 14. Check these for number of correct items recalled, and put score in right-hand column.

Each student should, preferably by reference to his answer on the S.P.I. (Appendix 7), write down his political preference.

TREATMENT OF RESULTS

1. Class results should be collected and each question should be recorded in tabular form thus:

	Number	
Q. . . .	*Correct*	*Incorrect*
Allegiance of students		
Conservative		
Labour		
Liberal		
Other		
TOTAL		

(These questions cover a wide range so that they will be suitable for different sizes and compositions of classes. Tables can be rejected or collapsed to suit the particular situation.)

2. Class discussion should then concentrate on deciding which questions successfully demonstrate political commitment in this instance, and *one* of these chosen for further treatment.

[1] The item and the questions are printed in the *Tutor's Manual*.

3. *The 2 × 2 Contingency Table.* The question agreed on should be collapsed to give only two rows (e.g. 'Conservative' and 'non-Conservative') and two columns (e.g. '2 items or less' and '3 items or more'), so that the chosen difference is highlighted.

Give title:............................

TABLE 1				TABLE 2			A
Observed frequencies	(x)	(non-x)	Total	Expected frequencies	(x)	(non-x)	Total
(y)				(y)	c	d	Total y =
(non-y)				(non-y)			
TOTAL				B TOTAL	TOTAL		G.T.

The question now to be considered is whether there is an association between the two variables or are they independent? Or, one might ask, is remembering (or perception of, etc.) these items associated with political commitment as stated in S.P.I.?

To complete Table 2: Fill in the total column A and total row B. Then, assuming that the variables are completely independent, complete the table of 'expected' frequencies.

Start by calculating the number for box *c*. This can be calculated, since, assuming that the variables are independent, one would expect box *c* to contain the same proportion of *x* as appears in the total *x* and non-*x*; i.e.

$$\text{box } c = \frac{\text{Total } y}{\text{Grand Total (G.T.)}} \times \text{Total } x$$

Each other box can be calculated in the same way, or alternatively by subtraction. For instance:

$$\text{box } d = \text{Total } y \text{ } minus \text{ box } c$$

The principle is now that the greater the difference between the figures in the boxes in Table 1 from those in Table 2, the more significant is the association between *x* and *y*. (Or, alternatively, the nearer the tables are to being identical, the *less* association there is between *x* and *y*.)

However, small differences could have occurred by chance. So we use a method of deciding whether the observed frequencies differ significantly from the expected frequencies – in this case the χ^2 (*chi*-square) test.

This is done by completing Table 3:

Observed frequencies O	*Expected frequencies* E	*[subtract]* $O-E$	*[square]* $(O-E)$	$\dfrac{(O-E)^2}{E}$

TOTAL $= \chi^2$

The total of the final column is the value for *chi*-square. The level of significance is then indicated below.

If χ^2 is over 10·8, the result could have happened by chance less than one in a hundred times.

If χ^2 is between 7·9 and 10·7, the result could have happened by chance less than one in two thousand times.

If χ^2 is between 6·6 and 7·8, the result could have happened by chance less than one in a hundred times.

If χ^2 is between 5·0 and 6·5, the result could have happened by chance less than one in forty times.

If χ^2 is between 3·8 and 4·9, the result could have happened by chance less than one in twenty times.

If χ^2 is between 2·7 and 3·7, the result could have happened by chance less than one in ten times.

If χ^2 is between 1·0 and 2·6, the result could have happened by chance more than one in ten times.

Note: For this elementary discussion of *chi*-square a number of refinements are not discussed, in particular:

1. Yates's correction for 2×2 tables.
2. Any discussion of degrees of freedom.
3. Any consideration of negative correlation ($\chi^2 =$ less than 1).
4. Discussion of larger tables and principles of collapsing them.
5. The principle of selecting 'significant' tables from a large number.

These can be considered in discussion or left for more sophisticated projects.

Further Work on Indirect Techniques
Depending on the results obtained and the time available, students may attempt to extend Fromme's pictorial technique (see below).

Each student should peruse newspapers and periodicals for a few days to find a suitable political cartoon for treatment. It should be amenable to several interpretations. Alternative captions should then be selected, with a careful consideration of the implicit attitudes between which the test is expected to discriminate. This can then be tested on a few other students and a complete report drawn up on the results, with notes on the student's conclusions on the use of this technique. How do the results compare with the class experiment?

If suitable, one or two of these tests can be selected by the tutor to be used in the laboratory class the following week, and the results treated as above and compared with the original project.

DISCUSSION

1. Look at your answers (particularly to Q. 11) and those of your friends in the class. What light do these throw on political commitment and attitude formation?

2. What assumptions are made by the users of these kinds of test? (For instance how do casual memories or interpretations reveal basic personality dimensions?)

3. Sorokin and other critics are concerned with the 'validity' of these tests (see Sorokin and Selltiz). What do they mean by this? What general criticisms would you make on the basis of this project?

4. Compare the advantages and disadvantages of these tests compared with direct, conscious methods of investigation?

5. Comment on the apparent political commitment of the class. What seem to be the principal factors which might account for it?

Further Reading

METHODOLOGY

Sorokin, P. A. (chap. 6, criticisms of the assumptions of projective techniques and comments on their use and validation)

Fromme, A. (pp. 425–59)

Frank, L. K.

Campbell, D. T.

Bartlett, F. C. (class experiment on the recall of pictorial materials and stories)

Newcomb, T. M.

Du Bois, C. (use of indirect methods in anthropology)

Madge, J. (1963) (chap. 11, commentary on the use of projective techniques especially as used by Adorno *et al.*)

Loveday, R. (1961) (pp. 55 ff. – introduction to 2 × 2 contingency tables and significance)

Moroney, M. J. (chap. 13, discussion of tests of significance – elementary presentation)

Project 24 **Utopias in Literature and Communication** Non-quantitative documentary analysis

OBJECTIVE

To investigate the conception of a utopia as expressed in a document by the systematic consideration of its content.

MATERIALS

Newspaper, biography, or other material with high evaluative and utopian content.

REFERENCES

Dahrendorf, R. 'Out of Utopia: Toward a Reorientation of Sociological Analysis' in Coser, L. A. and Rosenberg, B. M. (eds.), *Sociological Theory*.
Madge, J., *The Origins of Scientific Sociology* (chap. 3).

INTRODUCTION

For many purposes it is found necessary to use personal or historical data for sociological purposes. This is done extensively in the analysis of propaganda source material in anthropology and when studying children. The exchanges of letters in Polish families from which a member had emigrated to the United States comprise the major portion of the classic work by Thomas and Znaniecki. In Himmelweit's study of the effects of television on children and Veness's research on the aspirations of school leavers, personal documents were an important part of the data collected. Also a large proportion of historical data can be treated as new material for analysis in that they also reflect underlying norms and values. In this project this method is applied to utopian constructions in literature.

METHOD

The student should select a single short report, essay, historical document, etc. with a high normative or evaluative content orientated in particular towards some ideal state or social system. Suitable materials include: speeches, sermons, hymns, religious books, personal letters, diaries, social work case histories, records of court proceedings, profiles, biographies, etc. There are appropriate passages too in the works of writers such as Orwell, T. H. Huxley, Marx, H. G. Wells, Michael Young, etc. The length necessary for detailed analysis depends to a large extent on the nature of the work, but 1,000–2,000 words will normally be sufficient.

The exercise also provides experience in locating and using, for new research objectives, already available data. Here the student is merely concerned with inspecting the material for evaluative content and indicating lines he would pursue if there were to be a fuller investigation of this exploratory phase.

A thorough inspection of the material is necessary, although the exact method should be left to the ingenuity of the student. In particular, note may be made of the use of evaluative words or phrases ('vicious', 'rebel', etc.) euphemisms ('walk of life', 'passing away', 'scrvicc', etc.), basic assumptions (conformity as rewarding, etc.), and a variety of latent evaluations.

A full reference to the passage analysed should be given, or, if appropriate, the passage can be included in the laboratory file.

RESULTS

Give: 1. Title and reference.
2. Method of investigation.
3. Results and conclusions.

DISCUSSION

1. What kinds of material are most amenable for this type of sociological investigation?

2. How far does the character of historical data invalidate historical comparisons in sociology?

3. Compare the technique developed for this project with Content Analysis as used in Project 25 (or see Berelson, B. in References to Project 25).

4. There has been some research designed to discover actual responses to propaganda. Merton (see Further Reading) describes one, 'the boomerang effect'. Another is that people respond selectively so as to reinforce their current attitudes and sentiments. Suggest a method of response-analysis which would investigate the actual effect of the material you have been considering.

5. Several investigators suggest that the role of propaganda is too often exaggerated. In the light of what you have read and done, comment on this statement.

Further Reading

DOCUMENTARY ANALYSIS

Merton, R. K. (esp. chap. 14, discussion of some studies of domestic propaganda)

Festinger, L. and Katz, D. (chap. 7, methods in the use of documents, records, census materials and indices)

Duverger, M. (part 1, chap. 1, general outline of the problems and techniques of documentary analysis)

Madge, J. (1953) (chap. 2, discussion of use of documents, in particular personal documents, in social science)

Himmelweit, H. T. et al. (note the use of children's essays)

Veness, T. (research method and use of personal documents)

Halloran, J. D. (survey of major work on the effects of mass communication, in particular, television)

Thomas, W. I. and Znaniecki, F.

Boskoff, A. and Cahnman, W. J.

Orwell, G.

UTOPIAS

Mannheim, K.; Mumford, L.; Buber, M.; Popper, K. R.

Project 25 The Relationship of Content and Readership of Periodicals Analysis of communication – content analysis

OBJECTIVE

The comparison and analysis of the content of one issue of two contrasting periodicals.

MATERIALS

One copy each of two popular magazines for each pair of students. (Optional) Completed S.P.I. cards and Mailed Survey cards.

REFERENCES

Berelson, B. *Content Analysis in Communication Research* (shortened version in Lindzey, G. (ed.), *Handbook of Social Psychology*).
Hoggart, R. *The Uses of Literacy* (esp. chaps. 7 and 8).

INTRODUCTION

The use of documents as the principal data in any investigation leaves a great deal of room for distortion. Conclusions are frequently based merely on impressions of the material as perceived and recalled in an unsystematic fashion. One method of refining the description of the content of documents is to use a research technique called Content Analysis which is objective, systematic and quantitative. This technique uses the manifest elements of a text (or communication) which are classified according to predetermined categories. Various elements can be selected – words, phrases, paragraphs, whole documents, etc. – and then categorised to test a hypothesis. In this project the simplest kind of application is suggested.

METHOD

Students should work in pairs and each student should obtain or be provided with one issue of a popular magazine which contains a proportion of material of a non-specialised kind, for example *Romeo*, *The Lady*, *Woman's Realm*, *Secrets*, *Punch*, *Country Life*, *Reader's Digest*, *Honey*, *Woman's Weekly*, etc. Each pair of students should then compare one item or a range of items in each of two contrasting magazines. Much tedious work can be avoided by a thorough review of each magazine before any analysis begins. For instance, some journals could be compared by analysis of the themes in their contents page, others by a sample of advertisements or illustrations within them, and others by comparing only items included in a serial story or correspondence column.

Students are advised to select (by small-scale trials if necessary) only *one* characteristic to investigate. The nature of this will vary according to the pair of magazines chosen, but possibilities are: age, sex, marital status, nationality, occupation, class position, activities, political or social goals, etc. With complex characteristics (such as class position or goals), the symbols should be clearly identified at the outset – for instance, kind of house, occupation, dress, style of life, social activities, or the 'problems' answered, appeals to social mobility, economic goals, etc.

The texts should then be read carefully and each relevant item classified and enumerated (in terms of number of occurrences, column inches, etc.). It may be necessary to examine the *context* of each item to see, for instance, whether it is treated favourably or unfavourably.

At a later stage the class can investigate the readership of the periodicals read by the respondents to a mail survey as an auxiliary exercise in card sorting, and their conclusions discussed in relation to the results of this project.

Some variations in this project can be introduced by comparing current with early copies of the same periodical, or by using overseas editions or foreign publications.

DISCUSSION

1. Describe in one paragraph your method of selecting categories and carrying out the analysis. Give the dates and titles of the periodicals used.

2. Give in one paragraph the main conclusions you come to on the basis of your findings. What kinds of reader would you expect to purchase the magazines?

3. Suggest what should be the next stage in an investigation of this issue.

4. How far does the content of these magazines represent the real world of the (expected) reader? How far does it provide him with a model with which to compare himself?

5. Look up what is meant by a 'reference group' in sociology and then end with a short discussion of the influence on the reader of magazines of the type studied.

Further Reading

METHODOLOGY

Duverger, M. (part 1, chap. 1, esp. section 3 which is a simple introduction to the method of content analysis)

Festinger, L. and Katz, D. (chap. 10, discussion of methods of analysis of qualitative material)

Madge, J. (1953) (chap. 2, esp. part 5, a discussion of the reliability of procedures for the interpretation of documentary data)

Cicourel, A. V. (chap. 6, clear discussion of the assumptions in content analysis and an appraisal of its usefulness)

Merton, R. K. (pp. 512–16)

COMMUNICATION AND MASS CULTURE

Rosenberg, B. and White, D. M. (a reader; contributions on mass popular literature)

Berelson, B. and Janowitz, M. (reader on communication, theory and practice)

Klapper, J. T.; McClelland, W. D.

REFERENCE GROUPS

Merton, R. K.

Project 26 **The Ecology of the City**
Analysis of patterns of spatial distribution of social characteristics

OBJECTIVE

To examine some of the social characteristics of different regions of the city using a simple ecological technique.

MATERIALS

1. Street map of the city, preferably with ward boundaries indicated.

2. Lists of approximate addresses of population taken from certain lists, etc. (see p. 143).

REFERENCES

Morris, T. *The Criminal Area or*
Reissman, L. *The Urban Process* (chaps. 4 and 5) *or*
Summary in chap. 9 of Broom, L. and Selznick, P. *Sociology.*

INTRODUCTION

The distinctive characteristic of the ecological approach is its emphasis on the spatial or distributive relationships of individuals and social phenomena, and the principles that determine these relationships. In spite of many of its less satisfactory characteristics, ecology can still provide a basis for a systematic theory of the city, and has produced many suggestive studies in the fields of criminology and epidemiology.

Human ecology is concerned with the 'typical constellations of persons and institutions', and developed a more sophisticated body of theory than other workers in the field of urban studies. (See for comparison 'Social area analysis', reference below.) As a concept it has been borrowed from the field of biology, and was first used as a basis for a sociological theory by R. E. Park and his associates at the University of Chicago in the 1920s. A large number of studies based on his ideas were published during this period (see Anderson, Thrasher, Wirth and Shaw below, for example). They developed a number of concepts: 'symbiosis', 'community', 'axiate growth', 'zones', 'gradient' and, in particular, 'natural areas' (see Morris, T., and Reissman, in References).

A number of different schemes were devised, of which one of the best known is the 'concentric zone theory'. This suggests that a city can be divided into a number of circular zones, each one larger than the one before it and all with a common centre, the outer ones surrounding the central business district, (1) the 'zone of transition', (2) working men's homes, (3) flats, and (4) suburbia.

METHOD

1. Each student should collect or use two lists of addresses of people with some known characteristic which can be drawn from any available local source, either by a representative of the class or by each student individually. Each list should contain 200–250 addresses (by a sampling procedure if necessary), but no names or even *exact* details are required – merely the name of the road in which each person lives.

The choice of social factor to be considered can be made to suit the tutor and class. However, suggestions which are generally possible are addresses of:

   i. People appearing before the city's magistrates during a recent week or weeks (these can be broken down into motoring and non-motoring offences).

  ii. Members of certain local clubs, associations, trade unions, etc.

 iii. Members of some occupational or professional groups.

 iv. Members of local political parties, religious groups.

  v. Addresses of people with telephones, or of boys or girls at the grammar or private school.

 vi. Property with a high (or low) rateable value (taken from the rating records of the local rating officer). Property with a high price (taken from the list of a local house agent).

vii. Jurors (in the electoral register).

viii. People attending at the hospital out-patient clinic or casualty department.

2. The student should then use two or three lists and spot the addresses on the city map, using distinctive colours for different lists. Long streets present a problem and may have to be omitted in extreme cases, or addresses spaced at random along them. Full details and a key should be given for all conventions used.

3. Optional extension. Each student should collect the *same* data in his home town or city during the vacation and prepare another scatter map for comparison with the first one prepared in the laboratory class.

TREATMENT OF RESULTS

1. The student can use the resulting map to indicate whether there appear to be any apparent concentrations, and to consider possible explanations for them.

2. If the distribution(s) seem suitable, the student can use the map to indicate certain possible 'natural areas', or consider possible zones by drawing concentric rings round the centre of the city if the zone theory seems more appropriate.

3. If the map used shows ward boundaries, the population of each ward should be obtained from the city records and a rate/10,000 population calculated. The wards with highest and lowest rates can be shaded on the map.

4. Class results and results from previous years should be compared, and copies filed in the laboratory reference library. Over several years a cumulative ecological profile of the city will be produced which can be used as background material for other research work in the locality.

DISCUSSION

1. List the technical difficulties of the ecological method as experienced in this project.

2. What are the uses of the ecological approach in practice?

3. What are the major *boundaries* between different neighbourhoods? Comment on the major divisions indicated on your scatter map. (For instance, does a river, railway, park, etc., divide areas of different social characteristics?)

4. Give a short sociological account for the existence of 'natural areas' in a city.

5. 'In Britain local authority housing policy and town planning make the ecologist's generalisations invalid.' Comment.

Further Reading

Madge, J. (1963) (chap. 4, history and outline of the approach of the Chicago School)

Shaw, C. H. and McKay, H. D. (1929) *or*
(1942) (classic research on criminal areas)

Gurvich, G. D. and Moore, W. E. (see article by Llewellyn and Hawthorn, 'Human Ecology')

Young, P. V. (chap. 16, introduction to the research techniques in human ecology)

Hawley, A. H. (modern defence of ecology)

Schnore, L. F. (part i – links ecology with Durkheim's 'social morphology' and suggests the former is a form of macro-sociology)

Alihan, M. A. (an early critique of conventional ecological theory)

Mannheim, H. (study of ecological distribution of juvenile crime in Cambridge)

Gist, N. P. and Halbert, L. A. (chapters on ecology)

Boggs, S. L. (relates occurrence of crime to environmental opportunities)

Theodorson, G. A.

Swedner, H. (esp. chap. 3, this is a sophisticated and thorough attempt to extend ecology to rural sociology)

Shevky, E. and Bell, D. (a parallel approach to 'urban subcommunities' based on census data, and census measures combined into various indices)

Project 27 **Political Opinion Polls**
Types of sample design

OBJECTIVE

To gain familiarity with polling techniques and to compare random and quota sampling methods by conducting a poll on voting intentions in a local constituency.

MATERIALS

1. Background information from *Whitaker's Almanack* and latest Census.

2. Sample of about 250 names and addresses will be drawn from electoral roll.

REFERENCES

Moser, C. A. *Survey Methods in Social Investigation* (chap. 6).
Benney, M. *et al. How People Vote.*

INTRODUCTION

Although political attitudes of the members of a large population cannot readily be quantitatively measured in all their complexity, diversity and intensity, certain aspects of these attitudes and some range of intensity can be assumed through recording certain key activities or measuring certain key opinions. Political attitudes can be studied in retrospect by an investigation of the influences acting on people recorded as voting for a particular candidate in an election. One important approach which attracts a great deal of public attention is that of national opinion polls, involving frequent surveys of voting intentions and allied subjects, particularly with a view to predicting election results. These election predictions have often been substantially correct, and provide useful data for the political scientist – despite the minority of inconsistent voters or waverers, who frequently 'decide' the result.

METHOD

A large number of methodological issues are raised by the opinion polls as actually conducted. Some of the major ones are as follows:

1. The selection of the sample (see below) – in particular, the sampling frame, interval and size.

2. Interview techniques and interviewer training.

3. The questions asked, and their position in the schedule.

4. The treatment of those respondents who at first are 'undecided', 'don't know', 'will not vote', or refuse to give any indication of their intentions.

5. Checking for interviewer bias or falsification.

6. Procedure followed if selected respondent has moved or is impossible to contact. Some investigators interview substitutes, such as neighbours, others do not.

7. Processing and analysis. In particular, treatment of answers by respondents with no clear voting intention.

8. The 'confidence limits' of the results. (Frequently small variations, translated into 'scorings', appear significant without being large enough to satisfy statistical tests of significance.)

Types of Sample Design
The basic distinction in modern sampling theory is between *probability* and *non-probability* sampling. The essential characteristic of the former is that one can specify for each element of the population the probability that it will be included in the sample. (The simplest case is where each element has the *same* probability of being included – the 'simple random sample'). In non-probability sampling there is no way of estimating the probability that each element has of being in the sample.

The major forms of probability samples are:
a. Simple random samples.
b. Stratified random samples.

   c. Cluster samples.
   d. Multi-stage samples.
   e. Multi-phase samples.

The most common form of non-probability sampling is *quota* sampling.

A simple random sample. Using the electoral register and a table of random numbers a sample can be drawn using the serial numbers of electors.

A stratified random sample. Stratification is a means of using knowledge of the population to increase the representativeness and precision of the sample. For instance, to ensure that a minority group are correctly represented in the sample, they can be separated from the majority before any selection takes place, *then* the sample taken from each section. In addition, if the minority is particularly important yet very small, it can be over-sampled, and the larger size allowed for in the analysis of results.

Cluster samples. In practice some advantage can be gained by taking *clusters* of names from each randomly selected place in the sampling frame. (For instance, National Opinion Polls use this procedure on which the first sample in this project is based.)

Multi-stage sampling. Here further clusters are selected from within each cluster and so on. For instance, a sample of constituencies could then be used for a further sampling of electors.

Multi-phase sampling. Some economies can often be made by conducting an enquiry in several stages on varying fractions of the population. For example, a rapid enquiry might be conducted on voting intentions and the results of this used to restrict the size of a further enquiry following up in depth.

The quota method has two stages. First the general characteristics of the population are examined; then each interviewer is given appropriate 'quotas' of people to interview – so many men, young, working class, etc. In quota sampling *the actual choice of people to interview* (in contrast to all the earlier methods) *is left to the interviewers.* This has great advantages in simplicity and speed, but has been severely criticised on many occasions (see Further Reading for consideration of its use, e.g. by Gallup and B.B.C. Audience Research).

Method

1. The class should be divided into two groups matched as far as possible, with one group approximately four times the size of the other. Then a leader elected by each group.

2. *a. Cluster sample of electors* (larger group – Group A)

One group leader should select a sample from the complete electoral register (obtainable from the local registration officer) as follows:

   i. Using some statistically random method he should select a number of electors equal to the number of students in his group.
   ii. Each student should then copy down the name and address of the elector allocated to him on the *Cluster Sample Log Sheet* (Appendix 9); then he should take down on the log sheet the same details for every *seventh* elector until he has ten names and addresses for his cluster. This will give him a list of *ten electors* to be interviewed for the project.

b. Quota sample of electors (smaller group – Group B)

The other group leader should examine the most recent Census County Report for the area, and calculate the proportions of the population which are (i) male/female, and (ii) in the age groups 20–29, 30–44, 45–64, and 65 +, and (iii) in the Registrar-General's five social classes (see *Socio-Economic Group Tables*, H.M.S.O., 1966). From these he can calculate the quotas needed for his group's interviews. These should be written on each *Quota Sample Log Sheet* (Appendix 9).

3. *a. Group A.* Students should visit the electors in their homes, ask the questions and record the answers as shown on the Cluster Sample Log Sheet. Much time can be saved if the initial visit is after 4.30 p.m. or during the weekend, when people are more likely to be at home. If time allows, one or more recalls (decided on before starting the interviews) should be attempted where the initial attempt was unsuccessful. Only the actual elector on the log sheet should be interviewed. *No* substitutes should be selected.

b. Group B

Students should go out into different parts of the constituency and attempt to ask the questions on the Log Sheet. Each contact should be a resident in the constituency, but the actual interviews may be obtained in any way – calling at houses or approaching people in the streets. However, permission should be obtained before interviewing in a café, store, station, etc. The age and social class of each contact should be discovered by tactful questions as appropriate. The middle class can be taken as Registrar-General's Classes I and II, i.e. all professional and managerial occupations including teachers, employers, shopkeepers, etc. Working class (III, IV and V) refers to junior office workers, transport, skilled and unskilled occupations. Check in the *Classification of Occupations 1960* (H.M.S.O.), if necessary.

Treatment of Results

Draw up and complete Tables 1 and 2 – Class results.

Table 1

Proportion of electors supporting various political parties
(take only those expressing preference)

	Previous election		Group A cluster sample		Group B quota sample	
	Votes	%	Number	%	Number	%
Conservative						
Labour						
Liberal						
Other						
Total		100		100		100

Table 2

Combined Assessment (Groups A and B)

	Project assessment		Previous election		Latest national poll	
	Number	%	Number	%	N.O.P.	Gallup
Conservative						
Labour						
Liberal						
Other						
Total		100		100	100	100

Discussion

1. Account for the results obtained and compare them with the result at the previous election and the latest national opinion polls. What prediction could you make on the basis of the results?

2. What in your view are the main factors which might account for the difference between the results produced by the two groups?

3. List the advantages and disadvantages of the two methods in note form for group A and group B.

4. Take one of the disadvantages you have listed, and suggest any way in which its effect could be lessened or measured – for instance how could the influence of the 'not contacted' be measured, or how could one investigate the claim that the quota method tends to avoid certain kinds of elector?

5. Comment on the methods, as far as you know them, of *one* of the national polling organisations (not necessarily one of those referred to above).

Further Reading

SAMPLE DESIGN

Moroney, M. J. (chaps. 10, 11, 12, general introduction to the statistical theory of sampling)

Chein, I. (non-statistical discussion of considerations involved in different methods of sampling)

Festinger, L. and Katz, D. (chap. 5, general treatment of sample selection techniques)

Parten, M. (esp. chaps. 7 and 8, full discussion of types and procedures for drawing samples)

Cantril, H. (part 3, general principles of sampling)

Stephan, F. J. and McCarthy, P. J. (esp. chaps. 9 and 10, full description of the principal types of sample in particular cluster and quota)

Corlett, T. and Edwards, F. (this article gives a good introduction to stratification and quota controls)

B.B.C. Audience Research (use of quota sampling in audience measurement)

POLITICAL OPINION POLLS

Berelson, B. and Janowitz, M. (basic reader on wide variety of issues including theory and methodology of public opinion; useful)

Butler, D. E.; Rose, R. (1965); Abrams, M.; Plowman, D. E. G. (1962); Lazarsfeld, P. F. *et al.* (intensive study of pre-election voting intentions); Gallup, G.; Albig, W.; Moser, C. A. (chap. 2, introduction to the field of market, audience and opinion research in Britain)

There are also frequent articles in the weekly and daily press on Opinion Poll results. See, in particular,

Rose, R. (1962); Rose, R. (1964); Plowman, D. E. G. (1964); Kelvin, R. P.

Project 28 **The Classification and Quantification of Data** Editing, coding and transferring data on to punched cards

OBJECTIVE

To examine the procedures for classifying and quantifying responses to questionnaires by editing and coding some selected examples and punching the results on IBM/ICT cards.

MATERIALS

    1. Completed S.P.I.s for whole class (Appendix 7).
    2. Registrar-General's *Classification of Occupations, 1960.*
    3. (optional) Tape used in Project 15.
    4. Card punch.
    5. Card verifier (optional).

REFERENCES

Selltiz, C. *et al. Research Methods in Social Relations* (chap. 11).
Moser, C. A. *Survey Methods in Social Investigation* (chap. 14).

INTRODUCTION

The selection of a system of measurement and classification of objects, statements or events, once imposed, transforms them into data. With fixed-choice questions the form of the question is an integral part of this process, but with less structured methods much of this is left until after the fieldwork has at least begun.

Apart from the procedures of editing and transferring data on to punched cards described briefly below, two issues are of particular methodological importance at this stage: classification and coding.

Classification involves resolving the whole body of new data into components or elements – of place, time, relationships, behaviour or function, or attitudes. The procedures used are frequently based on implicit common-sense assumptions about the situation involved. For instance the researcher often begins with only broad dichotomies, which he expects the raw data to fit. He then may elaborate these categories as seems necessary. The relationship between observation and category is based upon what seem obvious rules which might be easily used by anyone. However, it is probably at this stage that implicit notions most influence the final results. For instance, a vague answer may have an implicit meaning which may or may not be clear to the researcher. Alternatively the same response could be classified in a number of ways, dependent on the classificatory framework in use.

Ideally the classification of any one set of responses should be concerned with only one principle at a time – for instance 'mentioning negroes', or 'social distance', 'favourability expressed towards the police', etc. It should also use a set of categories which are exhaustive, each of which should be mutually exclusive; i.e. every response (etc.) should have one category which fits. However, there is no reason why the same data should not be used for any number of classifications at different stages in the research.

The less structured the material, the more complicated is the task of classification. In particular the establishment of principles is especially difficult in exploratory studies, since these do not start with explicit hypotheses. The investigator is not yet clear what aspects may turn out to be the most important or significant. There are several methods for dealing with this situation, one of which is to sort the cases into groups that seem to belong together, or alternatively sorting out responses which seem to contradict common-sense or theoretical expectations.

The second issue, coding, is primarily the transformation of the classification into symbols (usually numbers) that are amenable to mechanical handling processes. Each response is categorised and then assigned an appropriate number or numbers on a coding frame. Normally the suitability of the frame is tested by examining a representative sample of the completed schedules and testing the frame on these.

The coding of answers can be carried out by (i) the respondent, (ii) the interviewer or (iii) the research worker in the office. But whoever codes and even assuming an adequate frame, coding requires the exercise of considerable judgment. There is inevitably scope for personal bias and for differences between coders – quite apart from errors due to carelessness. The variability in coding is often not measured, and a number of experiments have shown that even experienced coders appear to have a low reliability, as substantial discrepancies were revealed between coders and for the same coder at different times (see Moser above). This can be minimised by extensive training, conducting trial runs and making periodic consistency checks.

METHOD

Each student should consider the following schedules for this exercise:

1. His own completed Student's Personal Inventory.

2. Twelve completed copies of the mail questionnaire (Appendix 10).

3. The completed interview schedule on marriage used in Project 18.

4. Any other completed questionnaires used or devised during the course of earlier projects (e.g. Projects 15, 16, 17, etc.).

1. *Editing.* Each student should look through the completed schedules and check the following points in particular:

Completeness. Are all questions answered? Can the incomplete items be completed on the basis of other responses? Are they incomplete because the respondent refused to answer, the interviewer forgot to ask the question or record the answer, or the question was not applicable?

Legibility and correct coding. In spite of instructions, precoded questions are often treated incorrectly (e.g. number underlined instead of ringed). This should be corrected. (Also, normally, illegible answers may be interpreted in the context of other replies.)

Accuracy. Check for clear inconsistencies (these can be used as deliberate checks in some investigations).

Uniformity between interviewers is also usually noted, especially treatment of refusals, 'not applicable', etc.

2. *Classification and Coding*

General. By a preliminary examination of the completed schedules each student should suggest a framework for classifying not more than six of the responses to those questions which are not coded in the schedule. A brief note should be made on the reason for using this system. This should be laid out in tabular form thus:

Question No.	Suggested coding frame – Maximum *10* categories (Code: 'not applicable' X 'refusal' *Y*)	Reason for this frame
Code	Category of Response	
0		
1		
2		
3		
4		
5		
6		
7		
8		
9		

Occupational grading for social-class position. As a guide to social-class position the occupation of the head of household can be classified using the *Classification of Occupations 1960* produced by the Registrar-General. His five social classes I to V can be coded 1 to 5 (Q. 11, 12 and 42 on S.P.I. and Q. 14 on M.Q.).

3. *Punching.* The tutor will arrange for the class to transfer their S.P.I. and mail questionnaire responses on to punched cards (it is assumed that these will normally be of the ICT/IBM 80-column variety).

Standard punched cards have 80 vertical columns, each of which has twelve punching positions – 0, 1, . . . 9, X, Y.[1] Special machines similar to typewriters punch the cards, so that the coded responses to 80 questions can be fitted on to one card.

4. *Verification* (if possible). In a normal data processing establishment each card is *verified* on a similar machine, and this should be carried out here, and repunching done if errors have occurred. (If no verification facilities are available, the S.P.I. should be punched *twice*

[1] 10 and 11, or 11 and 12 on some machines.

as a check, and the M.Q. cards visually checked.) Each student will now have a card representing his S.P.I. and twelve cards representing some of the responses to the mail questionnaire. These should be labelled and retained for treatment in later projects (especially Nos. 29, 30 and 31).

5. The student should then note his own identification number for retrieval, and the complete set of S.P.I. cards should be reproduced for each pair of students.

6. *Consistency in coding full responses* (optional exercise). The recording used for Project 15 can be played back to the class (or by students individually) after classifications have been agreed. Comparisons of actual classifications of the same response can be made.

DISCUSSION

1. Criticise the classificatory system used in one questionnaire in the light of your experience in this project.

2. At what stage in an investigation is it best to start formulating the coding frame? Note whether there are any particular circumstances which would affect this.

3. What are the advantages and disadvantages of the coding being carried out by the interviewer during the interview rather than leaving this to be done by a specialist coder?

4. Select one cause of unreliability in the classification and quantification of this data, and suggest how this could be reduced.

5. What is gained and what is lost when raw data of this kind are transferred to punched cards for a mechanical handling process?

Further Reading

Cicourel, A. V. (chaps. 1 and 4, consideration of the processes of measurement, classification and quantification in sociological research)

Lazarsfeld, P. F. and Barton, A. H.

Parten, M. (esp. chap. 13, practical instructions on classification and coding)

Edwards, F. (see articles on coding by Downham and Harris)
     (*Alternatives*: Downham, J. S. *and* Harris, A. I.)

Hammond, P. E. (see in particular Udy's approach to classification and coding, chap. 7)

Project 29 **A Study of Differential Academic Motivation** Factor control in ex post facto experiments; card sorting

OBJECTIVE

To investigate factors associated with different levels of academic motivation within the class.

MATERIALS

1. Student's Personal Inventory (S.P.I.) completed and punched on to cards.
2. Card sorter.

REFERENCES

Differential Motivation
Lipset, S. M. and Bendix, R. *Social Mobility in Industrial Society* (chap. 9, 'Intelligence and Motivation') *or*
see 'Social Mobility' in any introductory sociology text.

Ex post facto *experiments, etc.*
Greenwood, E. *Experimental Sociology* (chap. 6, 'The Technique of Control in Experimental Sociology') *or*
Madge, J. *The Tools of Social Science* (chap. 5).

INTRODUCTION

The structure of opportunities confronting an individual, and his capacity to take advantage of such opportunities (i.e. his achievement motivation as well as ability) are related phenomena which must be considered in a study of social mobility.

This project is specifically concerned with achievement motivation, and is focused on educational goals in the academic sphere. Lipset and Bendix point out that educational achievement is the main source of occupational achievement in a bureaucratised industrial society. However, it should be remembered that at every stage the preference for an alternative goal in the same or other spheres may be as 'rational' a strategy for actual social mobility as preoccupation with academic success. In the project the class should decide on any factor(s) that they consider may be associated with academic motivation among themselves.

Festinger considers that the basis of experimental method lies in observing the effect on the dependent variable of the manipulation of the independent variable under controlled conditions. The mode of control may be either direct or indirect. In the latter case manipulation is of data rather than direct manipulation of subjects (e.g. random selection).

The question is whether it is an equally acceptable scientific procedure to trace in the after-the-fact manner from the given records the relationship between two factors under conditions of control. If the 'ex post facto' method in which, as Greenwood points out, 'we work backward, by controlling after the stimulus has already operated, thereby reconstructing what might have been an experimental situation' is valid, it offers wide possibilities for sociology. (Students should look at the further reading to make up their minds on this point. It is to be remembered that the ex post facto design used here has given rise to considerable discussion, and has in particular been criticised by Merton on the grounds that post factum explanations do not lend themselves to nullifiability.)

The conclusiveness of an experimental result depends on how far it deviates from similar results expected on a purely chance basis, i.e. the design must ideally ensure that the operation of all other relevant variables is by chance and thus the influence of the experimental stimulus is not by chance. After *factor equation* (the balancing of each factor in the experimental group with a corresponding factor in the control group) has been utilised to the maximum, steps are taken to ensure that inequitable factors are randomised among the members of experimental and control groups. In Projects 6, 8 and 9 different forms of *randomisation* were used.

If a research project is to be concerned with an explicit hypothesis the attempt to validate it can either be by wide-ranging inquiry into 'typical' cases or by an analysis of *deviant* cases. Here an intensive study of a case which deviates from the general pattern, rather than being explained away, plays a positive role in qualifying or refining the hypothesis. It is suggested that in some cases 'deviant case analysis' could be considered within the framework of this project.

METHOD

Students may work in pairs using the cards representing the class responses to the questions in the Student's Personal Inventory, and should investigate the factors associated with relatively high and low academic motivation as follows:

1. Count and sort the cards on column 41, and complete Table 1.

TABLE 1

Distribution of students by motivation as measured in the S.P.I.

	Motivation Code										
	(low)							(high)	Rejects or	
	0	1	2	3	4	5	6	7	8	other	Total
No. of students:											

2. Note the code number of any single extreme or deviant case for later consideration.

3. Divide the cards into two roughly equal groups – with 'low' and 'high' motivation scores – by taking an arbitrary dividing line somewhere along the scale. (Reject 'others' and 'rejects'.)

4. Keeping these two piles separate, count the cards on appropriate columns. Draw up and complete Table 2.

5. Consider these results. Do these suggest any obvious association between age, sex or marital condition and motivation score? If there is, you must now attempt to match the two groups for that variable. Use either 'one for one' matching or a frequency method so that the method you devise produces two groups of about equal size having the same age, sex or marital distribution. Note how many cases have to be discarded in this process.

6. Now investigate a number of possible hypotheses of your own choosing, by sorting on the appropriate column. You might start

with social class background, last secondary school, religious attendance, etc. Give *all* figures you obtain, only collapsing the tables at a later stage.

TABLE 2

Basic differences between students with high and low motivation scores

Col. 8 Sex and marital state Code	High	Low	Total	Col. 7 Age Code	Age	High	Low	Total
Male,								
married 1								
single 2								
wid/sep/div 3								
Female,								
married 4								
single 5								
wid/sep/div 6								
other code and								
rejected cards								
TOTAL								

7. (optional) If the groups are large enough, you may try to match on one further factor where you find there is an association with motivation. Note how many further cases have to be discarded and continue.

8. Deviant Case. Compare the deviant case selected for very high or low motivation with the rest of the class by sorting on columns of your own choice. (Choose with reference to your earlier hypotheses.)

TREATMENT OF RESULTS

Gather your results together and write a short account of your findings. You should be able to answer the question: What factors are associated with academic motivation in the class? Give clear collapsed tables where factors appear associated.

DISCUSSION

1. Comment on the use of the hypothetical situations described in the questions on which the motivation score was based. Suggest alternative methods of producing such a score.

2. Describe the technique of matching as you evolved it in

F   W.S.I.

practice. Note the pitfalls and disadvantages of matching as a method of factor control.

3. How did you make use of the deviant case? How far is the technique of deviant case analysis useful in sociology, and for what purposes?

4. Is it legitimate to use tests of significance (such as *chi*-square) for factors differing between two matched groups? Explain your answer.

5. What is the place of the *ex post facto* experiment in sociology?

Further Reading

MOTIVATION, EDUCATION AND MOBILITY

Glass, D. V.; Turner, R. H. (1964); Corwin, R. G. (chap. 7, pp. 207 ff. – 'The Problem of Motivation'); Reissman, L. (1949); Veness, T. (motivation and aspiration in schoolchildren); Turner, R. H. (1961) (a comparison of kinds of mobility patterns in U.S. and British educational systems)

FACTOR CONTROL, EXPERIMENT AND DEVIANT CASE ANALYSIS

Selltiz, C. *et al.* (chap. 4, 'Studies testing causal hypotheses')

Festinger, L. and Katz, D. (chap. 7 on matching)

Thomlinson, R. (pp. 34 ff. and 67 ff. – experiment and matching)

Stephan, F. J. and McCarthy, P. J. (chap. 4.2 – 'Models of selection procedures')

Riley, M. W. (unit eleven – experimental design, with examples of various types)

Moser, C. A. (chap. 1.5, brief discussion of the ways in which the experimenter can control his independent variables)

Chapin, F. S.

Cicourel, A. V. (chap. 7, experimental design in sociology)

Sorokin, P. A. (chap. 9, critical account of experiment and factor control in sociology)

Wilkins, L. T. (1964) (appendix 1 – matching)

Merton, R. K. (chap. 2, pp. 93 ff. – criticisms of *post factum* explanations)

Kendall, P. L. and Wolf, K. H.

Lipset, S. M. *et al.* (classic study of a 'deviant case')

Project 30 **Population Structure**
Card-sorting technique, graphical presentation of results; checks on the representativeness of survey respondents

OBJECTIVE

To examine, using graphical methods, the structure of the response population in a postal survey.

MATERIALS

Cards from Mail Survey (Project 20; see also Project 28)[1]; co unter-sorter.

REFERENCES

Davis, K. *Human Society* (chap. 20, 'The Demographic Equation').
Cicourel, A. V. *Method and Measurement in Sociology* (chap. 5, 'The Demographic Method').

INTRODUCTION

Demography is the numerical portrayal of a human population. The basic procedures are largely statistical and are principally concerned with the behaviour of the aggregate rather than the behaviour of individuals or social groups. In particular the demographer studies (i) the composition of the population concerned and (ii) changes that occur during some period of observation. Its data are similarly divided into two kinds – that provided by enumeration (such as the Census) and the statistics of certain vital events (usually during one year, month, etc.) such as births, deaths, migrations and marriages.

[1] Available in Data Pack from publishers.

Its techniques are concerned with obtaining answers to three questions:

   i. What is the frequency of occurrence of some behaviour event in the population (birth-rates, proportion married, etc.)?

   ii. How far has this changed over a period?

   iii. Are there patterns of variation within the population?

Topics which particularly concern demographers are therefore such issues as fertility, migration, and life tables. However, their interest is often more concerned with explanations of demographic 'facts' without explicitly linking them to cultural influences. (Cicourel suggests 'The understanding of why and how persons go about their daily life, which produces what are recorded as "demographic facts", requires an appreciation of how everyday common-sense meanings are normatively governed.')

This project uses one of the most frequent graphic devices employed in population studies – the population pyramid – to indicate the age and sex distributions within a population. Although some of the data for the comparison (the returns from a postal survey) were collected in a manner more common in sociology than in strict demography, the method of analysing it can be exactly the same. Examples of population pyramids will be found in a wide variety of studies, and these data are normally considered vital to any description of a population under investigation. Comparison of the sample successfully interviewed (etc.) with census data on these lines often provides one method of checking the representativeness of the final sample. In some cases the primary demographic description can itself provide the basis for a sociological explanation of wider significance (see Riesman in Further Reading, for instance).

METHOD

   1. Use the cards from the Mail Survey in Exeter (or from your own local mail survey) and the counter-sorter to draw up and complete Table 1. The simplest method is to conduct the first sort on column 12 (Sex) and then, *keeping the two piles separate*, sort both again on column 11 (Age) to give figures for the first part of the table. Students may work in pairs.

Keeping the two piles (sexes) separate, repeat for Marital Status (column 13) and then for Household Size (column 10).

TABLE 1

Returns from mail survey – breakdown by sex, age, marital status and household size

	Code	Total	Age group (Col. 11) 1234567890X other	Marital status (Col. 13) 123 other	Household size (Col. 10) 123456 other
Male	1				
Female	2				
Rejects, others, etc.					
TOTALS					

2. Now put all the cards together and sort on column 13 (Marital Status) and sort cach pile on columns 10 and 11 to complete Table 2.

TABLE 2

Returns from mail survey – breakdown by marital status, age and household size

	Code	Total	Household size (Col. 10) 123456 other	Age group (Col. 11) 1234567890X other
Single	1			
Married	2			
Wid/div/sep	3			
Rejects, others, etc.				
TOTAL				

3. Put all cards together and sort on column 10 then column 11. Complete Table 3.

TABLE 3

Returns from mail survey – breakdown by age and household size

	Code	Total	Age group 1234567890X other
Live alone	1		
One other	2		
Three altogether	3		
Four altogether	4		
Five altogether	5		
Six or more	6		
Rejects, other, etc.			
TOTAL			

Repeat all sorts when totals do not tally.

4. Look up comparable figures in the *Annual Abstract of Statistics for England and Wales* and for the population of the town or city surveyed in the mail survey in the County Report of the most recent census. Draw up and complete Table 4.

TABLE 4

Census Returns – Population by sex, age groups, age and marital status, England and Wales and . . . . . . (name of town, etc.)

	Total	Age group	Marital status	Household size
Male				
Female				
TOTAL				

TREATMENT OF RESULTS

1. Using the same axes, plot histograms in the form of population pyramids for (1) the mail survey respondents, (2) the whole city (etc.), (3) England and Wales (or Scotland, etc., if more appropriate), and (4) your own mail survey (if conducted). The form of the pyramid will be seen in most texts on population studies and some census reports (see Census General Report, P.E.P., Barclay, Coontz, etc.):

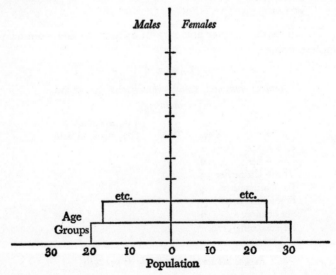

2. Using whatever conventions you choose, devise one or more other graphic representations of the populations to indicate differences in age, sex, marital status and household size.

3. (optional) Look up comparative figures for 1901 and 1931 and consider changes as shown in population pyramids.

DISCUSSION

1. Summarise the main differences between the respondents in the mail survey and the census figures for the population that they are supposed to represent.

2. How did these differences arise? (Note in particular, sampling frame, sampling methods, completion of questions, etc.) See Project 20 for details of the process distribution of questionnaires. All returns were transferred to punched cards.

3. What further characteristics do you feel should ideally be used to make such a comparison more useful?

4. Suggest in note form some effects of changes in the sex and age distribution in the population of a country.

5. Comment on the different theoretical approaches of sociology and demography to the study of a population. What has each to offer the other?

Further Reading

Moser, C. A. (chaps. 6 and 7, sample design)

Barclay, G. W. (see in particular chap. 1, 'The Nature of Demography', and chap. 7)

Hauser, P. M. and Duncan, O. D. (comprehensive reader, see chap. 3 on data and methods)

Duncan, O. D. and Spengler, J. J. (1956a)

General Report Census 1951 (chap. 4 gives data and age pyramids for England and Wales, 1951)

Political and Economic Planning (P.E.P.) (esp. chap. 2, general picture of population in Great Britain and related policy issues)

Cox, P. R. (general introduction. See chap. 11 for use of population pyramids in an account of population of Great Britain)

Coontz, S. H. (useful introduction to population theories since Malthus)

Duncan, O. D. and Spengler, J. J. (1956*b*)

Riesman, D. *et al.* (1953) (one example of the use of demographic data as the basis for a sociological 'theory')

Project 31 **Indicators of Social Class Position** The processing and analysis of data; use of counter-sorter; regression and correlation

OBJECTIVE

To compare and evaluate some different indices of social class position.

MATERIALS

Counter-sorter; punched cards from mail survey and S.P.I.

REFERENCES

Stratification Scales (for more elementary introductions see Broom and Selznick or Toby, under Further Reading).

Barber, B. *Social Stratification* (esp. chap. 8, 'Indices of Social Class Position') *or*

Gordon, M. M. *Social Class in American Sociology* (chap. 7, 'The Logic of Stratification Scales') *or*

Caplow, T. *The Sociology of Work* (chap. 2, 'The Measurement of Occupational Status').

Processing and Analysis
Selltiz, C. *et al. Research Methods in Social Relations* (chap. 11).

INTRODUCTION

Social Class Indices
Sociological literature contains reports of large numbers of research projects in which individuals are allocated to social classes and whose behaviour is then related to some other phenomenon on the

basis of this allocation. Concern over producing adequate indices of social position or 'stratification scales' has been translated, particularly in the United States, into a number of empirical studies of the indices themselves. Several different techniques are in general use. All are open to some theoretical and methodological criticisms. However, research suggests that, despite this, gross class differences can be successfully investigated using several of them.

1. *Reputational ratings.* This technique, particularly suited to small communities, is associated with the name of Lloyd Warner. In his study of 'Elmtown', for instance, the status rating for an individual hinges on the votes he receives from other members of the community, polled by the research worker.

2. *Self-placement* (The 'subjective approach'). Two limitations of the reputational approach – necessary size and nature of the community, and compatibility – do not apply where the respondent is expected to assess his own standing in society. One of the earlier measures of this kind was developed by Centers for inclusion in surveys conducted by polling organisations. The basis of the scale was the respondent's reply to 'If you were asked to use one of these four names for your social class, which would you say you belonged in: the middle class, lower class, working class, or upper class?'

3. *Evaluation of social symbols.* People are sometimes classified by the symbols associated with one social group or another. Opinion polls may use interviewer ratings of rank, based on style of dress, manner of speech or the furnishings of the home, for instance. This approach has been furthered by Chapin in America and Chapman in Britain.

4. *Ratings based on the single item of occupation.* In contemporary industrial society the most commonly used single item scale is based on occupational position. This is relatively easy to ascertain, not being considered private, and considerable research has suggested that there is some consensus of opinion amongst the population on how different jobs are rated (although problems arise where jobs cover a wide range – farmer or civil servant – where people are ignorant about some occupations, or where a predominantly lower class group does the ranking). In America Edwards's and the Minnesota Occupational Scale are best known. In Britain the Hall-Jones Scale is the best validated, but the Registrar-General's scale the most widely used.

5. *Other single indices.* Other status characteristics can be used to

provide scales for particular purposes – in particular amount of income, house type, cost and ownership, dwelling area, kind or length of formal education.

6. *Multiple factor indices.* Using more than one indicator makes an index more complicated and costly, but can increase its validity significantly. Warner used indices of this type in Yankee City and Jonesville; for instance his Index of Status Characteristics is based on occupation, source of income, house type and dwelling area, with rankings of each assigned different weights in the final calculation.

Regression and Correlation

When working with more than one variable at once, the sociologist will normally at some stage be concerned with the possible associa-tion between them. He will be interested in 'correlation'. This situation calls for one or more of the following processes:

1. Graphing a *scatter diagram.* This is a set of dots portraying simultaneously the individual scores according to two variables as described below.

2. If a trend is discernible in this diagram, it may be summarised geometrically by a *regression line*, which represents the scattered dots with a single straight or curved line coming as close to as many of the dots as possible.

3. *Correlation coefficients* (which normally vary from -1 to $+1$) state the amount of statistical association that would be evident in a scatter diagram – i.e. it measures co-variation (but does *not* prove causation).

In addition, one of the major functions of statistics is to assess the investigator's grounds for confidence in maintaining that this apparent co-variation is not due to chance factors admitted by the procedure of sampling. The *chi*-square test is the most generally used (and misused) measure of whether a given difference is significant. Instructions for its use are given on pages 132–3, but for a detailed discussion of the issues involved the student should look at the appropriate references given in Further Reading.

Multivariate Relationships

More difficult statistical techniques are involved where a number of variables have to be considered in conjunction. Quite apart from attempting to combine several observations into one index, it might be important to take into account a number of variables simultaneously in order to interpret an established relationship. This approach is called 'multivariate analysis'. The statistical techniques are beyond the scope of this project, but interested students may follow this up in the references given on pages 175–6.

METHOD

1. *Simple counting and sorting*

Students may work in pairs. The class will have two groups for analysis: (a) the cards punched on the basis of their own replies to the Student's Personal Inventory, with one card representing the reply of each member of the class, and (b) a stack of 100 or more cards representing the replies in the Mail Survey (M.S.). Arrangements will be made so that each pair of students has the use of the complete packs of S.P.I. cards and M.S. cards, which should be kept separate throughout. Each pair will be allocated time (about an hour) on a ICT/IBM counter sorter, where a hand punch is available for repunching damaged cards.

The class should be given a demonstration of the sorter in action and then individual pairs can follow the instructions below, preferably with some supervision by the punch card section staff as necessary.

S.P.I. cards. Sort and count the cards on the columns indicated below.

In the early stages check total on counter with total each time. Count the number of cards falling into each pocket (numbers 0, 1, etc., to 8, 9, X and Y) and total in each case. Draw up a table showing a general breakdown of S.P.I. Cards for the class answering the following questions:

1. Registrar-General's classification – Column 42.
2. Self-selected occupational classification – Column 10.
3. Self placement – Column 31.
4. Family's gross income – Column 29.
5. Home ownership – Column 32.
6. Father's terminal education – Column 13.
7. Mother's terminal education – Column 14.
8. Paternal grandfather's occupational classification – Column 11.
9. Maternal grandfather's occupational classification – Column 12.

M.S. cards. Sort and count the cards and complete another table (as above). It may be possible at this stage to cut out the sorting mechanism so that the sorter counts all cards and rejects them all into the same pocket. Students should check on this with their tutor since it will speed up the process. This table should allow for:

1. Registrar-General's classification – Column 14.
2. Self placement – Column 19.
3. Family's gross income – Column 21.
4. Home ownership – Column 20.
5. Terminal age of education – Column 17.
6. Educational experience – Column 16.

(Note that in column 16 and other columns where double punching has been used – where more than one answer is possible – the *sorting* procedure is more complicated. However, *counting* can continue as above, but totals will not tally.)

2. *Internal breakdown of population*
Each pair of students should select two of the variables used above for an initial comparison within the S.P.I. and M.S. cards, not using at this stage a column where there is double punching. They should then *sort* on one of these columns, and, keeping the piles separate, sort each of them on the second column chosen. Tables for the S.P.I. and M.S. cards can then be drawn upon the following lines:

TABLES 1 and 2

S.P.I./M.S.

Variable 1

	0	1	2	3	4	5	6	7	8	9	X	Y	Total
Variable 2													
0													
1													
2													
3													
4													
5													
6													
7													
8													
9													
X													
Y													
TOTAL													

Treatment of Results

1. *Scatter diagram* (grouped). From Tables 1 and 2 draw a scatter diagram on graph paper to suggest any possible association.

2. *Regression line.* Suggest any possible straight (or curved) line which comes as close as possible to the dots on the scatter diagrams.

3. *Coefficient of Correlation for Grouped Data*

Draw up and complete Table 3 using figures from Table 1 (omit values coded X and Y; for simplicity restrict variables to five values each as a maximum; combine categories if necessary to achieve this). Use a large sheet of paper.

TABLE 3

S.P.I. Correlation of

Variable y (take midpoint as origin)	\-2	\-1	0	1	2	f_y	$f_y y$	$f_y y^2$
\-2								
\-1								
0								
1								
2								
f_x						$=\Sigma f$	$=\Sigma f_y y$	$=\Sigma f_y y$
$f_x x$						$=f_x x$		
$f_x x^2$						$=\Sigma_x x^2$		
Vertical total of xy						$=\Sigma fxy$		

Column heading: *Variable x (take midpoint as origin)* spans columns \-2, \-1, 0, 1, 2.

Calculation and completion of table:

For each *cell*:

1. Put frequency (f) of the pair of values in Table 1 in *centre* of cell.
2. In the *upper left-hand corner* of each cell put the product xy of the x, y values for that cell.
3. In the *lower right-hand corner* put the 'product-moment' fxy of the cell found by multiplying the central number (f) by the upper left-hand number (xy).

For each *row*:

1. Calculate the horizontal totals for each value of y ($=f_y$).
2. Calculate the first moment of each value of y ($=f_y y$).
3. Calculate the second moment of each value of y ($=f_y y^2$).

For each *column*:

1. Repeat as for *y*, calculating $f_x, f_x x$, and $f_x x^2$ for each value of *x*.
2. Calculate the vertical totals of product moments (the numbers in the lower right-hand corners of each cell).

The Coefficient of Correlation can then be calculated by substituting the values obtained in the formula:

Coefficient of Correlation

$$(r_{xy}) = \frac{(\Sigma f_{xy}/\Sigma f) - (\Sigma f_x x/\Sigma f)(\Sigma f_y y/\Sigma f)}{\sqrt{[(\Sigma f_x x^2/\Sigma f) - (\Sigma f_x x/\Sigma f)^2]} \times \sqrt{[(f_y y^2 \Sigma/\Sigma f) - (\Sigma f_y y/\Sigma f)^2]}}$$

(*Caution*: This procedure assumes *linearity* and should be used with care; also notice that many uses of the results may assume normal distribution of *x* and *y* in the population, and thus would normally only be used for normally distributed data. It is used here as a purely descriptive measure.)

4. *The use of* chi-*square in testing contingency tables*

Where data are not necessarily linear (that is the scatter diagram does not tend to show a straight line), where no assumptions about the normality of its distribution can be made, and where the data are the result of some sampling process, the most convenient method is to use the *chi*-square test when investigating the possible relationship between two variables. (See Project 23 for elementary use.[1])

Complete Tables 4a and 4b using data from Table 2, collapsing table to at most five rows and five columns.

TABLE 4a

Observed Frequencies

	Variable *x*	Total
Variable *y*		
TOTAL		

Procedure for considering whether there is an association between *x* and *y* evident from the figures. Fill in the total (column *A*) and total (row *B*) in Table 4b. Then, assuming that the variables are independent, complete the table of expected frequencies (see Project

[1] The argument behind the χ^2 test is strictly valid only if none of the class frequencies are very small.

TABLE 4*b*

Expected Frequencies

		A
y	*x*	*Total*

B TOTAL

23 for details). Then tabulate Observed and Expected frequencies in Table 5 and calculate χ^2.

TABLE 5

O	E			
Observed frequencies	*Expected frequencies*	$O-E$	$(O-E)^2$	$\dfrac{(O-E)^2}{E}$

TOTAL $=\chi^2$

The value for χ^2 is clearly dependent on the size of the table. To allow for this in assessing the result, count the number of 'Degrees of Freedom' in 4*a* by using the formula:

$$D \text{ of } F = (h - 1)(k - 1),$$

where h is the number of rows, and k the number of columns. The level of significance can then be determined from a table of the percentage points of the χ^2 distribution to be found in statistical tables or at the end of many statistical textbooks (e.g. Loveday).
Complete: In Table 4 the value of $\chi^2 = \ldots \ldots$; with $\ldots \ldots$ degrees of freedom the difference is significant at the $\ldots \ldots$ per cent level (or)/is not significant.

5. If time is available, students may conduct further breakdowns of the S.P.I. or M.S. data and calculate correlations between the different indices. Alternatively they might start to consider how several of the variables might be combined into one index.

6. Another extension to this project would be for the class to plan a further analysis of the S.P.I. results and the returns from the mail

questionnaire. The S.P.I. returns would give a complete picture of the class and of previous classes and could be written up as a report. The M.S. analysis would enable the student to compare the people responding in a mail survey with the population as a whole (using for comparison census returns for the population surveyed).

DISCUSSION

1. Discuss the different indices of social class position used in the S.P.I. and M.S., noting the extent to which individuals occupy similar positions on different scales. Suggest an improved stratification scale which might be used in surveys of this type. With which dimension(s) of stratification is this scale concerned?

2. Either from observation or from your calculations decide which pairs of indices seem to produce the highest correlation, which the lowest? Explain why this is so.

3. Discuss two of the major methodological issues which emerge during the project. The following are suggested as possibilities:

   i. The problem of non-response in a mail survey.
   ii. The practice of collapsing contingency tables before conducting a test of significance.
   iii. The extent to which a product-moment coefficient or correlation can be used in social research.
   iv. The uses and limitations of the *chi*-square test of significance in social research (read Selvin and Lipsct *et al.* below).

Further Reading

INDICES OF SOCIAL CLASS POSITION

Toby, J. (chap. 7 gives introduction to the various techniques)

Broom, L. and Selznick, P. (chap. 6 gives elementary treatment of methods of studying social stratification)

Hall, J. and Jones, D. Caradog (introduction to the Hall-Jones scale)

Classification of Occupations, 1960 (all occupations coded for classification as in Census reports)

Chapman, D. (British example of scale based on evaluation of social symbols)

Centers, R. (American ditto)

Hatt, P. K. (review of problems and methods of stratification scales)
Warner, W. L. and Lunt, P. S. (Elmtown Reputational approach)
Warner, W. L. *et al.* (Warner's 'I.S.C.' and 'E.P.' indices)
Glass, D. V. (use of Hall-Jones scale in unique programme of
    research in Britain)
Young, M. and Willmott, P.
Reiss, A. J. *et al.* (research on ranking occupations in United States,
    includes useful chapter by Hatt)
North, C. C. and Hatt, P. K. (brief summary of NORC research on
    status of occupations)

There are also a number of studies of occupational rankings in
different countries. For instance, see Tuckman on Canada in
Canadian Journal of Sociology, vol. 1, no. 2; Hutchinson on Brazil in
British Journal of Sociology, vol. 8, no. 2, 1951.

For a good general introduction to the theory of social stratification
see Bottomore, T.

For other references see footnotes in Barber, B. (chaps. 5–8) and
Caplow, T. (chap. 2), etc.

STATISTICAL ANALYSIS OF DATA

Madge, J. (1953) (pp. 66 ff., 'The Guidance of Statistics')
Moser, C. A. (chap. 15, summary of analytical procedures)
Loveday, R. (1961) (chap. 7, elementary statistics of the use of χ^2)
Tate, M. W. (chap. 7, correlation and regression – a full introduction
    to the statistics)
Thomlinson, R. (chap. 5, statistical operations in sociology)
Selvin, H. C. (1957/8)
Lipset, S. M. *et al.* (appendix 1 – a defence of the deliberate omission
    of tests of significance)
Lazarsfeld, P. F. and Rosenberg, M. (section 2, 'Multivariate
    Analysis')

Project 32 **Distribution of Human Variables** The comparison and measurement of variability and an introduction to the principle of sampling

OBJECTIVE

To compare the frequency distribution curves of various data and to discuss the meaning of the differences revealed.

REFERENCES

Vernon, P. E. 'Measurement of Abilities, Attitudes and Personality Traits' in Welford, A. T. *et al.* (eds.), *Society*.

Young, P. V. *Scientific Social Surveys and Research* (chap. 13).

INTRODUCTION

Frequency distributions in actual practice not only vary in range but also in the shape of the resulting curve. Two aspects of the shape of the distribution are particularly important here: (1) The extent to which values on the whole differ from the mean value and (2) the degree of asymmetry or 'skewness' of the curve. In this project the class will be producing a number of frequency distributions, the differences in shape of which can then be interpreted in sociological terms.

METHOD

There follow four suggestions for producing four frequency distributions which should be used at the tutor's discretion.

1. *The distribution of 'heads' on 20 tosses of 5 coins*
   The student should use five coins tossed twenty times to complete Table 1 as below.

TABLE I

Distribution of 'heads' on 20 tosses of 5 coins

Frequency
of occurrence

All five	HHHHH	
4 out of 5	HHHHT	
3 out of 5	HHHTT	
2 out of 5	HHTTT	
1 out of 5	HTTTT	
All tails	TTTTT	

TOTAL FREQUENCY

The smoothed frequency polygon can then be drawn (for method see Project 4).

2. *The distribution of scores on a numerical problem-solving test*
Here is a row of numbers that go in a certain order.

19 : 18 : 17 : 16 : 15 : 14 : 13 : 12 : 11

Here is the same row but with two numbers missing.

19 : 18 : 17 : 16 : 15 :   :   : 12 : 11

The items of the test are like this. Your task is to find out how the numbers are arranged and to write in the missing numbers. The first item of the Practice Test below has been done to show you how. Not all the items have their numbers in a simple sequence. For example in this next row each number is repeated. The missing numbers are 6 and 8.

2 : 2 : 4 : 4 : 6 :   :   : 8 : 10

Now do the rest of the Practice Test in the same way.

Practice Test

1 : 3 : 5 : 7 : 9 : (11) : (13) : 15 : 17
10 : 20 : 30 : 40 : 50 : (60) : (70) : 80 : 90
5 : 4 : 6 :   : 7 :   :   : 7 : 9
1 : 2 : 1 : 3 : 1 :   :   : 5 : 1

The real test over the page is done like these. If you come to an item you cannot work out, do not leave it out: just guess as near as you can and go on with the next item. Work as quickly as you can but be careful not to make mistakes.

In each row write in the missing numbers. *You have 5 minutes.*[1]

```
 2:  4:  6:  8:10:—:—:16:  18
90:80:70:60:50:—:—:20:  10
 1:  1:  2:  2:  3:—:—:  4:   5
 6:  2:  6:  4:  6:—:—:  8:   6
 4:  6:  5:  7:  6:—:—:  9:   8

81:72:63:54:45:—:—:18:   9
 6:  7:10:11:14:—:—:19:  22
 1:  3:  2:  3:  3:—:—:  3:   5
20:19:16:15:12:—:—:  7:   4
 3:  7:  5:  9:  7:—:—:13:  11

 6:  7:  8:  7:  8:—:—:  9:  10
 4:  2:  6:  3:  8:—:—:  5:  12
 2:  4:  3:  9:  4:—:—:25:   6
 8:  1:  6:  2:  4:—:—:  4:   0
 6:13:11:18:16:—:—:28:  26

 4:  5:  7:10:14:—:—:32:  40
 2:  6:  4:  8:  6:—:—:12:  10
 1:  2:  0:  2:  3:—:—:  4:   0
110:90:72:56:42:—:—:12:   6
 2:  4:  6:  4:  6:—:—:  8:  10

45:36:28:21:15:—:—:  3:   1
37:31:29:23:21:—:—:  7:   5
 2:24:  4:12:  6:—:—:  3:  10
 1:  0:  9:  0:25:—:—:  0:  81
 1:  1:  2:  3:  5:—:—:21:  34

 2:  6:12:20:30:—:—:72:  90
 1:  4:  8:11:22:—:—:53:106
48:  7:35:  6:24:—:—:  4:   8
100:10:50:64:  8:—:—:  6:  18
 5:  3:  8:  6:14:—:—:24:  50
```

The class will be given the correct answers. Each student's total score should then be used to complete Table 2, from which the smoothed frequency polygon can be drawn.

[1] Alternatively, *you have until first person finishes.*

TABLE 2

Distribution of class scores on numerical problem-solving test

Scores (count one for each number given correctly)

Scores	Mid interval	Frequency of occurrence
0–4	2	
5–9	7	
10–14	12	
15–19	17	
20–24	22	
25–29	27	
30–34	32	
35–39	37	
40–44	42	
45–49	47	
50–54	52	
55–59	57	
60 (All correct)		
TOTAL FREQUENCY		

Note: In a small class, intervals should be 0–9, 10–19, etc.

3. *The distribution of scores on a biblical knowledge test*
There follows a short test of biblical knowledge. Students may have a reasonable amount of time to complete it.

Biblical Knowledge Test

Complete the following:
   1. Which Book of the Old Testament follows Judges?
   2. Who, in the Gospel according to Matthew, asked for John the Baptist's head on a charger?
   3. Complete the quotation: 'Give not that which is holy unto the
............'
   4. How many Epistles to the Corinthians appear in the Bible?
   5. 'Were there not ten cleansed? But where are the nine?' What were the nine?
   6. 'For as I passed by, and beheld your devotions, I found an altar with this inscription *To The Unknown God*.' Who passed by?
   7. Whom was he addressing?
   8. Who or what 'was more subtle than any beast of the field'?

9. 'I am distressed for thee, my brother . . . .'

10. In which Book of the Bible does it say 'Wisdom is better than rubies'?

11. 'Remember now thy Creator in the days of thy youth while the . . . . days come not.' Which days?

12. 'I charge you, O Daughters of Jerusalem, if ye find my beloved, that ye tell him, that I am sick of love.' Who is sick of love?

13. 'Even Solomon in all his glory was not arrayed like one of these.' What are 'these'?

14. 'Fear ye not, therefore, ye are of more value than many . . . .'

15. 'Wist ye not that I must be about my Father's business?' Whose father?

16. Which Gospel starts 'In the beginning was the Word'?

17. Who said 'What is truth?'?

18. 'Now Barabbas was a . . . .'

19. 'Behold, a virgin shall conceive, and bear a son, and shall call his name . . . .'

20. Complete: 'Mene, mene, tekel . . . .'

21. 'All wickedness is but little to the wickedness of a . . . .'

22. 'How can he get wisdom (etc., etc.) whose talk is of . . . .'

23. Who 'Shall be called the children of God'?

24. '. . . . ., because thou hast seen me, thou hast believed.' Who?

25. Who wrote, 'If a woman have long hair, it is a glory to her'?

26. Which 'is the greatest' (of faith, hope and charity) according to one of the Epistles?

27. What was St Luke's occupation?

28. 'Be swift to hear, slow to . . . ., slow to wrath.'

29. 'Perfect love casteth out . . . .'

30. Who 'saw the holy city, new Jerusalem, coming down from God out of heaven'?

31. 'For I feared thee, because thou art an austere man.' Who was 'an austere man'?

32. How many mites did the poor widow cast into the treasury?

33. What are the words of the shortest verse in the Bible?

34. Who was Ananias's wife?

35. 'To be carnally minded is . . . .'

36. '. . . . . is the fulfilling of the law.'

37. 'Only Luke is with me.' With whom?

38. 'Give honour unto the wife as unto the weaker vessel.' Who wrote this?

39. Who was 'the son of Nun'?

40. Who said 'Repent ye, for the Kingdom of heaven is at hand.'?

The class will be given the correct answers. Only these answers count as 'correct' for the purposes of this exercise. Each student's total score should then be used to complete Table 3, from which the smoothed frequency polygon can be drawn.

TABLE 3

Distribution of class scores on biblical knowledge test

As Table 2. Score: count 1 for each answer given correctly.

4. *The distribution of scores on an objective test of sociological knowledge*
Students will be given a reasonable amount of time to complete the test.

1. The word sociology appeared first in ....'s writings.

2. K. R. Popper emphasises that the poverty of .... generally lies in the inability to imagine a change in the conditions of change – a criticism which is levelled in particular at the work of Marx.

3. Durkheim, in his discussion of method, said that sociologists should study ...., and that they should study them as things (*comme les choses*).

4. '.......... are these objective consequences contributing to the adjustment or adaptation of the system which are intended and recognised by participants in the system.' (Merton).

5. Weber's discussion of social stratification distinguishes between class and ....

6. .... challenged the belief that sex differences in behaviour are a simple function of biology by interpreting the contrasts, between the Arapesh, Mundugumor, Tchambuli, and Americans, in the behaviour of the two sexes, to mean that differential behaviour of men and women everywhere is the result of differential socialisation.

7. C. H. Cooley coined the term .... and defines it as characterised by intimate face-to-face association and co-operation.

8. R. Linton defines a . . . . as a position in a pattern of social relations; it is a collection of rights and duties, or of norms.

9. 'Experience tends universally to show that the purely . . . . type of administrative organisation . . . is, from a purely technical point of view, capable of attaining the highest degree of efficiency.' (Weber).

10. The . . . . factor refers to the size, distribution and composition of the population.

11. According to . . . . 'the history of all hitherto existing society is the history of class struggles.'

12. Davis and Moore proposed a theory of . . . . based on the assumption that all societies face the dual problems of placement – getting people to fill statuses – and performance – getting them to act out the associated roles.

13. A . . . . is an agricultural collective in Israel, whose main features include communal living, collective ownership of all property, and the communal rearing of children.

14. Burnham's thesis was that industrial . . . . is becoming the new controlling elite in society.

15. Sutherland's . . . . 'theory' of criminal behaviour is in terms of an excess of definitions favourable to violation of law over definitions unfavourable to violation of law.

16. Crimes committed by the upper and middle classes in the course of their occupations have been called by Sutherland . . . .

17. According to . . . . religion essentially is a society's classification of some things as sacred and of other things as profane.

18. Merton states that . . . . is the practice of interpreting data by establishing their consequences for larger structures in which they are implicated.

19. Complete Michels' 'Iron Law': 'Who says organisation says . . . .'

20. . . . . is a lifelong process whereby a person learns social values and social roles of the culture.

21. A diagram of informal relations within a group is referred to as a . . . .

22. Status that a person receives by virtue of his birth is . . . . status.

23. Prescribed religious acts that are sacred in themselves, and also symbolise the sacred, are called . . . .

24. . . . . is legitimated power.

25. One way to study social stratification is to ask people how they classify one another. This method is called, by Lloyd Warner, the .... approach.

26. .... describes the 'I' and the 'me' as two components of self: the acting self he terms the 'me', while the part of the self that is an organisation of the internalised attitudes of others is the 'I'.

27. According to David Riesman, modern man is primarily ....-directed.

28. According to G. H. Mead, ... precedes language, mind and self-consciousness.

29. .... emphasised that as a result of change, non-material aspects of a cultural item lag behind changes in the material aspect pertaining to that item.

30. Folkways are norms with .... sanctions.

31. .... refers to man's total social heritage – all the knowledge, skills, beliefs and customs he acquires as a member of society.

32. Durkheim used the term '.......... solidarity' to describe solidarity which was characterised by specialisation, division of labour, and interdependence.

33. In Durkheim's terminology, ... is a social state of 'deregulation', – where there is a lack of clear-cut norms.

34. An individual's .... group(s) provide(s) him with standards by which to judge his own behaviour.

35. Generally the .... is the major agency through which socialisation takes place.

36. Merton maintains that the sociology of .... came into being with the signal hypothesis that even truths were to be held socially accountable, and were to be related to the historical society in which they emerged.

37. Merton uses the device of the analytical .... for presenting codified materials (e.g. in dealing with functional analysis), in the belief that they display the array of assumptions, concepts and basic propositions employed in sociological analysis.

38. According to Max Weber's analysis the .... ethic contributed significantly to the development of capitalism in the Western world.

39. .... groups, Weber maintained, are communities, unlike classes; they are groups where the members consider each other to be equals and evaluate their group in terms of 'honour'.

40. Who wrote *The Social System*?

TABLE 4

Distribution of class scores on an objective test of sociological knowledge

As Table 2

The class will then be given the correct answers and results processed as before.

TREATMENT OF RESULTS

1. Using the results obtained above, draw the smoothed frequency polygons so that they can be compared.
2. Compare the dispersions of any pair of these graphs by the use of (*a*) the mean deviation and (*b*) the standard deviation for each.

Calculation of Mean Deviation
This is a measure of dispersion which makes use of all the observations of a group (cf. Range and Interquartile Range).

1. Calculate the median value.
2. Draw up and complete Table 5, columns 1–4.

TABLE 5

1 Mid Values	2 Deviations from the median value (take all as +ve) *x*	3 Frequency (from earlier table) *f*	4 Multiply deviation by frequency *fx*	5 Calculate (col 2 × col 4) *fx²*
TOTAL		Σf=	Σfx	Σfx²=

3. Find the mean of the deviations by dividing the total of the *fx* column by the total frequency.

Repeat for other set(s) of readings.

∴ Mean Deviation 1 =   2 =   from Median.

Calculation of Standard Deviation
1. Complete column 5.
2. Calculate standard deviation using formula:

$$S.D. = 5 \times \sqrt{\left[\frac{\Sigma fx^2}{\Sigma f} - \left(\frac{\Sigma fx}{\Sigma f}\right)^2\right]}$$

Note 1: The mean deviation can be taken from mode, median or mean. The standard deviation *must* be taken from the mean. In this experiment we have done this by applying the term

$$- (\Sigma fx/\Sigma f)^2$$

as a correcting factor.

Note 2: 5 in the formula is the interval between mid values.

$$\therefore \text{ S.D. } 1 = \qquad 2 =$$

Discussion

1. Compare your frequency polygons, and attempt to account for the differences in their distributions and shapes. What type of function do you expect to be normally distributed? For instance, compare inherited with learned characteristics.

2. Problem-solving tests are widely used in the testing of native intelligence. Upon what assumptions? Are these justified?

3. On the basis of this project write a paragraph to suggest how you would go about testing a hypothesis comparing innate ability and social conditioning.

Further Reading

Methodology

Loveday, R. (1958) (chap. 4, elementary introduction to method of calculating mean deviation and standard deviation)

Tate, M. W. (chap. 4, more advanced discussion of variability and its measurement)

Moroney, M. J. (chaps. 5 and 9, non-technical treatment of distribution)

Inherited and Acquired Characteristics

Douglas, J. W. B.; *Fifteen to Eighteen* (The Crowther Report); Floud, J. E. *et al.*

Project 33 A Kinship Universe
Genealogical charts as an example of the use of organisation charts

OBJECTIVE

To develop for comparative purposes a diagrammatic method of representing the structure of kinship.

REFERENCES

Parsons, T. 'The Kinship System of the Contemporary United States', in *Essays in Sociological Theory*.
Firth, R. (ed.), *Two Studies of Kinship in London* (esp. pp. 42–58).
Bott, E. *Family and Social Network*.

INTRODUCTION

There has been little systematic research into how significant kin ties are for individual and family behaviour. In Britain this research has been mainly concerned with the working class. In this project the student is to attempt to represent the structure of his own extended family diagrammatically for comparison with one or more other members of the class.

Although social anthropologists' genealogical charts may be used as a basis at the start, it is envisaged that the final diagrams may use quite different conventions and techniques, and also represent *social* relationships as distinct from consanguinity alone.

METHOD

Note: Although Firth's definitions are given here, students may prefer to use those given by Bott (chap. 5).

1. Working alone each student should list all his or her recognised kin (see Firth above: 'all persons who are recognised by the informant as related to him by consanguinity (blood relationship) or affinity (relationship by marriage) whether known by name or not'. For reference some identifying characteristic, such as job or place of residence, can be noted.

2. The list should then be inspected for *nominated* kin (those whose Christian or surnames are specifically known and remembered). These should be underlined in the list.

3. Within the range of nominated kin, Firth distinguishes between 'effective' and 'non-effective' kin. 'By effective is meant all kin with whom some social contact is maintained, as by correspondence, occasional visits or attendance at family ceremonial.' Decide on an exact criterion of this (e.g. those present at a recent marriage or funeral, or mutual exchange of Christmas cards) and put X next to their names on your list.

4. The final distinction is between peripheral and intimate effective kin. ('With the latter, social contact is purposeful, close and frequent. With the former, it is distant, accidental or sporadic' (Firth).) Again decide on an exact criterion; then circle those who, in your case, are intimate effective kin.

5. Starting in rough, each pair of students should then attempt to develop a diagram to represent their individual kinship networks as systems of social relationships. As a guide, it will probably be convenient to start with *ego* in the centre of the page and use conventions of distance, thickness of line (etc.) on the diagram to represent different aspects of the structure.

Apart from the distinctions indicated by Firth, Parsons considers the household unit and the pattern of inheritance of property as important to his analysis. Other factors which might be considered are: holidays shared, economic dependency, services rendered (e.g. on birth of child, illness, etc.), attendance at family festivities, etc. In some cases conflicts, ideological splits, etc. may be indicated.

The final diagram should be transferred to graph paper (or plain paper if preferred).

TREATMENT OF RESULTS

Compare diagrams with partner or another student, and, if possible in discussion, draw up your conclusions about your extended family or those of the class as a whole. (For instance compare it with the generalisations of Parsons, Goode or another sociologist.)

Calculate the percentage of your 'recognised' kin that were

1. 'Nominated' (including effective and intimate).
2. 'Effective' (including intimate).

Also the percentage of 'nominated' that were

1. 'Effective' (including 'intimate').
2. 'Intimate'.

And the percentage of 'effective' kin that are 'intimate'.

DISCUSSION

1. Discuss Young and Wilmott's assertion that the extended family is a bridge between the nuclear family and the wider society.

2. 'Most family systems of the world are moving towards a conjugal system' (Goode 1963). 'While sense of obligation to kin and the lack of firm rules about behaviour to such kin bothers some families, the possibility of *selected* relationships among kin is one of the ways by which industrial/urban influences towards individuation and impersonal isolation are counteracted' (Firth 1964). Can you see evidence for either of these trends in your family? Comment.

3. Which ratio calculated above might provide the most useful index of the extent to which your family approaches the conjugal pattern?

4. What aspects of the family structure would you consider that might not appear or be understated in the research into kinship?

5. What are the main functions of this kind of diagrammatic presentation of social organisations? What are their main limitations?

Further Reading

Schusky, E. L.; Radcliffe-Brown, A. R. (1960); Schneider, D. M. and Homans, G. C.; Goode, W. J. (1963) (esp. chap. 2, para. 9, and comparisons with Arabic Islam, Sub-Saharan Africa, India, China and Japan); Sampson, A. (chap. 3); Goode, W. J. (1964*b*); Goode, W. J. (1964*a*).

Project 34 **Full-time Miscreants**
Accounting for the results of an empirical investigation

Objective

To compare the student's interpretation of sociological data with that of the investigator.

References

Merton, R. K. *Social Theory and Social Structure* (chaps. 2 and 3, 'The Bearing of Sociological Theory on Empirical Research' and 'The Bearing of Empirical Research on Sociological Theory').

Mack, J. 'Full-time miscreants, delinquent neighbourhoods and criminal networks', *British Journal of Sociology* (to be referred to *after* project has been completed).

Introduction

Interpretation of research data can often be no more than common-sense reading of simple tables and explanation in logical terms of the figures within them. Where sampling has been involved, this may be set in the context of sampling errors, and where complicated indices and relationships are involved this may involve highly sophisticated analysis. But whatever the nature of the data, some interpretation is necessary, and in some cases it could be considered the most important stage in the inquiry. It is never possible to leave the reader to select his own interpretation from raw data – and in most cases (especially where the investigator's own acquaintance with the subject is considerable) his own conclusions on the data are the most valuable product of the research.

Problems of analysis and interpretation differ in different study designs and normally they present greatest difficulties in exploratory, non-experimental investigations, where the search for the broader meanings of the findings had led to the investigator's greater reliance on hazardous post-factum interpretations.

Rose (see Further Reading) distinguishes five points at which 'choice-making' enters into scientific research. He suggests that 'scientific method is not completely determined, but leaves open many "arbitrary" choices for the scientist to make, and that the scientist's choices at these points are not mere random expressions of his free will but reflect his general cultural and scientific background.' The five points are:

1. The choice of problem for research.
2. The range of admissible hypotheses.
3. The concepts used to formulate problems.
4. The techniques of research.
5. The form of conclusion.

'These points at which scientists must make choices are so important that they lead us to a recognition that science can never be value-free but must contain a strong strain of cultural and individual choices.' There are many possible forms for presenting the same data, all of which may be equally compatible under the canons of science.

Normally there are two *main* considerations when data are interpreted. First the results are linked with those of other studies in an effort to establish *continuity*. Secondly, the interpretation is an attempt to produce an *explanation*. Thus it becomes involved with *theory*.

A theory may have played a part in the original choice of a research topic, and it undoubtedly on many occasions stimulates research and enhances the meaning of the findings. On the other hand, research also serves to test existing theories and provide a basis for new ones. Where few theories are worked out in sufficient detail or not operationalised, research has an alternative function of contributing to the development of theories – by their progressive refinement or reformulation in particular. In addition, empirical research can lead to the clarification of theoretical concepts and the refocusing of theoretical interests.

The particular type of interpretation used in this project, called post factum or 'effect-to-cause' interpretation, calls for particular comment. This is where data are collected and interpretations are

G W.S.I.

subsequently applied – in contrast to the empirical testing of a predesignated hypothesis. This approach is attractive since the explanations used are bound to be consistent with the data. Explanations which are found not to be so are neglected. Thus the procedure can really only reach the level of plausibility, and cannot disprove a hypothesis. It does not lend itself to nullifiability. Several interpretations may seem equally plausible.

METHOD

Each student should read Appendix 11. This is the first part of John Mack's article, giving his findings in the initial stages of a research programme. After this he should write (1) a summary of the results, and (2) his own conclusions as if he were completing the article.

TREATMENT OF RESULTS

Each student should look at Mack's summary and conclusions and compare them with his own and those of one other member of the class, using appropriate categories. Use three columns as follows: Your Interpretation; Mack's Interpretation; Other Students' Interpretations.

DISCUSSION

1. How is it possible to choose between competing interpretations? Suggest some principles and illustrate from this project.

2. In your comparison, what was the chief influence which seemed to produce difference in interpretation? Knowledge, values?

3. Write a few paragraphs linking this project to the sociology of knowledge applied to sociologists.

4. What do you think should have been the next stage of Mack's research project?

Further Reading

Selltiz, C. *et al.* (chap. 14, research and theory); Rose, A. M.; Kendall, P. L. and Lazarsfeld, P. F. (interpretation procedures in *The American Soldier*); Komarovsky, M. (1955).

Project 35 Household Incomes and Expenditure Patterns Simple calculations with calculating machines (using secondary data)

OBJECTIVE

To compare patterns of expenditure of households with different incomes, using calculating machines.[1]

MATERIALS

Simple calculating machines.[1]

REFERENCE

Ministry of Labour *Family Expenditure Survey, Report for 1963.*

INTRODUCTION

Each year a sample of about 5,000 addresses is selected by the Ministry of Labour and visited in rotation throughout the year. The households at these addresses are asked to co-operate in maintaining detailed expenditure records for fourteen consecutive days, and in providing interviewers with information about the household, the members' incomes and regular payments. The selection procedure is a two-stage probability sample – a random selection of names from the Register of Electors in a stratified sample of local authority areas in the United Kingdom. Hotels, boarding-houses, etc., and families who have moved are excluded. Of the effective sample, 29 per cent contained one or more members who refused to co-operate or could

[1] *Note:* If calculating machines are not available a possible alternative is to use approximations and slide rules. It is important, however, that the student should learn a swift method of mechanical calculation.

not be contacted, leaving a final number of 3,415 households in the survey (see *Family Expenditure Survey*, pp. 2 ff., for general description of these households).

The project uses some of the data collected in this survey for an analysis of patterns of expenditure among households with different sizes of income.

METHOD (Students are to work in pairs)

1. Learn basic routines of calculating machine to be used: simple addition, subtraction, multiplication and division. Also squares, cubes, etc. (This may be covered by a demonstration by your tutor or computing staff.)

2. Complete Table 1.

TABLE 1

Expenditure on selected items in three selected income groups

(from *Family Expenditure Survey* 1963, table 2)

	'low' £4 but under £6		'medium' £20 but under £25		'high' £40 – more	
1. TOTAL NUMBER OF HOUSEHOLDS	203		555		284	
	s.	d.	s.	d.	s.	d.
2. Average weekly household *income*	97	3·2	447	1·9	1,180	11·3
3. Convert row 2 into decimal parts of shilling	s.		s.		s.	
	s.	d.	s.	d.	s.	d.
4. Average weekly household *expenditure* (less 'other payments', income tax, national insurance contributions, etc.)	112	5·7	400	1·6	822	6·0
5. Convert into decimal parts of a shilling	s.		s.		s.	
6. Excess (+ or –) of 'income' over 'expenditure'	s.		s.		s.	
	s.	d.	s.	d.	s.	d.
7. Expenditure on housing	21	4·1	40	7·9	81	3·0
8. Convert into decimal (etc.)	s.		s.		s.	
	s.	d.	s.	d.	s.	d.
9. Expenditure on fuel, light, and power	16	4·4	24	0·1	36	2·4
10. Converted	s.		s.		s.	

	'low' £4 but under £6		'medium' £20 but under £25		'high' £40 – more	
	s.	d.	s.	d.	s.	d.
11. Expenditure on food	40	11·7	122	8·8	187	7·0
12. Converted	s.		s.		s.	
	s.	d.	s.	d.	s.	d.
13. Expenditure on alcoholic drink	2	0·2	15	2·5	36	2·5
14. Converted	s.		s.		s.	
	s.	d.	s.	d.	s.	d.
15. Expenditure on tobacco	4	0·0	25	8·3	35	3·9
16. Converted	s.		s.		s.	
	s.	d.	s.	d.	s.	d.
17. Expenditure on clothing and footwear	7	6·5	34	9·3	89	9·9
18. Converted	s.		s.		s.	
	s.	d.	s.	d.	s.	d.
19. Expenditure on durable household goods	2	3·5	20	6·1	56	3·3
20. Converted	s.		s.		s.	
	s.	d.	s.	d.	s.	d.
21. Expenditure on other goods (periodicals, toys, cosmetics, cleaning materials, flowers, etc.)	8	0·8	26	9·9	55	11·6
22. Converted	s.		s.		s.	
	s.	d.	s.	d.	s.	d.
23. Expenditure on transport and vehicles	2	8·1	55	7·0	106	10·7
24. Converted	s.		s.		s.	
	s.	d.	s.	d.	s.	d.
25. Expenditure on other services (postage, telephone, domestic help, hairdressing, sport, etc.)	7	2·4	32	4·4	132	6·3
26. Converted	s.		s.		s.	
	s.	d.	s.	d.	s.	d.
27. Miscellaneous	0	0·1	1	9·4	4	5·3
28. Converted	s.		s.		s.	

3. Calculate figures from this table to answer the following questions:

    i. Which income groups spend the highest and lowest proportions of their weekly income on each of the following: housing, fuel (etc.), food, alcohol, tobacco, clothing, durable household goods, and transport? Show your results in tabular form.

ii. What are the ratios of the high income group's expenditure to the low income group's expenditure on the same items?

4. (*optional*) From the full results of the survey, calculate which individual items are the most significant in the weekly budget of the low income households.

5. (*optional*) Compare some of the figures obtained in the 1963 Survey with figures from one earlier or more recent survey, and draw up your conclusions on changing patterns of expenditure (*a*) in all households and (*b*) one particular income group.

DISCUSSION

1. Which items might be under- or over-recorded in this survey? Why?

2. Some figures in the full tables are marked as having a 'relatively high sampling error'. What does this mean, and what precautions should the reader take when using figures so marked?

3. On which groups of items do the higher income groups tend to spend their additional incomes? Suggest one sociological explanation for this.

4. Comment on the methodology of the *Family Expenditure Survey* (in particular on sampling procedure, non-response and recording procedure). Suggest improvements to increase the validity of the findings.

5. Suggest how questions on expenditure could be used in an investigation of sociological differences between urban and rural families.

Further Reading

COMMENTS AND STATISTICS ON SOCIAL CONDITIONS

Carr-Saunders, Sir A. M. *et al.*; Marsh, D. C.; Central Statistical Office; Richmond, A. H.; Ministry of Labour (1957); Ministry of Labour (1961, 1962, 1963)

Project 36 **The Computer in Sociology** The use of the computer

OBJECTIVE

A demonstration of an elementary application of the digital computer in the analysis of sociological data.

MATERIALS

1. About one hour booked on the university/college computer.
2. Demonstration program.
3. Spare data tape.

REFERENCE

Thomlinson, R. *Sociological Concepts and Research* (chap. 6, an introduction to the applications of the computer to sociological analysis).

INTRODUCTION

At present most techniques of mathematical analysis in use in sociology are relatively simple and require no advanced mathematical knowledge. Equipment such as slide rules and calculating machines are normally quite adequate for the purpose. However, other methods of analysis are being introduced which can only be used by specialists in this field, and here the use of computers is extending rapidly.

The basic computer has five components: input, store, arithmetic unit, output and control unit. The input unit introduces information and instructions into the machine by means of punched cards, punched paper tape or magnetic discs, tape or ink. The store merely memorises the information ('data') and instructions ('program'), awaiting an order to start from the control unit. The

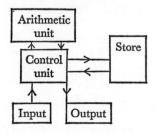

arithmetic unit (or 'processing' unit) carries out simple arithmetic on this information in accordance with the instructions. The output unit then prints or punches out the results. The whole process is in principle simple. The arithmetic does not involve more than addition, subtraction, multiplication and division. It is the combination of extreme speed in the arithmetic unit with the large store of information and instructions which creates the illusion of intelligence. The programmer has to supply a minutely detailed list of specific instructions in a language that the computer can understand, and it merely follows them exactly and undeviatingly. Once these simple principles have been grasped, the impressive technical arrangements are relatively unimportant, since the purpose of the project is more to understand what the computer can do rather than precisely how it does it.

The computer enables the sociologist to do a variety of things with his data, in particular (i) perform a large number of simple operations on a large body of data; (ii) conduct sophisticated and complex operations on a small (or large) amount of data; or (iii) simulate elements of social behaviour.

(i) In many cases the sociologist uses the computer to carry out a large number of relatively simple operations, such as correlations between pairs of variables, calculating percentages and laying out tables. Here he is making use of the computer's phenomenal speed and large memory to save a great deal of clerical work and its attendant liability to errors.

(ii) On the other hand other methods of analysis (such as factor analysis) are considerably more complex, and their repeated use would require a good deal of expense and expert assistance. However, once the correct program has been written, with a computer each set of data can be analysed with little skilled assistance.

(iii) Some of the problems of experimental design in sociology can be overcome by making the computer perform a function related to that of a mathematical model – with the added advantage that many more variables may be interrelated because of the computer's high speed. It can simulate a social process or event, making manipulation a real possibility. For this the sociologist has to be able to state assumptions which not only include precise definitions of relevant variables and their interrelationships but also can be assigned numerical values. He can then program the computer to determine the *expected* outcome of some events, based on his assumptions. This can then be compared to the *actual* outcome of the observed events. The requirements for computer simulation are approximated in relatively few areas of sociological research, but both voting behaviour and small group interaction have been studied using simulation techniques (see Bales, Hare and McPhee below). However, each set of results provides a basis for improving the researcher's assumptions, seeking additions to the model and refining the mathematical representation of the prediction process.

The potential of the use of computers is very great. The constant restriction upon sociological research of the difficulty of handling the large number of variables in their complex interrelationships as they exist in even the simplest social system may gradually be overcome. It has been suggested further that in this way the sociologist may no longer need to be continually narrowing his research focus, but by an imaginative use of these developments he may widen his scope and aim at macro-sociological syntheses rather than narrow statements on partial and limited findings. Coleman (in Hammond, P. E.) suggests that the computer will radically influence even the kind of data collected. The computer needs precise formulations, 'a more intimate mixture of analysis and synthesis than occurs in our old techniques', and something more rigorous than 'a vague and unreliable model in the researcher's head'.

METHOD

1. Each student should complete the questionnaire on family size, household occupation and family income (Appendix 12).

2. The completed questionnaires will be punched by the computer staff on to cards or tape for feeding into the computer. Meanwhile the tutor or a member of the computer staff will introduce the class to the machine, its language and component parts. Students should note in particular:

a. The method(s) of input.

b. The capacity of the store (+ backing store).

c. The method(s) of output.

d. The estimated speed of calculation.

e. The speed of reading in data.

f. the speed of output (1) in printed form and (2) in other form(s).

3. A demonstration program will be run as an indication of the speed and performance of the computer on a simple statistical task.

The program is intended to investigate a hypothesised relationship between density of household occupation and family income among the members of the class. The spare data tape can be used as an alternative if the class is small. On the basis of the data provided, the computer will calculate the 'space factor' for each individual's home as a measure of the density of occupation of his home. The formula used is:

$$\text{Space factor} = \frac{(2a+b)100}{2c+d+\frac{1}{2}e},$$

where a = number of bedrooms

b = number of other rooms

c = number of adults

d = number of children

e = number of small children

The computer will then lay out the results in the form of three tables as on page 203.

4. Another more sophisticated program can be demonstrated if time is available.

TREATMENT OF RESULTS

Each student should complete the tables using the figures produced by the computer, and write a short paragraph of interpretation.

TABLE I (*etc.*)

*Distribution of urban students' homes by income and
space factor*

Income £ p.a.	Space factor under 60	60–120	120–180	180–240	240–300	over 300	Total
under 500							
500–1000							
1000–1500							
1500–2000							
over 2000							
TOTAL							

Mean space factor =
Mean income =
Correlation coefficient =

DISCUSSION

1. What further statistical tests might be used to interpret these results? Would any qualification be needed when commenting on the correlation coefficients produced?

2. List some of the more important techniques of analysis that you know where a computer might be used with advantage (compared with card sorting, see Projects 30 and 31).

3. 'One of the virtues of computer simulation is that the computer is a hard master for the sociologist' according to Hare and to Thomlinson. Why, in particular?

4. What are the functions of models in science? Describe an example from modern sociology.

Further Reading

GENERAL

Borko, H. (general introduction to computers and data processing systems)

Coleman, J. S. (1964*a*) (a book for the mathematically sophisticated, but chap. 1 gives a useful survey of the uses of mathematics in sociology)

Hagood, M. J. and Price, D. O. (chap. 11)

Riley, M. W. (unit 10, commentary on 'dynamic' studies and the use of the computer)

The Gentle Computer (series of articles on computers and applications first published in *New Scientist*, 14 Oct.–25 Nov. 1965).

Coleman, J. S. (1964*b*) (commentary on this research with outline of the processing of the data)

COMPUTER SIMULATION

Hare, A. P. (1961) (an early attempt at computer simulation)

McPhee, W. N. (another early attempt at computer simulation)

Bales, R. F. (1959) (comment on computer simulation)

Gullahorn, J. T. and Gullahorn, J. E. (computer model of five propositions from Homans' *Social Behavior*)

Pool, I. de Sola and Abelson, R.

Coleman, J. S. (1965) (this number of the Journal is devoted to articles on computer simulation)

Appendix 1

Letter of Introduction

For use wherever information is required from members of the public

University of ....

.... College

Department of ....

Date:

Research Methods in Sociology
To whom it may concern

.... is a student at this University/College.

As part of the course, each student has to take part in some exercises in social research, and I hope that you will be able to help us by answering a few questions.

Of course we use no names and your replies will be treated in confidence. However, if you have any doubts, do not hesitate to get in touch with me personally.

.... (signed)
Class Tutor

Appendix 2 – for Project 4

Results should be tabulated on this form:

Title:.............

Category of action (e.g. less than 5 mins., ignored sign, etc.)	Record of actions as observed (put 1 for each occurrence in appropriate category	Total frequency of occurrence

Appendix 3 – for Project 7 Problem Children Three Cases

There follow brief notes on three local delinquents. Please discuss them each in turn and try to agree on what treatment you feel would be most appropriate for them. You have about *one hour*; so do not take much more than 20 minutes for each of them.

Case 1   **Case of Michael**

Family concerned
Mr *B*, 38 years, vegetable cook in hotel; earns £14.
Mrs *B*, 35 years, housewife.
Elizabeth, 9 years.
Michael, 8 years.
Nicholas, 7 years.
Paula, 5 years.

Referred to Children's Department by Education Welfare
Michael is a problem in school – soiling and enuretic – all children inadequately dressed and dirty. Family previously known to Children's Department when, a year ago, children admitted to care for three weeks, when Mrs *B* confined. (Baby died after 2 days.) Since then, Child Care Officer had visited monthly and had given help with clothing. Family described by Child Care Officer and Health Visitor as needing 'interminable support to manage at a level, physically only just acceptable for the children, but real warmth and a feeling for life being worth living'. School described children as being lively, except Michael, who was reported to be tense and nervous in school and often complaining of pains in his stomach. He had been referred to the hospital and no physical cause was found for stomach pains, soiling or enuresis.

In this area the Child Guidance Officer offers only a diagnostic and referral service, mainly for ascertainment as to maladjustment or educational subnormality for special schooling.

Group decision (if agreement achieved):

Case 2   Case of Rosina

Family concerned
Mother: Mrs *J*.
Daughter: Rosina – 14 years.

Offence
Mrs *J* and Rosina had been in the public library together; Rosina took a distinctive handbag from a table and Mrs *J* saw her do this and did not stop her. Together they spent some of the £10 they found in the bag, which Rosina then used. The father of the loser of the handbag saw Rosina in the town, recognised the bag and notified the police. When questioned, neither Mrs *J* nor Rosina denied taking the bag and before appearing at the Magistrates' Court, Mrs *J* had returned the bag, contents and all the money to the loser.

Home background
A two-bedroomed cottage facing on to an inner courtyard in some old and dilapidated 'buildings' scheduled for demolition. Furnishings poor, but everything very clean. Mrs *J* and Rosina sleep in a double bed in one of the bedrooms, the other is used as a playroom by Rosina. Rent: 13s. 2d. per week. Council may re-house within next two years. Income is Supplementary Allowances £6 10s. 0d. No other income. Mrs *J* does not work.

Group decision (if agreement achieved):

Case 3   Case of Gordon

Boy concerned
Gordon, aged 18½.

Offence
Breaking and entering, larceny.

Previous offences
Traffic offences, bodily harm, broken bail (three months spent in prison as a result of this while awaiting trial at a Quarter Sessions).

Background
Gordon lived with his mother, aged 40, a housewife, his stepfather, aged 37, a lorry driver, and three younger, full siblings. His own father had died three years previously, but had left the home when Gordon was 8, although had been in touch with the family until Gordon was 14. Gordon had three

changes of primary school, won a scholarship and attended grammar school until he was 16, when he left without G.C.E. Since then he had had five changes of labouring jobs. In his spare time he drank heavily, associated with unsatisfactory companions and married women.

After the court Gordon and his mother and stepfather were seen by the Probation Officer. The meaning and purpose of the order were explained. His mother seemed relieved that he was placed on probation and was very maternal in her attitude. His stepfather was undemonstrative and uncritical. Gordon was 'off-hand'.

A week later Gordon did not report and a message was later received to say that he had been sent to prison by another court for driving a van without insurance; he had pleaded guilty and refused to appeal against the sentence.

Group decision (if agreement achieved):

Appendix 4 – for Project 8

Name ....

Decision Form 1

Situation	Minimum odds of success demanded	Score
1		
2		
3		
4		
5		
6		
TOTAL SCORE		

(prepare Decision Forms 2, 3 and 4 as required)

Appendix 5 – for Project 9

Name ....   *First* Ranking

Ten Characteristics – 1
to be ranked by the extent to which they are
socially restrictive

	Rank order
Blind	
Deaf-mute	
Feeble-minded	
Half-caste	
Heir Apparent (to the throne)	
Illegitimate	
Jew	
Midget	
Orphan	
Transvestite	

(The second and third rankings should be given on separate but similar forms.)

Appendix 6 – for Project 18

.... University/College Survey of Family and Marriage

NO NAMES ARE TO BE RECORDED
No prompting except where specified

QUESTIONNAIRE
(Interview Schedule)

Engaged/Married? [underline]

If engaged, ask questions in this column:	*If married,* ask these questions:
Q. 1. Just to check, was it your name we found (in the local paper) recently?	Q. 1. Just to check, was it your name we found (in the local paper) recently?

Q. 2. When do you plan to get married? [Ring.]
1. Within a week
2. Over a week, within a month
3. Over a month, within a year
4. Over a year

Q. 3. Do you expect to live with (either) parents at first, when you are married?
1. Yes
2. No

Q. 4. Do you intend to go out to work at all after you are married? [Prompt: paid work?]
1. Yes, paid work
2. Yes, unpaid work
3. No

Q. 5. Do you think young wives should go out and work?
1. Yes
2. No

Q. 6. Why (not)? [Prompt.]

Q. 7. How would you like to spend the first year of your marriage?

Q. 8. What do you expect will be the main problems of married life for you?

Q. 9. What do you expect will be the *best* part of being married?

Q. 10. What will be the *most important* part for you?

Q. 11. How many times have you been out this week? [Prompt: how many evenings in the last week?]
1. None
2. One
3. Two or three
4. Four or five
5. Six or seven

Q. 12. How much do you earn each week?

Q. 13. How do you spend it?

Q. 2. When did you get married? [Ring.]
1. Less than a week ago
2. Over a week, within a month
3. Over a month, within a year
4. Over a year ago

Q. 3. Are you living with parents?
1. Yes
2. No

Q. 4. Do you go out to work at all? [Prompt: paid work?]
1. Yes, paid work
2. Yes, unpaid work
3. No

Q. 5. Do you think young wives should go out and work?
1. Yes
2. No

Q. 6. Why (not)? [Prompt.]

Q. 7. How would you like to spend the first year of your marriage?

Q. 8. What are the main problems of married life for you?

Q. 9. What is the best part of being married?

Q. 10. What is the *most important* part for you?

Q. 11. How many times have you been out this week? [Prompt: how many evenings in the last week?]
1. None
2. One
3. Two or three
4. Four or five
5. Six or seven

Q. 12. How much do you earn each week?

Q. 13. How do you spend it?

Q. 14. Who will be boss in your home? | Q. 14. Who is boss here?

Q. 15. How long after getting married should a young couple start a family? [Prompt to get answer.] | Q. 15. How long after getting married should a young couple start a family? [Prompt to get answer.]

ALL

Do you agree or disagree with the following statements:

Q. 16. In marriage, being a mother is the most important thing for the woman.
1. Agree
2. Disagree

Q. 17. The normal wife prefers to stay in her home rather than go out to a job.
1. Agree
2. Disagree

Q. 18. In marriage it is the man who is really the head, he 'wears the trousers'.
1. Agree
2. Disagree

Q. 19. A married woman should go out several evenings each week with her husband.
1. Agree
2. Disagree

Q. 20. How old are you?
1. Under 17; 2. 17/18; 3. 19/20; 4. 21/22; 5. 23/24; 6. 24/25; 7. Over 25.

Q. 21. What job had your (future) husband?

FOR COMPLETION AFTER INTERVIEWS

Number of interviews attempted:
Reasons for non-contact (giving number of recalls, etc.):
1.
2.
3.
4.
General comments on actual interviews:

Appendix 7 – for Project 20

Student's Personal Inventory (S.P.1.)

Complete this questionnaire and retain it for use in later projects. Do *not* put your name on it. Your tutor will give you an identification number. Start here by ringing the appropriate number:

	Identification Number:			*Date*
University or College No.		*Class*	*Student*	
Code:	$Q_{1, 2}$	Q_3	$Q_{4, 5}$	Q_6

Q. 7. How old are you?

    1. Under 16; 2. 16 or 17; 3. 18; 4. 19; 5. 20; 6. 21; 7. 22 or 23; 8. 24 or over.

Q. 8. Are you

    1. Male and married; 2. Male and single; 3. Male and widowed, separated or divorced; 4. Female and married; 5. Female and single; 6. Female and widowed, separated or divorced.

Q. 9. What kind of secondary school do you or did you (last) attend?

    1. Pre-1944 elementary only; 2. Grammar or 'high' school; 3. Independent or direct grant day; 4. Independent boarding; 5. Secondary modern; 6. Comprehensive; 7. Other, specify.

Q. 10. Into which of the following categories does your father's job fit? (If he is *retired*, please ring the number opposite the last kind of job he did: *if he is unemployed*, please ring the number opposite his usual job.)

    1. Professional – for example, doctors, teachers, managers of large or medium-sized firms, lawyers, accountants, architects, surveyors.

    2. Business – for example, managers of small firms, owners or managers of shops, business executives, farmers and farm managers.

    3. Clerical and sales – for example, local government officials, clerks, office workers, salesmen, insurance representatives, shop assistants, commercial travellers.

    4. Skilled workers and foremen – for example, fitters, toolmakers, qualified electricians, trained mechanics, joiners, bricklayers, masons, printers, painters, engine drivers, bus drivers, policemen, foremen in general.

    5. Semi-skilled workers – for example, machine-tool operators, miners, construction workers, furnacemen, process workers, farm workers, postmen.

    6. General workers – for example, labourers, window cleaners, casual workers, porters, messengers.

Q. 11. Last occupation of your father's father. Give appropriate number as in Q. 10.

Q. 12. Last occupation of your mother's father. Give appropriate number as in Q. 10.

Q. 13. At what age did your father finish full-time education?

    1. Under 13; 2. 13; 3. 14; 4. 15; 5. 16; 6. 17 or 18; 7. 19 or 20; 8. 21 or over; 9. Don't know.

Q. 14. At what age did your mother finish full-time education?

  1. Under 13; 2. 13; 3. 14; 4. 15; 5. 16; 6. 17 or 18; 7. 19 or 20; 8. 21 or over; 9. Don't know.

Q. 15. How many brothers and sisters have you?

  0. None; 1. One; 2. Two; 3. Three; 4. Four; 5. Five; 6. Six or more.

Q. 16. How far from college is your home?

  1. In this city; 2. Outside city but within 20 miles; 3. Over 20 but not more than 100 miles; 4. Over 100 miles but not more than 200 miles; 5. Over 200 miles; 6. Outside G.B.; 7. Not applicable.

Q. 17. Your religion?

  1. R.C.; 2. C. of E.; 3. Methodist; 4. Other non-conformist; 5. Non-christian religion; 6. Uncertain; 7. No religion; 8. Other, specify.

Q. 18. Have you attended a religious service within the last

  1. Week; 2. Month; 3. 12 months; 4. Not for more than a year.

Q. 19. Do you say prayers at home?

  1. Yes; 2. No.

Q. 20. Were you married or do you intend to marry in church?

  (0. I do not intend to marry) 1. In church; 2. Not in church; 3. Uncertain.

Q. 21. Are there any of the following people whom you think shouldn't be allowed in your church?

  1. Vagrants; 2. Convicted criminals; 3. Divorced people; 4. Members of other denominations; 5. Atheists; 6. Coloured people; 7. Any others, specify; 0. Everyone should be allowed in.

Q. 22. Do you own

  1. A car; 2. A motor-bike, scooter, etc.; 3. A bicycle; 0. None of these.

Q. 23. Are you living

  1. In a college hall of residence; 2. In lodgings; 3. In a flat; 4. At home; 5. Other, specify.

Q. 24. How many books on sociology do you own?

  1. None; 2. A few (more than 1, less than 20); 3. 20–50; 4. Over 50.

Q. 25. How many books on sociology have you bought or borrowed in the last month?

  0. None; 1. One; 2. Two; 3. Three; 4. Four; 5. Five or six; 6. More than six.

Q. 26. It is often said that most people commit offences against the law at some time during their lives. Ring those which have technically applied to you.

  1. Stealing (e.g. apples, poaching, road signs, etc.); 2. Deliberate damage (e.g. school property); 3. Murder, homicide (or attempted);

4. Wounding or causing injury; 5. Assault (e.g. fighting); 6. Sexual offence; 7. Forgery (signature etc.); 8. Driving offence (no L plates, speeding, parking, etc.); 9. Drunkenness; 0. I cannot remember having done any of these things.

Q. 27. What is the size of your home town (etc.)?

1. Less than 10,000 population; 2. 10,000 but under 25,000; 3. 25,000 but under 100,000; 4. 100,000 but under 500,000; 5. 500,000 but under one million; 6. Over a million.

Q. 28. When did you last see your mother?

1. Over a year; 2. Within a year but over a month; 3. Within a month but over a week; 4. Within a week but over 24 hours; 5. Within last 24 hours.

Q. 29. Estimate your family's gross weekly income (if necessary divide annual income by 50).

1. Under £5; 2. £5 but under £10; 3. £10 but under £15; 4. £15 but under £20; 5. £20 but under £30; 6. £30 but under £50; 7. £50 but under £100; 8. £100 or more.

Q. 30. If there were an election tomorrow I would (like to) vote

1. Conservative; 2. Labour; 3. Liberal; 4. Other, specify; 0. I would not want to vote.

Q. 31. To which social class does your family belong?

1. Lower or working class; 2. Middle class; 3. Professional or executive class; 0. There are no social classes.

Q. 32. Is your family home

1. Owned by your parents; 2. Rented by you from a private landlord or company; 3. Rented from the council.

Q. 33. How much grant do you get from your county this year?

1. £50 or less; 2. £50–£99; 3. £100–£149; 4. £150–£199; 5. £200–£249; 6. £250–£299; 7. £300–£349; 8. £350–£399; 9. £400–£449; 10. £450 or over.

Q. 34. Why did you come to university/college? (ring one or more)

1. For future career; 2. For broader education; 3. Nothing else to do; 4. Family's wish; 5. Social life at college; 6. Never thought about it; 7. Employer's wish; 8. Other, specify.

Q. 35. If you had a serious problem (e.g. broken engagement) to whom do you think you would turn for advice?

Ring *one* only.

1. Your parent(s); 2. A relative; 3. Friend of opposite sex; 4. A member of university/college staff; 5. Friend of same sex; 6. The college chaplain; 7. A doctor; 8. Student health or advisory service; 9. Other, specify.

Q. 36. Do you pay a subscription to any department club or society in the university/college?

1. One only; 2. 2 or 3; 3. 4 or more.

Consider the following incidents. Then indicate which of the given alternatives you feel is the best course of action for the student involved (imagine that you are advising him).

Q. 37. A student leaves home and comes to a provincial university on a full grant. His father, a coal miner, is incapacitated in a pit disaster leaving his wife to look after a four-year-old child. They will be dependent on Supplementary Allowances. The student may

    1. Work all the harder on his degree, and visit home as often as possible;
    2. Stay at home for a term only, to straighten things out;   3. Give up his degree course.

Q. 38. A second-year female student finds that her worries about her boy-friend interfere with her work. When working for her terminal examinations, she writes to him every day but gets very depressed. Her boy-friend, whom she hopes to marry, says that she should immediately join him at Sheffield University so that he can revise for his finals more effectively. The student may

    1. Decide not to see him, write or phone until after their examinations;
    2. Carry on as before;   3. Join him in Sheffield, take a job and give up her degree.

Q. 39. The son of a chartered accountant marginally fails his Part I examination but is allowed to repeat the year. His father is unwilling to support him because he feels that this indicates his lack of academic talent and that he should join the family firm straight away on a salary of £1,000 p.a. He may

    1. Take a job in term and during the vacation to keep himself and continue course;   2. Leave the university.

Q. 40. A first-year social science student finds she is very worried at getting low marks in tests and essays. Accidentally she notices on her professor's desk that according to the selection test her I.Q. is 95. She may

    1. Worry but continue the course;   2. Go and discuss her ability with the professor and take his advice;   3. Apply for diploma and professional training.

Q. 41. Add up your scores on Qs. 37–40. Ring your *code* here:

Score	3	4	5	6	7	8	9	10	11
Code	0	1	2	3	4	5	6	7	8

Q. 42. Father's occupation.

Appendix 8 – for Project 20

Mail Survey – Questionnaire

University of Exeter

Department of Sociology

SURVEY

Improvements in the Social Services

DEAR SIR *or* MADAM,

We are carrying out a small survey in this area on what you feel about these services. Your replies will help us to decide what services are needed and which should be improved if possible.

We enclose a few questions for you (or your wife) to answer. It would be a great help and save our interviewer calling if you would complete it yourself and send it back to us in the envelope provided.

You need not sign your name, as your answers will be confidential and your name is not known to us. Please let me know if you have any questions or want to receive a summary of our conclusions in due course.

We are most grateful for your help.

Yours truly

JOHN WAKEFORD

(*Lecturer in Sociology*)

RING THE NUMBER(S) NEXT TO THE ANSWER(S) THAT APPLY TO YOU

Q. 1. Has the City changed much since you have been here?

1. Yes; 2. No.

Q. 2. Which of the following are most in need of improvement? (Ring more than one number if you wish.)

1. Medical services; 2. Treatment of criminals; 3. Roads and transport; 4. Services for elderly; 5. Child welfare; 6. Animal welfare; 7. Recreation facilities; 8. Education; 9. Other, specify.

Q. 3. State any view you have on any one of these in particular.

Q. 4. What changes should there be in the tax system to pay for this?

Q. 5. In this City there should be more provision of:

1. Shops; 2. Pubs; 3. Council houses; 4. Bowling alleys; 5. Cinemas; 6. Bingo halls; 7. Allotments; 8. Other, specify.

Q. 6. If there were an election next week would you vote:
  1. Labour; 2. Conservative; 3. Liberal; 4. Other; 5. Not vote.

Q. 7. Which daily newspapers do you take at home?
  1. *Express*; 2. *Mirror*; 3. *Mail*; 4. *Telegraph*; 5. Other national paper; 6. Local paper; 7. None.

Q. 8. Have you ever read a copy of any of these?
  1. *Punch*; 2. *Weekend*; 3. *Romeo*; 4. *Honey*; 5. *Country Life*; 6. *The Lady*; 7. *Woman's Weekly*; 8. *Reader's Digest*.

Q. 9. What opportunities for employment are there for young people in this area?

Q. 10. How many are there in your family at home?
  1. You live by yourself; 2. One other; 3. Three altogether; 4. Four; 5. Five; 6. Six or more.

Q. 11. How old are you?
  1. Under 25; 2. 25–29; 3. 30–34; 4. 35–39; 5. 40–44; 6. 45–49; 7. 50–54; 8. 55–59; 9. 60–64; 10. 65–69; 11. 70 or over.

Q. 12. Are you: 1. Male; 2. Female.

Q. 13. Are you:
  1. Single; 2. Married; 3. Widowed/divorced/separated.

Q. 14. What is the exact occupation of the head of your household? (If retired, give last occupation; if housewife give husband's occupation.)

Q. 15. Were you born in this City?
  1. Yes; 2. No, but within 10 miles; 3. No, more than 10 miles away.

Q. 16. What sort of schools and colleges have you attended? (ring the number beside *every* answer that applies to you.)
  1. Primary or elementary school; 2. Secondary school or technical school; 3. Grammar school; 4. Private school; 5. Technical or training college for degree or diploma; 6. University; 7. Apprenticeship; 8. Day release or part-time classes for a certificate; 9. Sandwich course; 10. Other college, etc., specify.

Q. 17. What age did you finish *full-time* education?
  1. Under 15; 2. 15; 3. 16; 4. 17; 5. 18; 6. 19; 7. 20; 8. 21 or more.

Q. 18. Do you have any qualifications or school certificates?
  0. None; 1. Training at work; 2. Others, specify.

Q. 19. What class do you belong to?
  1. Working; 2. Middle; 3. Upper; 4. No class; 5. Other (give name).

Q. 20. What kind of house/flat do you live in?
  1. Owner-occupier; 2. Council; 3. Private rented; 4. Other.

Q. 21. How much money is earned by your family?
  1. Less than £5 a week; 2. £5–£9; 3. £10–£19; 4. £20–£39; 5. £40–£79; 6. Over £80.

Please add any other comments you have here.

Now put this in the envelope provided and send it to John Wakeford, Department of Sociology, The University, Exeter, Devon.

Appendix 9 – for Project 27

Group A   **Cluster Sample Log Sheet**

Q. 1. (a) *If there were a general election tomorrow, which party would you support?*
or, if election date known:

(b) *How do you think you will vote in the General Election/by-election on* ....?

If refuse, or undecided ask:

Q. 2. *Which party are you most inclined to support?*

		Answer to	
Name	*Address*	*Q. 1*	*Q. 2*

Calculate totals:
Conservative   Labour   Liberal   Other | *Total* | 'Would not vote' or *Refuses to say*

Group B   **Quota Sample Log Sheet**

Q. 1. (a) *If there were a General Election tomorrow, which party would you support?*
or, if election date known:

(b) *How do you think you will vote in the General Election/by-election on*
............?

If refuse, or undecided, ask:

Q. 2. *Which party are you most inclined to support?*

Quota controls	Sex		Age Group				Social Class		Total (for sex, age and social class)
	M	F	20 –29	30 –44	45 –64	65 +	'Middle' R-G's Classes I and II	'Working' R-G's Classes III–V	
Con-stituency quotas:									30

Inter-view number	Put X in appropriate columns								Answer to	
									Q. 1	Q. 2
1 2 etc. to 30										
(check) TOTAL										

Calculate totals:
Conservative   Labour   Liberal   Other | *Total* | 'Would not vote' or *Refuses to say*

Appendix 10 – for Project 28

Twelve completed Mail Survey questionnaires

(Answers indicated in bold type)

Questionnaire 1

Q. 1. Has the City changed much since you have been here?
    1. **Yes;**   2. No.

Q.2. Which of the following are most in need of improvement? (Ring more than one number if you wish.)

1. Medical services; 2. Treatment of criminals; **3. Roads and transport;** 4. Services for elderly; 5. Child welfare; 6. Animal welfare; 7. Recreation facilities; 8. Education; 9. Other, specify.

Q.3. State any view you have on any one of these in particular:

8. Consider at least 50 per cent of expenditure on education at present collected by rate should be collected through income tax so as to share this over a wider personnel.

Q.4. What changes should there be in the tax system to pay for this?

3. Road Fund tax restored to Ministry of Transport in its entirety as before.

8. See Q.3.

Q.5. In this City there should be more provision of:

1. Shops; 2. Pubs; 3. Council houses; 4. Bowling alleys; 5. Cinemas; 6. Bingo halls; 7. Allotments; **8. Other, specify.**

Restaurants and good class cafés open in evenings.

Q.6. If there were an election next week would you vote:

1. Labour; **2. Conservative;** 3. Liberal; 4. Other; 5. Not vote?

Q.7. Which daily newspapers do you take at home?

1. *Express*; 2. *Mirror*; 3. *Mail*; 4. *Telegraph*; **5. Other national paper; 6. Local paper;** 7. None.

Q.8. Have you ever read a copy of any of these?

1. Punch; 2. *Weekend*; 3. *Romeo*; 4. *Honey*; *5. Country Life;* 6. *The Lady*; 7. *Woman's Weekly*; *8. Reader's Digest.*

Q.9. What opportunities for employment are there for young people in this area?

Not enough but appears to be increasing.

Q.10. How many are there in your family at home?

1. You live by yourself; 2. One other; 3. Three altogether; 4. Four; 5. Five; 6. Six or more.

Q.11. How old are you?

1. Under 25; 2. 25–29; 3. 30–34; 4. 35–39; 5. 40–44; 6. 45–49; 7. 50–54; 8. 55–59; 9. 60–64; 10. 65–69; **11. 70 or over.**

Q.12. Are you: **1. Male;** 2. Female?

Q.13. Are you:

1. Single; 2. Married; 3. Widowed/divorced/separated/**widower**?

Q.14. What is the exact occupation of the head of your household? (If retired, give last occupation; if housewife, give husband's occupation.)

Transport Engineer and Manager (rtd.).

Q.15. Were you born in this City?

1. Yes; 2. No, but within 10 miles; **3. No, more than 10 miles away.**

Q.16. What sort of schools and colleges have you attended? (Ring the number beside **every** answer that applies to you.)

1. Primary or elementary school; 2. Secondary school or technical school; 3. Grammar school; 4. **Private school;** 5. Technical or training college for degree or diploma; 6. **University;** 7. Apprenticeship; 8. Day-release or part-time classes for a certificate; 9. Sandwich course; 10. **Other college, etc., specify.**
Public school.

Q. 17. What age did you finish *full-time* education?
1. Under 15; 2. 15; 3. 16; 4. **17;** 5. 18; 6. 19; 7. 20; 8. 21 or more.

Q. 18. Do you have any qualifications or school certificates?
0. None; 1. Training at work. 2. Others, specify.
Matriculation; Member of Inst. of Transport Engineering.

Q. 19. What class do you belong to?
1. Working; 2. **Middle;** 3. Upper; 4. No class; 5. Other (give name).

Q. 20. What kind of house/flat do you live in?
1. **Owner-occupier;** 2. Council; 3. Private rented; 4. Other.

Q. 21. How much money is earned by your family?
1. Less than £5 a week; 2. £5–£9; 3. £10–£19; 4. £20–£39; 5. £40–£79; 6. Over £80.
Retired on pension.

Please add any other comments you have here.

Questionnaire 2

Q. 1. Has the City changed much since you have been here?
1. **Yes;** 2. No.

Q. 2. Which of the following are most in need of improvement? (Ring more than one number if you wish.)
1. **Medical services;** 2. Treatment of criminals; 3. **Roads and transport;** 4. Services for elderly; 5. Child welfare; 6. Animal welfare; 7. **Recreation facilities;** 8. Education; 9. Other, specify.

Q. 3. State any view you have on any one of these in particular:
Worst road surfaces in the West Country. Too great a use of 'No Waiting' signs as substitute for parking: should be more '20 Minute' signs and perhaps a system of traffic wardens to control this.

Q. 4. What changes should there be in the tax system to pay for this?

Q. 5. In this City there should be more provision of:
1. Shops; 2. Pubs; 3. Council houses; 4. **Bowling alleys;** 5. Cinemas; 6. Bingo halls; 7. Allotments; 8. **Other, specify.**
(*a*) **Theatres;** (*b*) **Ice rink;** (*c*) **Night clubs;** (*d*) **Car-racing track for South-West.**

Q. 6. If there were an election next week would you vote:

    1. Labour; **2. Conservative;** 3. Liberal; 4. Other; 5. Not vote?

Q. 7. Which daily newspapers do you take at home?

    1. *Express*; 2. *Mirror*; 3. *Mail*; ***4. Telegraph;*** 5. Other national paper; **6. Local paper;** 7. None.

Q. 8. Have you ever read a copy of any of these?

    1. Punch; 2. Weekend; 3. *Romeo*; 4. *Honey*; ***5. Country Life;*** 6. *The Lady*; 7. *Woman's Weekly*; ***8. Reader's Digest.***

Q. 9. What opportunities for employment are there for young people in this area?

INADEQUATE. Little opportunity without having to move to the large industrial cities. The Youth Employment Service in Exeter is of little help.

Q. 10. How many are there in your family at home?

    1. You live by yourself; 2. One other; 3. Three altogether; **4. Four (Inc. Cat!);** 5. Five; 6. Six or more.

Q. 11. How old are you?

    1. Under 25; **2. 25–29;** 3. 30–34; 4. 35–39; 5. 40–44; 6. 45–49; 7. 50–54; 8. 55–59; 9. 60–64; 10. 65–69; 11. 70 or over.

Q. 12. Are you: **1. Male;** 2. Female?

Q. 13. Are you: **1. Single;** 2. Married; 3. Widowed/divorced/separated.

Q. 14. What is the exact occupation of the head of your household?

Civil Service.

Q. 15. Were you born in this City?

    1. Yes; 2. No, but within 10 miles; 3. No, more than 10 miles away.

Q. 16. What sort of schools and colleges have you attended?

(Ring the number beside *every* answer that applies to you.)

    1. Primary or elementary school; 2. Secondary school or technical school; 3. Grammar school; **4. Private school; 5. Technical or training college for degree or diploma;** 6. University; 7. Apprenticeship; **8. Day-release or part-time classes for a certificate;** 9. Sandwich course; **10. Other college, etc., specify.**

College of Art.

Q. 17. What age did you finish *full-time* education?

    1. Under 15; 2. 15; 3. 16; **4. 17;** 5. 18; 6. 19; 7. 20; 8. 21 or more.

Q. 18. Do you have any qualifications or school certificates?

    0. None; **1. Training at work;** **2. Others, specify.**

G.C.E. 5 'O' Levels.

Q. 19. What class do you belong to?

    1. Working; **2. Middle;** 3. Upper; 4. No class; 5. Other (give name).

Q. 20. What kind of house/flat do you live in?

    1. Owner-occupier; 2. Council; 3. Private rented; 4. Other.

Q. 21. How much money is earned by your family?

1. Less than £5 a week; 2. £5–£9; 3. £10–£19; 4. £30–£39; 5. £40–£79; 6. Over £80.

Please add any other comments you have here.

Questionnaire 3

Q. 1. Has the City changed much since you have been here?
1. Yes; 2. No.

Q. 2. Which of the following are most in need of improvement? (Ring more than one number if you wish.)
1. Medical services; 2. Treatment of criminals; 3. Roads and transport; 4. **Services for elderly;** 5. Child welfare; 6. Animal welfare; 7. Recreation facilities; 8. **Education. More and better-class teachers;** 9. Other, specify; 10. **Police; more, especially at night and evenings.**

Q. 3. State any view you have on any one of these in particular:
Ref. No. 10. Reasons: A. Uncouth youths – in gangs of three or more and shouting insults and pushing people off pavements. Magistrates to 'back' police more – in assault cases on police or public. B. Prevent C.N.D. people from causing obstruction of public, etc. or wrecking of political speeches by organised interruptions. Ref. No. 8. Reasons: Teach manners. Eradicate dialects. All schools to have homework from age of 10 upwards (to make better teenagers).

Q. 4. What changes should there be in the tax system to pay for this?
Tax tables to be published start of year after budget. Tax to be paid according to income. Less allowances for wife, 3 children, mortgage interest, private sick fund, etc. Do away with rates. Council to submit for expenses. *No Council* **houses for rent. All** *must* **buy – poor on long-term basis (transferable). (They will then look after them.) Pay tax once a year.**

Q. 5. In this City there should be more provision of:
1. Shops; 2. Pubs; 3. Council houses; 4. Bowling alleys; 5. Cinemas; 6. Bingo halls; 7. Allotments; 8. Other, specify.
Beautify river banks, make walks, gardens, boats, sun-glass shelters. All for council revenue to offset rates.

Q. 6. If there were an election next week would you vote:
1. **Labour;** 2. Conservative; 3. Liberal; 4. Other; 5. Not vote?

Q. 7. Which daily newspapers do you take at home?
1. Express; 2. Mirror; 3. *Mail; 4. Telegraph;* 5. **Other national paper** – *Sun;* 6. **Local paper** – *Ex. and Echo;* 7. None.

Q. 8. Have you ever read a copy of any of these?
1. Punch; 2. *Weekend;* 3. *Romeo;* 4. *Honey;* 5. *Country Life;* 6. *The Lady;* 7. *Woman's Weekly;* 8. *Reader's Digest.*

Q. 9. What opportunities for employment are there for young people in this area?

Expand tourist industry. Earn valuable dollars. Designate Devon and Cornwall as tourist areas *only.* *Keep* **narrow winding roads. Part of attraction. More all-first-class rail coaches. State tours by rail. Fixed price. Cater for wealthy retired folk to invest in safety.** *Light* **clean industry only. This would give ample employment to all.**

Q. 10. How many are there in your family at home?

1. You live by yourself; 2. One other; 3. Three altogether; 4. **Four;** 5. Five; 6. Six or more.

Q. 11. How old are you?

1. Under 25; 2. 25–29; 3. 30–34; 4. 35–39; 5. 40–44; **6. 45–49;** 7. 50–54; 8. 55–59; 9. 60–64; 10. 65–69; 11. 70 or over.

Q. 12. Are you: **1. Male;** 2. Female?

Q. 13. Are you: 1. Single; **2. Married;** 3. Widowed/divorced/separated?

Q. 14. What is the exact occupation of the head of your household?

State Registered Psychiatric Nurse.

Q. 15. Were you born in this City?

1. Yes; 2. No, but within 10 miles; **3. No, more than 10 miles away.**

Q. 16. What sort of schools and colleges have you attended? (Ring the number beside **every** answer that applies to you.)

1. Primary or elementary school; 2. Secondary school or technical school; 3. Grammar school; 4. Private school; **5. Technical or training college for degree or diploma. Electrical Eng.;** 6. University; **7. Apprenticeship. Electrical;** 8. Day-release or part-time classes for a certificate; **9. Sandwich course;** 10. Other college, etc., specify.

Q. 17. What age did you finish *full-time* education?

1. Under 15; 2. 15; 3. 16; 4. 17; 5. 18; 6. 19; 7. 20; 8. 21 or more.

Q. 18. Do you have any qualifications or school certificates?

0. None; **1. Training at work;** 2. Others, specify.
A. S/Reg. Psych. Nurse. B. Qualified Electrician and Service Engineer. C. Qualified Automobile Electrician.

Q. 19. What class do you belong to?

1. Working – Surely 99 per cent work? Wrong designation names. 2. Middle; 3. Upper; 4. No class; **5. Other (give name).**

Q. 20. What kind of house/flat do you live in?

1. Owner-occupier; 2. Council; 3. Private rented; 4. Other.

Q. 21. How much money is earned by your family?

1. Less than £5 a week; 2. £5–£9; 3. £10–£19; 4. £20–£39 £26 10s. 0d.; 5. £40–£79; 6. Over £80.

Please add any other comments you have here.

Ref. Q. 19. **Should be much wider grouping and according to: interests, type reading, and off-duty occupations, speech (classless) what one finds funny, swearing habits and where, manners, where one dines when out.**

Questionnaire 4

Q. 1. Has the City changed much since you have been here?
    1. Yes; 2. No.

Q. 2. Which of the following are most in need of improvement? (Ring more than one number if you wish.)
    1. Medical services; 2. Treatment of criminals; **3. Roads and transport; 4. Services for elderly;** 5. Child welfare; 6. Animal welfare; 7. Recreation facilities; 8. Education; 9. Other, specify.

Q. 3. State any view you have on any one of these in particular:
Separate roads for lorries, or tracks (or railway tracks used for them). More free car space for shoppers (especially locals, who have to shop in Exeter often for victuals).

Q. 4. What changes should there be in the tax system to pay for this?
A government tax (not local), payable by persons 21 to retiring age.

Q. 5. In this City there should be more provision of:
    1. Shops; 2. Pubs; 3. Council houses; 4. Bowling alleys; **5. Cinemas;** 6. Bingo halls; 7. Allotments; 8. Other, specify.
Civic Hall and Theatre.

Q. 6. If there were an election next week would you vote:
    1. Labour; 2. Conservative; 3. Liberal; 4. Other; **5. Not vote.**

Q. 7. Which daily newspapers do you take at home?
    1. *Express*; **2. *Mirror*;** 3. *Mail*; 4. *Telegraph*; 5. Other national paper; **6. Local paper;** 7. None.

Q. 8. Have you ever read a copy of any of these?
    1. *Punch*; *2. Weekend;* 3. *Romeo*; 4. *Honey*; 5. *Country Life*; *6. The Lady; 7. Woman's Weekly; 8. Reader's Digest.*

Q. 9. What opportunities for employment are there for young people in this area?
Not many, except for dead-end jobs, though I think things are improving. Of course there are government posts for some.

Q. 10. How many are there in your family at home?
    1. You live by yourself; 2. One other; 3. Three altogether; 4. Four; 5. Five; 6. Six or more.

Q. 11. How old are you?
    1. Under 25; 2. 25–29; 3. 30–34; 4. 35–39; 5. 40–44; 6. 45–49; 7. 50–54; 8. 55–59; **9. 60–64;** 10. 65–69; 11. 70 or over.

Q. 12. Are you: 1. Male; **2. Female?**

Q. 13. Are you: 1. Single; 2. Married; **3. Widowed/divorced/ separated?**

                                                           W.S.I.

Q. 14. What is the exact occupation of the head of your household?
Clerk.

Q. 15. Were you born in this City?
1. Yes; 2. No, but within 10 miles; **3. No, more than 10 miles away.**

Q. 16. What sort of schools and colleges have you attended?
1. Primary or elementary school; 2. Secondary school or technical school; 3. Grammar school; 4. Private school; 5. Technical or training college for degree or diploma; 6. University; 7. Apprenticeship; **8. Day-release or part-time classes for a certificate;** 9. Sandwich course; 10. Other college, etc., specify.

Q. 17. What age did you finish *full-time* education?
1. Under 15; **2. 15;** 3. 16; 4. 17; 5. 18; 6. 19; 7. 20; 8. 21 or more.

Q. 18. Do you have any qualifications or school certificates?
0. None; 1. Training at work; 2. Others, specify:
Scholarship to secondary school. S. of Arts – French, Writing, Violin, Shorthand.

Q. 19. What class do you belong to?
1. Working; **2. Middle;** 3. Upper; 4. No class; 5. Other (give name).

Q. 20. What kind of house/flat do you live in?
1. Owner-occupier; 2. Council; 3. Private rented; 4. Other.

Q. 21. How much money is earned by your family?
1. Less than £5 a week; **2. £5–£9;** ~~3. £10–£19; 4. £20~~–39;
5. ~~£40–£79; 6. Over £80.~~

Please add any other comments you have here.

Questionnaire 5

Q. 1. Has the City changed much since you have been here?
1. Yes; 2. No.

Q. 2. Which of the following are most in need of improvement? (Ring more than one number if you wish.)
1. Medical services; 2. Treatment of criminals; 3. Roads and transport; **4. Services for elderly;** 5. Animal welfare; 6. Child welfare; **7. Recreation facilities;** 8. Education; 9. Other, specify.

Q. 3. State any view you have on any one of these in particular:
Widows working over 60 years should not be made to pay income tax on earnings.

Q. 4. What changes should there be in the tax system to pay for this?

Q. 5. In this City there should be more provision of:
1. Shops; 2. Pubs; 3. Council houses; 4. Bowling alleys; 5. Cinemas; 6. Bingo halls; **7. Allotments;** 8. Other, specify.

Q. 6. If there were an election next week would you vote:
1. Labour; 2. Conservative; 3. Liberal; 4. Other; 5. Not vote?

Q. 7. Which daily newspapers do you take at home?

1. *Express*; 2. *Mirror*; *3. Mail;* 4. *Telegraph*; 5. Other national paper; **6. Local paper;** 7. None.

Q. 8. Have you ever read a copy of any of these?

1. *Punch*; 2. *Weekend*; 3. *Romeo*; 4. *Honey*; 5. *Country Life*; *6. The Lady;* 7. *Woman's Weekly*; *8. Reader's Digest.*

Q. 9. What opportunities for employment are there for young people in this area?

Factories chiefly.

Q. 10. How many are there in your family at home?

1. You live by yourself; 2. One other; 3. Three altogether; 4. Four; 5. Five; 6. Six or more.

Q. 11. How old are you?

1. Under 25; 2. 25–29; 3. 30–34; 4. 35–39; 5. 30–44; 6. 45–49; 7. 50–54; 8. 55–59; **9. 60–64;** 10. 65–69; 11. 70 or over.

Q. 12. Are you: 1. Male; 2. Female?

Q. 13. Are you: 1. Single; 2. Married; **3. Widowed/divorced/ separated?**

Q. 14. What is the exact occupation of the head of your household? (If retired, give last occupation; if housewife, give husband's occupation.)

Q. 15. Were you born in this City?

1. Yes; 2. No, but within 10 miles; 3. No, more than 10 miles away.

Q. 16. What sort of schools and colleges have you attended? (Ring the number beside *every* answer that applies to you.)

1. Primary or elementary school; 2. Secondary school or technical school; 3. Grammar school; 4. Private school; 5. Technical or training college for degree or diploma; 6. University; 7. Apprenticeship; 8. Day-release or part-time classes for a certificate; 9. Sandwich course; 10. Other college, etc., specify.

Q. 17. What age did you finish *full-time* education?

1. Under 15; 2. 15; 3. 16; **4. 17;** 5. 18; 6. 19; 7. 20; 8. 21 or more.

Q. 18. Do you have any qualifications or school certificates?

0. None; 1. Training at work; 2. Others, specify.

Q. 19. What class do you belong to?

1. Working; **2. Middle;** 3. Upper; 4. No class; 5. Other (give name).

Q. 20. What kind of house/flat do you live in?

1. Owner-occupier; 2. Council; 3. Private rented; **4. Other.**

Q. 21. How much money is earned by your family?

1. Less than £5 a week; **2. £5–£9;** 3. £10–£19; 4. £20–£39; 5. £40–£79; 6. Over £80.

Please add any other comments you have here.

Questionnaire 6

Q. 1. Has the City changed much since you have been here?

    1. Yes; 2. No.

Q. 2. Which of the following are most in need of improvement? (Ring more than one number if you wish.)

    1. Medical services;   2. Treatment of criminals;   **3. Roads and transport;** 4. Services for elderly; 5. Child welfare; 6. Animal welfare; 7. Recreation facilities; 8. Education; 9. Other, specify.

Q. 3. State any view you have on any one of these in particular:

Need for direct bus services between all parts of the City and the railway stations and bus station. Changing in the City centre should be eliminated.

Q. 4. What changes should there be in the tax system to pay for this?

None necessary.

Q. 5. In this City there should be more provision of:

    1. Shops;   2. Pubs;   3. Council houses;   4. Bowling alleys; 5. Cinemas; 6. Bingo halls; 7. Allotments; **8. Other, specify.**

Social, i.e. community centres, also cafés.

Q. 6. If there were an election next week would you vote:

    1. Labour; 2. Conservative; 3. Liberal; 4. Other; 5. Not vote.

Q. 7. Which daily newspapers do you take at home?

    1. *Express*; 2. *Mirror*; **3. *Mail*;** 4. *Telegraph*; 5. Other national paper; **6. Local paper;** 7. None.

Q. 8. Have you ever read a copy of any of these?

    1. Punch; 2. Weekend; 3. *Romeo;* 4. *Honey; 5. Country Life; 6. The Lady;* 7. *Woman's Weekly;* **8. *Reader's Digest.***

Q. 9. What opportunities for employment are there for young people in this area?

Q. 10. How many are there in your family at home?

    1. You live by yourself;   2. One other;   **3. Three altogether;** 4. Four; 5. Five; 6. Six or more.

Q. 11. How old are you?

    1. Under 25; 2. 25–29; 3. 30–34; 4. 35–39; 5. 40–44; 6. 45–49; 7. 50–54; **8. 55–59;** 9. 60–64; 10. 65–69; 11. 70 or over.

Q. 12. Are you: **1. Male;** 2. Female?

Q. 13. Are you: 1. Single; **2. Married;** 3. Widowed/divorced/separated?

Q. 14. What is the exact occupation of the head of your household?

Depot Manager.

Q. 15. Were you born in this City?

    1. Yes; 2. No, but within 10 miles; **3. No, more than 10 mile away.**

Q. 16. What sort of schools and colleges have you attended? (Ring the number beside **every** answer that applies to you.)

1. **Primary or elementary school;** 2. Secondary school or technical school; 3. **Grammar school;** 4. Private school; 5. Technical or training college for degree or diploma; 6. University; 7. Apprenticeship; 8. Day-release or part-time classes for a certificate; 9. Sandwich course; 10. Other college, etc., specify.

Q. 17. What age did you finish **full-time** education?

1. Under 15; 2. 15; 3. 16; 4. **17;** 5. 18; 6. 19; 7. 20; 8. 21 or more.

Q. 18. Do you have any qualifications or school certificates?

0. None; 1. Training at work; 2. **Others, specify.**
Oxford Senior.

Q. 19. What class do you belong to?

1. **Working;** 2. Middle; 3. Upper; *or* 4. **No class;** 5. **Other** (give name).
I don't accept class distinction.

Q. 20. What kind of house/flat do you live in?

1. **Owner-occupier;** 2. Council; 3. Private rented; 4. Other.

Q. 21. How much money is earned by your family?

1. Less than £5 a week; 2. £5–£9; 3. £10–£19; 4. £20–£39; 5. £40–£79; 6. Over £80.

Please add any other comments you have here.

It is difficult to follow the relevance of some of these questions.

Questionnaire 7

Q. 1. Has the City changed much since you have been here?

1. Yes; 2. **No.**

Q. 2. Which of the following are most in need of improvement? (Ring more than one number if you wish.)

1. Medical services; 2. Treatment of criminals; 3. Roads and transport; 4. Services for elderly; 5. Child welfare; 6. Animal welfare; 7. **Recreation facilities;** 8. Education; 9. Other, specify.

Q. 3. State any view you have on any one of these in particular.

Q. 4. What changes should there be in the tax system to pay for this?

Q. 5. In this City there should be more provision of:

1. Shops; 2. Pubs; 3. Council houses; 4. Bowling alleys; 5. Cinemas; 6. Bingo halls; 7. Allotments; 8. Other, specify.

Q. 6. If there were an election next week would you vote:

1. **Labour;** 2. Conservative; 3. Liberal; 4. Other; 5. Not vote?

Q. 7. Which daily newspapers do you take at home?

1. *Express*; 2. *Mirror;* 3. *Mail;* 4. *Telegraph*; 5. Other national paper; 6. **Local paper;** 7. None.

Q. 8. Have you ever read a copy of any of these?

1. *Punch*; **2. Weekend;** 3. *Romeo*; 4. *Honey*; **5. Country Life;** 6. *The Lady*; 7. *Woman's Weekly*; **8. Reader's Digest.**

Q. 9. What opportunities for employment are there for young people in this area?

Q. 10. How many are there in your family at home?

1. You live by yourself; 2. One other; 3. Three altogether; 4. **Four;** 5. Five; 6. Six or more.

Q. 11. How old are you?

1. Under 25; 2. 25–29; 3. 30–34; 4. 35–39; 5. 40–44; 6. 45–49; 7. 50–54; 8. 55–59; 9. 60–64; 10. 65–69; 11. 70 or over.

Q. 12. Are you: 1. Male; 2. **Female?**

Q. 13. Are you: 1. Single; **2. Married;** 3. Widowed/divorced/ separated?

Q. 14. What is the exact occupation of the head of your household? **Postman.**

Q. 15. Were you born in this City?

1. Yes; **2. No,** but within 10 miles; 3. **No,** more than 10 miles away. **Yes.**

Q. 16. What sort of schools and colleges have you attended? (Ring the number beside **every** answer that applies to you.)

1. **Primary** or elementary school; 2. **Secondary school** or technical school; 3. Grammar school; 4. Private school; 5. Technical **or** training college for degree or diploma; 6. University; 7. Apprenticeship; 8. Day-release or part-time classes for a certificate; 9. Sandwich course; 10. Other college, etc., specify.

Q. 17. What age did you finish **full-time** education?

1. **Under 15;** 2. 15; 3. 16; 4. 17; 5. 18; 6. 19; 7. 20; 8. 21 or more.

Q. 18. Do you have any qualifications or school certificates?

o. None; 1. Training at work; 2. Others, specify.

Q. 19. What class do you belong to?

1. **Working;** 2. Middle; 3. Upper; 4. No class; 5. Other (give name).

Q. 20. What kind of house/flat do you live in?

1. Owner-occupier; 2. Council; 3. Private rented; **4. Other.**

Q. 21. How much money is earned by your family?

1. Less than £5 a week; 2. £5–£9; **3. £10–£19;** 4. £20–£39; 5. £40–£79; 6. Over £80.

Please add any other comments you have here.

Questionnaire 8

Q. 1. Has the City changed much since you have been here?

1. **Yes;** 2. No.

Q. 2. Which of the following are most in need of improvement? (Ring more than one number if you wish.)

    1. Medical services; 2. Treatment of criminals; 3. Roads and transport; 4. Services for elderly; 5. Child welfare; 6. Animal welfare; 7. Recreation facilities; 8. Education; 9. Other, specify.

Q. 3. State any view you have on any one of these in particular.

I think we have a fairly good supply of each.

Q. 4. What changes should there be in the tax system to pay for this?

Q. 5. In this City there should be more provision of:

    1. Shops;   2. Pubs;   3. Council houses;   4. Bowling alleys; 5. Cinemas; 6. Bingo halls; 7. Allotments; 8. Other, specify.

Q. 6. If there were an election next week would you vote:

    1. Labour; 2. Conservative; 3. Liberal; 4. Other; 5. Not vote?

Who I thought most suitable to fill the post.

Q. 7. Which daily newspapers do you take at home?

    1. *Express*; 2. *Mirror*; *3. Mail*; 4. *Telegraph*; 5. Other national paper; 6. Local paper; 7. None.

Q. 8. Have you ever read a copy of any of these?

    1. Punch; 2. *Weekend*; 3. *Romeo*; 4. *Honey*; *5. Country Life;* 6. *The Lady*; *7. Woman's Weekly; 8. Reader's Digest.*

Q. 9. What opportunities for employment are there for young people in this area?

Could do with more.

Q. 10. How many are there in your family at home?

    1. You live by yourself; **2. One other;** 3. Three altogether; 4. Four; 5. Five; 6. Six or more.

Q. 11. How old are you?

    1. Under 25; 2. 25–29; 3. 30–34; 4. 35–39; 5. 40–44; 6. 45–49; 7. 50–54; 8. 55–59; 9. 60–64; 10. 65–69; **11. 70 or over.**

Q. 12. Are you: 1. Male; **2. Female?**

Q. 13. Are you: **1. Single;** 2. Married; **3. Widowed/divorced/ separated?**

Q. 14. What is the exact occupation of the head of your household? (If retired, give last occupation; if housewife give husband's occupation.)

Q. 15. Were you born in this City?

    1. Yes; 2. No, but within 10 miles; 3. No, more than 10 miles away.

Q. 16. What sort of schools and colleges have you attended? (Ring the number beside **every** answer that applies to you.)

    1. Primary or elementary school; 2. Secondary school or technical school; 3. Grammar school; **4. Private school;** 5. Technical or training college for degree or diploma; 6. University; 7. Apprenticeship; 8. Day-release or part-time classes for a certificate; 9. Sandwich course; 10. Other college, etc., specify.

Q. 17. What age did you finish **full-time** education?

1. Under 15; 2. 15; 3. 16; 4. 17; 5. 18; 6. 19; 7. 20; 8. 21 or more.

Q. 18. Do you have any qualifications or school certificates?

0. None; **1. Training at work;** 2. Others, specify.

Q. 19. What class do you belong to?

1. Working; 2. Middle; 3. Upper; 4. No class; 5. Other (give name). **Ordinary.**

Q. 20. What kind of house/flat do you live in?

1. Owner-occupier; 2. Council; **3. Private rented;** 4. Other.

Q. 21. How much money is earned by your family?

1. Less than £5 a week; 2. £5–£9; 3. £10–£19; 4. £20–£39; 5. £40–£79; 6. Over £80.

Please add any other comments you have here.

Questionnaire 9

Q. 1. Has the City changed much since you have been here?

1. Yes; **2. No.**

Q. 2. Which of the following are most in need of improvement? (Ring more than one number if you wish.)

1. Medical services; 2. Treatment of criminals; **3. Roads and transport; 4. Services for elderly;** 5. Child welfare; 6. Animal welfare; 7. Recreation facilities; 8. Education; 9. Other, specify.

Q. 3. State any view you have on any one of these in particular:

I feel that a lot of elderly people do not take up their rights because of their dislike of National Assistance. They feel this service is degrading.

Q. 4. What changes should there be in the tax system to pay for this?

Abolition of rates by dealing with this on a national level through income tax.

Q. 5. In this City there should be more provision of:

1. Shops; 2. Pubs; **3. Council houses;** 4. Bowling alleys; 5. Cinemas; 6. Bingo halls; 7. Allotments; 8. Other, specify.

Q. 6. If there were an election next week would you vote:

1. Labour; 2. Conservative; 3. Liberal; 4. Other; 5. Not vote?

Q. 7. Which daily newspapers do you take at home?

1. *Express*; **2. *Mirror*;** 3. *Mail*; 4. *Telegraph*; 5. Other national paper; 6. Local paper; 7. None.

Q. 8. Have you ever read a copy of any of these?

1. *Punch*; **2. *Weekend*; 3. *Romeo*; 4. *Honey*;** 5. *Country Life*; 6. *The Lady*; 7. *Woman's Weekly*; 8. *Reader's Digest*.

Q. 9. What opportunities for employment are there for young people in this area?

Not a lot.

Q. 10. How many are there in your family at home?

 1. You live by yourself; 2. One other; **3. Three altogether;**
4. Four; 5. Five; 6. Six or more.

Q. 11. How old are you?

 1. Under 25; 2. 25–29; 3. 30–34; 4. 35–39; 5. 40–44; 6. 45–49;
7. 50–54; 8. 55–59; 9. 60–64; 10. 65–69; 11. 70 or over.

Q. 12. Are you: 1. Male; **2. Female?**

Q. 13. Are you: 1. Single; **2. Married;** 3. Widowed/divorced/
separated?

Q. 14. What is the exact occupation of the head of your household?
Builder's labourer.

Q. 15. Were you born in this City?

 1. Yes; 2. No, but within 10 miles; **3. No, more than 10 miles away.**

Q. 16. What sort of schools and colleges have you attended? (Ring the
number beside **every** answer that applies to you.)

 1. Primary or elementary school; 2. Secondary school or technical
school; **3. Grammar school;** 4. Private school; 5. Technical or
training college for degree or diploma; 6. University; 7. Apprenticeship; 8. Day-release or part-time classes for a certificate; 9. Sandwich
course; 10. Other college, etc., specify.

Q. 17. What age did you finish **full-time** education?

 1. Under 15; 2. 15; **3. 16;** 4. 17; 5. 18; 6. 19; 7. 20; 8. 21
or more.

Q. 18. Do you have any qualifications or school certificates?

 0. None; 1. Training at work; 2. Others, specify.
 G.C.E. 2 'O' Levels.

Q. 19. What class do you belong to?

 1. Working; 2. Middle; 3. Upper; 4. No class; 5. Other (give
name).

Q. 20. What kind of house/flat do you live in?

 1. Owner-occupier; 2. Council; 3. Private rented; 4. Other.

Q. 21. How much money is earned by your family?

 1. Less than £5 a week; 2. £5–£9; **3. £10–£19;** 4. £20–£39;
5. £40–£79; 6. Over £80.

Please add any other comments you have here.

Questionnaire 10

Q. 1. Has the City changed much since you have been here?

 1. Yes; 2. No.

Q.2. Which of the following are most in need of improvement? (Ring
more than one number if you wish.)

 1. Medical services; 2. Treatment of criminals; 3. Roads and
transport; 4. Services for elderly; 5. Child welfare; 6. Animal
welfare; 7. Recreation facilities; 8. Education; 9. Other, specify.

Q.3. State any view you have on any one of these in particular:

Many more bed-sitting-room bungalows or flats should be built so that elderly people could live on their own and yet be within easy reach of a qualified nursing assistant or assistants.

Q.4. What changes should there be in the tax system to pay for this?

Very little change would be necessary.

Q.5. In this City there should be more provision of

1. Shops;   2. Pubs;   3. Council houses;   4. Bowling alleys;
5. Cinemas;   6. Bingo halls;   7. Allotments;   8. Other, specify.

Good concert hall – A good ballroom – theatre and first-class park with recreational facilities.

Q.6. If there were an election next week would you vote:

1. **Labour;**   2. Conservative;   3. Liberal;   4. Other;   5. Not vote?

Q.7. Which daily newspapers do you take at home?

1. *Express*;   2. *Mirror;*   3. *Mail*;   4. *Telegraph;*   5. Other national paper;   6. Local paper;   7. None.

Q.8. Have you ever read a copy of any of these?

1. *Punch;*   2. *Weekend*;   3. *Romeo*;   4. *Honey;*   5. *Country Life*;   6. *The Lady;*   7. *Woman's Weekly;*   8. *Reader's Digest.*

Q.9. What opportunities for employment are there for young people in this area?

Ample – according to local press adverts.

Q.10. How many are there in your family at home?

1. You live by yourself;   2. One other;   **3. Three altogether;**
4. Four;   5. Five;   6. Six or more.

Mother – brother – myself.

Q.11. How old are you?

1. Under 25;   2. 25–29;   3. 30–34;   4. 35–39;   5. 40–44;   6. 45–49;
7. 50–54;   8. 55–59;   9. 60–64;   10. 65–69;   11. 70 or over.

Q.12. Are you: 1. Male;   2. **Female?**

Q.13. Are you: 1. Single;   2. Married;   **3. Married/divorced/ separated?**

Q.14. What is the exact occupation of the head of your household?

Brother in business on own account. Myself – I was a secretary but am now looking after Mother, who is partially paralysed.

Q.15. Were you born in this City?

1. **Yes;**   2. No, but within 10 miles;   3. No, more than 10 miles away.

Q.16. What sort of schools and colleges have you attended? (Ring the number beside **every** answer that applies to you.)

1. Primary or elementary school;   2. Secondary school or technical school;   **3. Grammar school;**   4. Private school;   5. Technical or training college for degree or diploma;   6. University;   7. Apprenticeship;   8. Day-release or part-time classes for a certificate;   9. Sandwich course;   10. Other college, etc., specify.

Q. 17. What age did you finish **full-time** education?
1. Under 15; 2. 15; **3. 16**; 4. 17; 5. 18; 6. 19; 7. 20; 8. 21 or more.

Q. 18. Do you have any qualifications or school certificates?
o. **None;** 1. Training at work; 2. Other, specify.
Shorthand 130 w.p.m., typing 80 w.p.m.

Q. 19. What class do you belong to?
1. Working; 2. Middle; 3. Upper; 4. No class; 5. Other (give name).

Q. 20. What kind of house/flat do you live in?
1. Owner-occupier; 2. Council; 3. Private rented; 4. Other.

Q. 21. How much money is earned by your family?
1. Less than £5 a week; 2. £5–£9; 3. £10–£19; **4. £20–£39;**
5. £40–£79; 6. Over £80.

Please add any other comments you have here.

Questionnaire 11

Q. 1. Has the City changed much since you have been here?
1. Yes; 2. No.

Q. 2. Which of the following are most in need of improvement? (Ring more than one number if you wish.)
1. Medical services; 2. Treatment of criminals; 3. Roads and transport; 4. Services for elderly; 5. Child welfare; 6. Animal welfare; **7. Recreation facilities;** 8. Education; 9. Other, specify.

Q. 3. State any view you have on any one of these in particular:
No full use made of the river either for recreational boating or walking.

Q. 4. What changes should there be in the tax system to pay for this?
None.

Q. 5. In this City there should be more provision of:
1. Shops; 2. Pubs; 3. Council houses; **4. Bowling alleys;**
5. Cinemas; 6. Bingo halls; 7. Allotments; **8. Other, specify.**
Theatre or concert hall.

Q. 6. If there were an election next week would you vote:
1. Labour; 2. Conservative; 3. Liberal; 4. Other; 5. Not vote?

Q. 7. Which daily newspapers do you take at home?
1. *Express*; 2. *Mirror*; 3. *Mail*; 4. *Telegraph*; 5. Other national paper; **6. Local paper;** 7. None.
The Top People's Paper.

Q. 8. Have you ever read a copy of any of these?
1. Punch; 2. *Weekend;* 3. *Romeo;* 4. *Honey;* **5. Country Life; 6. The Lady;** 7. *Woman's Weekly;* **8. Reader's Digest.**

Q. 9. What opportunities for employment are there for young people in this area?

Ask the employment exchange.

Q. 10. How many are there in your family at home?

1. You live by yourself;   2. One other;   3. Three altogether; 4. Four;   **5. Five;**   6. Six or more.

Q. 11. How old are you?

1. Under 25; 2. 25–29; 3. 30–34; **4. 35–39;** 5. 40–44; **6. 45–49;** 7. 50–54;   8. 55–59;   9. 60–64;   10. 65–69;   11. 70 or over.

Q. 12. Are you: **1. Male;**   2. Female?

Q. 13. Are you: 1. Single;   **2. Married;**   3. Widowed/divorced/ separated?

Q. 14. What is the exact occupation of the head of your household?

If I told you I would identify myself.

Q. 15. Were you born in this City?

1. Yes;   2. No, but within 10 miles;   **3. No, more than 10 miles away.**

Q. 16. What sort of schools and colleges have you attended? (Ring the number beside **every** answer that applies to you.)

1. Primary or elementary school; 2. Secondary school or technical school;   3. Grammar school;   **4. Private school;**   5. Technical or training college for degree or diploma;   **6. University;   7. Apprenticeship;**   8. Day-release or part-time classes for a certificate;   9. Sandwich course;   10. Other college, etc., specify.

Q. 17. What age did you finish **full-time** education?

1. Under 15;   2. 15;   3. 16;   4. 17;   5. 18;   6. 19;   7. 20;   **8. 21 or more.**

Q. 18. Do you have any qualifications or school certificates?

0. None;   1. Training at work;   2. Others, specify.

Professional qualification.

Q. 19. What class do you belong to?

1. Working;   2. Middle;   3. Upper;   **4. No class;**   5. Other (give name).

Please define.

Q. 20. What kind of house/flat do you live in?

1. Owner-occupier;   2. Council;   3. Private rented;   4. Other.

Q. 21. How much money is earned by your family?

1. Less than £5 a week;   2. £5–£9;   3. £10–£19;   4. £20–£39; 5. £40–£79;   6. Over £80.

Please add any other comments you have here.

I can't help feeling that my answers, which are as full as I can make them, won't help you much. For instance, what is the value of Q. 1. unless you know how long I have lived here.

Questionnaire 12

Q. 1. Has the City changed much since you have been here?

  1. Yes, *for the worst*; 2. No.

Q. 2. Which of the following are most in need of improvement? (Ring more than one number if you wish.)

  1. Medical services; **2. Treatment of criminals;** 3. Roads and transport; **4. Services for the elderly;** 5. Child welfare; 6. Animal welfare; 7. Recreation facilities; 8. Education; 9. Other, specify.

Q. 3. State any view you have on any one of these in particular:

  Services for the elderly. Such as home helps going to people who really need them, especially the disabled, who have to do without so that able-bodied people can have them. There is nothing done for middle age and too much for children, single people who have fathers to keep them.

Q. 4. What changes should there be in the tax system to pay for this?

  I should like to speak to a genuine person about my questions.

Q. 5. In this City there should be more provision of:

  1. Shops;   2. Pubs;   3. Council houses;   4. Bowling alleys;
  5. Cinemas; 6. Bingo halls; 7. Allotments; **8. Other, specify.**
  Modern conveniences in our flats.

Q. 6. If there were an election next week would you vote:

  1. Labour; 2. Conservative; 3. Liberal; 4. Other; **5. Not vote? None.**

Q. 7. Which daily newspapers do you take at home?

  1. Express; 2. Mirror; 3. *Mail*; 4. *Telegraph*; 5. Other national paper; 6. Local paper; 7. None.

Q. 8. Have you ever read a copy of any of these?

  1. Punch; 2. *Weekend*; 3. *Romeo*; 4. *Honey*; *5. Country Life; 6. The Lady; 7. Woman's Weekly; 8. Reader's Digest.*

Q. 9. What opportunities for employment are there for young people in this area?

Q. 10. How many are there in your family at home?

  1. You live by yourself (my budgies); 2. One other; 3. Three altogether; 4. Four; 5. Five; 6. Six or more.

Q. 11. How old are you?

  1. Under 25; 2. 25–29; 3. 30–34; 4. 35–39; 5. 40–44; 6. 45–49;
  7. 50–54; 8. 55–59; **9. 60–64;** 10. 65–69; 11. 70 or over.

Q. 12. Are you: 1. Male; **2. Female?**

Q. 13. Are you: **1. Single;** 2. Married; 3. Widowed/divorced/separated?

Q. 14. What is the exact occupation of the head of your household? (If retired, give last occupation; if housewife, give husband's occupation.)

Q. 15. Were you born in this City?

1. Yes;   2. No, but within 10 miles;   **3.** No, more than 10 miles away.
No, thank goodness.

Q.16. What sort of schools and colleges have you attended? (Ring the number beside **every** answer that applies to you.)

1. Primary or elementary school;   2. Secondary school or technical school;   3. Grammar school;   4. Private school;   5. Technical or training college for degree or diploma;   6. University;   **7.** Apprenticeship;   8. Day-release course or part-time classes for a certificate;   9. Sandwich course;   10. Other college, etc., specify.

Q.17. What age did you finish **full-time** education?

1. Under 15;   2. 15;   3. 16;   4. 17;   5. 18;   6. 19;   7. 20;   8. 21 or more.

Q.18. Do you have any qualifications or school certificates?

0. None;   1. Training at work;   2. Others, specify.

Q.19. What class do you belong to?

1. Working;   2. Middle;   3. Upper;   **4. No class;**   5. Other (give name).

No class distinction now.

Q.20. What kind of house/flat do you live in?

1. Owner-occupier;   **2. Council;**   3. Private rented;   4. Other.

Council, much to my regret. I hate it. Have to live here until I can get one myself privately owing to ill health. It's damp and in shocking condition.

Q.21. How much money is earned by your family?

1. Less than £5 a week;   2. £5–£9;   3. £10–£19;   4. £20–£39;   5. £40–£79;   6. Over £80.

Please add any other comments you have here.

Appendix 11 – for Project 34

Full-time Miscreants, Delinquent Neighbourhoods and Criminal Networks[1]

JOHN MACK

(reprinted from *Brit. J. Soc.*, vol. 15, no. 1, 1964, with permission)

This paper is an interim report on some work now being done on systems of criminal activity. The first part describes the criminal output – in terms of

[1] Part of this paper was read to the Scottish branch of the B.S.A., in February 1963. The fieldwork for the Full-time Criminal and Network studies is the responsibility of M. Ritchie. The studies were financially assisted by the Scottish Home and Health Department to whom grateful acknowledgment is hereby made.

full-time practitioners – of an urban industrial territory. The second part describes a delinquent neighbourhood and sketches the wider criminal network which is today the more typical form of criminal sub-culture. The third part gives some interpretations of the data provided by these and other studies in the sociology of crime, and suggests some further lines of inquiry.

It should perhaps be emphasised that while the activities described here illustrate some of the basic and traditional sources of crime – professional criminals, organised criminals, and, in general, groups habituated to a criminal way of life – these activities provide no more than a fraction of the crimes which are made known to the police in the country as a whole, and which derive from a great variety of situations. The work described here is concerned with only a few of the many kinds of behaviour technically classified as criminal. This concentration on one thing at a time is a necessary condition of any inquiry which aims at the advancement of knowledge about criminals. The fact that many other types of crime and criminal are left unnoticed here does not imply that their existence is queried or denied.

1. Full-time Criminals

In Worktown, an urban territory of 100,000 population, there are twelve full-time criminals, of whom nine are full-time 'travelling' criminals: i.e. operating mainly outside their area of residence. The twelve have been thinned out from a longer list agreed by the police forces concerned. Eight of the twelve are heavy-weight or at least middle-weight operators; the remaining four are smaller fry. In the remainder of this section we shall confine ourselves in the main to the eight more formidable characters, six of whom are travelling criminals. It is a small group, but it constitutes the main contribution of the territory to the organised crime of the region and beyond.

The precise definition of 'full-time' criminal – a term we prefer to 'professional' criminal – is that although the people concerned have some nominal occupation which they practise more or less regularly, they are known to be engaged in or available for criminal activities at all times. Secondly, the main classes of crime in which they are engaged are crimes against property, or more generally, crimes of dishonesty. Some of them are also violent but the violence is marginal to their main activity. Thirdly, they have been engaged in continuous criminal activity for a considerable period to date. All of the twelve have so far had a criminal span, operating from this territory, of not less than seventeen years: i.e. the youngest is 34. Some younger men are still coming on but have not yet made the grade since they might conceivably give up.

The territory consists in the main of two towns; one large and one small. The bulk of the adult population are industrial workers or engaged in the usual services, transport and other, of an industrial area. All of the full-time criminals fall into the social-occupational classes of semi-skilled and un-skilled workers.

The eight more formidable characters fall into two distinct groups:

The first four (whom we shall call *AA, BB, CC,* and *DD*) are psycho-logically unremarkable. They show no signs of emotional unbalance. They appear to be above average intelligence. Their childhood home backgrounds are either unknown – two come from Ireland – or fairly respectable. Two of the four have a slight juvenile record – one with two periods of probation, the other one absolute discharge. Two have regular work records. The other two live mainly on public funds as well as on undisclosed sources of income. All four have a fairly stable family life, two being regularly and two irregularly married. All have children living regularly under the same roof with them.

Details of the four are as follows:

AA (*now 52*) arrived here from Ireland at about age 30. He has had occasional jobs as motor driver but is now mostly on relief. The police find him a friendly character, easy to get on with. His professional specialism is that of key-making and duplicating, particularly safe keys. He moves about all the time and is known for his specialism throughout the region. He looks sleepy and stupid, but participates in remarkable feats of organisation and planning on a small scale.

BB (*now 42*) arrived from Ireland when 19. He also is a motor driver to trade but is seldom in work. He is known to the police, who have a sneaking regard for him, as a friendly, sociable character with no violence in him. *BB* is an expert house-breaker, ranked high in ability by the police; he has many associates and travels widely throughout the region.

CC (*now 34*). *CC*'s life-style was transformed about age 24. Although he had one minor juvenile offence he came from a fairly respectable home. But he got into bad company in his late teens and hung around street corners with criminals. Now he is always clean and tidy, a home-lover, non-drinker, non-smoker, devoted to his children, a fairly regular worker, keen on physical fitness and to all outward appearances a good citizen. On the darker side of his ordinary life he is said to be a money-lender at his work on a considerable scale.

Underneath his fair-seeming surface he is a persistent house-breaker and safe-blower, is seldom inactive, travels widely, and has a wide range of criminal associates, including one or two connections in England. Quiet, reserved and uncommunicative, he is regarded by the police with a certain grudging respect, as a quite rational and able criminal who may conceivably stop when he has acquired a respectable modicum of capital.

DD (*now 37*). There is no information about *DD*'s early background. His present house is better than average; his children are well looked after. He is on the whole a steady worker but gambles a lot. Views on his temperament differ. Police in his own town find him cheerful and companionable, always smiling, salutes his police friends in the street. Police in the neighbouring town find him sullen and withdrawn. *DD* is an outstandingly able contriver and executant of burglaries big and small, based on complete information. He appears to be the ablest of these criminals. He may however be surpassed by *CC*, who never gives anything away. The two are thought to work together from time to time.

The second group (*WW*, *XX*, *YY* and *ZZ*) are thought to be not too bright. Two of them are markedly unbalanced characters; a third has a record of violence, including assaults on the police. All four have poor work records. All four are regarded by the police as surly, unsociable, unpleasant characters. Three had poor home backgrounds as children. Three have juvenile records, one including a term in an Approved School, one (post-16) a Borstal sentence, and one both Approved School and Borstal.

Details of the four are as follows:

WW (*now 38*) has no juvenile record but had a bad childhood home background. A violent and uncontrolled character. An excessive drinker and persistent drunkard, goes wild when drunk and suffers from persecution feeling and terror of renewed imprisonment. Has been known to threaten to murder police for putting him in prison but this indicates his horror of imprisonment rather than his likely behaviour. No record of assaults on police.

Poor work record; lives on public relief. Does not travel. Depredations all within area, mostly house-breakings.

XX (*now 36*). A lone wolf with magpie tendencies; mixes with no one; dour and unco-operative with the police. A non-stop house-breaker: seems unable to resist stealing anything on sight, including worthless articles which he hides on the hill-side. When *XX* is caught 'the police office looks like Woolworths'.

A difficult child; slept out; avoided school; mother alleged a fall as a small child resulting in a fractured skull.

Approved School at 12 for 10 thefts: released at $16\frac{1}{2}$ and committed 6 thefts in 2 months for which he was in quick succession admonished, fined, admonished, sent to Approved School, and returned to Approved School having absconded. Later was sent to Borstal.

No work record. Adult professional specialism is breaking into houses (in a vigilant area avoided by other criminals) when the owners are in residence but asleep. Main activity is local but has been convicted in London and elsewhere.

YY (*now 36*). Described by police as an evil and dangerous man – inclined to be violent – spat in general direction of police at last sentence. Has never been in regular employment. First came to the notice of the police at the age of 11 years and as a juvenile spent a period on probation and one in Approved School. Adult convictions consist mainly of theft by house-breakings with a sprinkling of assaults and breaches of the peace; his latest charge in 1960 involved the use of explosives; he has twice served terms of imprisonment in England (1 year and 3 years). Associate of ZZ.

ZZ (*now 35*) has the biggest public reputation. Taught safe-blowing when young in company with other young criminals including CC and DD, and in turn has passed on the teaching to others including WW. A persistent safe-blower on a large scale; undeterrable; 'no thrill like facing a safe at 2 a.m. and blowing it'. Slight juvenile record. 28 days Remand Home at 16. Immediately after sent to Borstal. Wide range of associates. Has been known through heartlessness or stupidity to require younger men to carry explosives at great personal risk to them. Seldom talks to the police. Active over a very wide area, including English Midlands.

The main difference between the two groups is shown in the table below. While it is known that the first group are continuously active, they are seldom caught or charged and seldom sent to prison. The second group are likewise continuously active during all the free time they have but they are frequently caught and are seldom out of prison.

The question arises – how do we know that the first group *are* full-time criminals? (The available evidence is by definition not sufficient to convict them in a court of law.) The claim is supported (*a*) by the knowledge of

Full-Time Miscreants – Time spent in prison

	Years at Risk (*from age 17 years*)	*Years in Prison* (*or Borstal*)
AA (52 years)	35	$1\frac{3}{4}$
BB (42 years)	25	$3\frac{2}{3}$
CC (34 years)	17	$3\frac{1}{3}$
DD (38 years)	21	$2\frac{3}{4}$
	98	$11\frac{1}{3}$

AA, BB, CC, DD: Proportion of adult years spent in prison, etc., 12 per cent

WW (38 years)	21	$11\frac{1}{4}$
XX (35 years)	18	$16\frac{3}{4}$
YY (36 years)	19	$7\frac{1}{3}$
ZZ (34 years)	17	15
	75	$50\frac{1}{3}$

WW, XX, YY, ZZ: Proportion of adult years spent in prison, etc., 64 per cent

Note (*i*) : No allowance is made in this table for remission of sentence.
Note (*ii*): ZZ is at present serving a sentence of 7 years imprisonment imposed on him in June 1963; this is not included in the above table.

various C.I.D. groups of a series of successful crimes by each; (*b*) by indications in their household spending of undisclosed sources of income; (*c*) by the discovery of one or the other in police road blocks and in other suspicious circumstances; and (*d*) by the disclosures of accomplices (after their capture) who tell all but whose evidence does not convict.

The next stage in the study of a group of criminals of this kind would be to trace the network of collaboration and information which links them together with each other and with lesser criminals in a social and economic system of communication and exchange, and which extends far beyond Worktown. There is *inter alia* a special link between Worktown and a town in the London area.

Methods of carrying out such a study are now under consideration. We go on meantime in this paper to discuss other examples of criminal interconnections in other parts of the country, not necessarily connected with Worktown.

II. Delinquent Areas and Criminal Networks

Existing studies of criminal sub-cultures are concerned in the main with territorial clusters of criminal-producing households – criminal areas or neighbourhoods.[1] Since these areas are usually quite small, we prefer the terms 'neighbourhood' or 'precinct'. There were in the past many examples of criminal neighbourhoods. But territorial location is becoming less and less important in modern society. Just as the nation is no longer composed of small socially self-contained towns and villages, but of cities and regions in which neighbours are less important than colleagues, so also with crime. The majority of persistent criminals today live in a neutral neighbourhood, or keep on the move. A criminal community may be predominantly a network of communications over a wide region with some kind of foothold in various neighbourhoods but not tied to these neighbourhoods. The important thing is no longer a place but a system of social relationships and functions, including a status system. These systems carry on, with changes of tempo and vigour, with ups and downs, a criminal way of life, an adaptable tradition that moves with the times.

There are in fact no *criminal* areas left, i.e. areas in which known criminals are known to reside in sizeable groups. This would make it too easy for the police, who are now able to go anywhere, by day or night. But there are in every conurbation a number of *delinquent* neighbourhoods. These are so defined because they produce delinquents (i.e. young offenders) in exceptionally large numbers of whom a very large selection go on to crime (that is

[1] See, for example, *Brit. J. Crim.*, vol. 3, editorial note, p. 209 (1962). See also T. Morris, *The Criminal Area*, London, 1957, chs. i–vi, for an effective summary of work in this field.

graduate from juvenile to adult offending).[1] Delinquent neighbourhoods
have therefore a strong connection with criminals, but most of these when
grown up use the place only as an occasional port of call, a part of a wider
network.

The distinguishing mark of these neighbourhoods is that their social tone
is directed against the values and practices of the wider society. The people
in them accept dishonesty and minor violence as a way of life. It is for most
of them a passive acceptance. The majority of households avoid being
convicted for criminal behaviour and the majority of these do so by not
behaving criminally.

One such neighbourhood we have begun to study in some detail. Most of
the work has still to be done. But some preliminary results are interesting.
We began by making a crime map of an urban territory. Twenty-seven
precincts, blocks of criss-crossing streets, stood out as having a high
delinquent content. Nineteen were located in older housing districts: 8 in
inter-war-built housing schemes: none in post-war housing schemes. These
latter schemes had not had time to build up the concentrations already
established in the older districts. The period covered is 1946–58. Of the
three precincts with the highest crime rating one is in an old near-central
district and the remaining two are in schemes built in the nineteen-thirties.
The figures were respectively: 23, 36 and 45 first offenders per year per
1,000 households on an annual average over twelve years.[2] Since houses
and households are much more tightly packed in the older area the actual
density of offenders and of offending households *per acre* is greater than in
the inter-war-built schemes. But the latter have still a long life in front of
them; the older areas are due for demolition and redevelopment.

The precinct with the highest crime-rate has been studied in more detail
up to 1960. It consists of a pocket of 1,100 houses – mainly the product of
slum clearance and 'rehousing' building policy. Measured for first *and
subsequent* offenders, i.e. *all* persons against whom charges are proved, the
sector has produced 110 offenders per thousand households, or 11 per 100
households, on an annual average for the 12 years 1948–60. The two highest
density streets (536 houses in all) have 16 offenders per 100 houses per year.
The highest density street (252 houses) produced 20 offenders per 100 houses
per year.

[1] Robert E. Forman discusses in *J. Criminal Law, Criminology and Police Science*,
vol. 54 (1963), pp. 317–21, the question of how delinquent an area must be to be
labelled delinquent.

[2] These and similar figures given here are of course official figures and therefore
exclude undetected offenders. R. E. Forman, op. cit., holds that although much
delinquency goes unrecorded in these high-rate areas, the more serious and
persistent delinquents do tend to receive official attention. 'This would imply that
rate differences between ecological areas probably reflect real differences in
behaviour' (p. 318).

How many of these households are actively criminal or delinquent at any one time? This has been calculated for the worst street, counting households producing *two or more offenders* over a period of ten years. The answer is 32 per cent. Another 7 per cent of households have a record of one offence only in the period. These are infectedly rather than actively criminal. In sum: three out of five households in the worst area in this region have no criminal record at all, and only one out of three is criminally active.

The most striking figure is that of those who graduate from delinquency to crime. Of the total of juvenile entrants into delinquency from the worst street in the 12 years 1946–58, viz. 135, no fewer than 39 or 29 per cent have become adult criminals. The national figure is probably well under 5 per cent. The degree of incorrigibility of the entry is shown by the Borstal figures. The two worst streets sent to Borstal a proportion of its young men at least ten times as high as the Scottish rate. The total was 27 in the period from the 532 houses. This is roughly 52 per 1,000 households which would if generalised for all Scotland give an annual Borstal entry of 5,000. The average annual entry into Borstal in 1958–60 was 400–500. Moreover this group shows an 80 per cent 'failure' compared with a general failure proportion of 50 per cent in the period (calculated over a period of 10 years after release).

Some sketches of life in this neighbourhood will illustrate its tone and atmosphere:

The Training of the Young
'Between the ages of 4 and 8 the main activity is to pick up the lumps of coal or other merchandise thrown on the sides of the track from the railway wagons by the older boys. The wee ones are hardly able to lift their feet over the wire, but they manage it. 8–12 they become very active: as Mr. *M.* observed, a 9-year-old could carry a hundredweight of coal on his back. 12 upwards the boys, young adults and adults are sometimes very agile. They wear a harness over their shoulders to keep their hands free. This is favoured particularly by the *D*——*'s* of 47 *X* Street. One 20 + very agile: was on a slowly moving truck when the police were closing in on him. He threw the bag full of coal on to the spikes of the railings about 7 ft away, jumped from the moving train on to the bag, then jumped down 12 ft and got away. Various devices were used to stop the trains some years ago. On several occasions the signals were interfered with. Drivers sometimes found sleepers across the rails; when they got out to remove the sleepers the coal-stealers swarmed on to the trucks. It was just like the Wild West. The coal-stealers threw the coal either in between the middle rails, or on the side next to *X* street. They then go and reclaim their own coal from where they have thrown it, having a strong sense of private property in what they steal.'

A Moral Improvement

'The Railway Police dogs had a considerable effect on the inhabitants of this area. Before the dogs came they used to steal whisky from the bonded store and sell it to the people in the nearby pub. The dogs made this much more difficult. The thieves were thrown back from the railway on to the street. After that the whisky was stolen from the pub, which was a slight moral improvement on the former situation. This pub has now been demolished.'

Rude Social Health

'The place gives an impression of rude social health. The young in particular have an active life with plenty of recreational activity and room to play in. One gets the impression of a thoroughly self-contained community going about its business with great vigour. As one observer remarked, it is just like a big tinker encampment. Although the excitement was quite marked when we were there, the whole place was very quiet.'

This impression of rude social health is perhaps mistaken. The factors[1] in the area report that they have requests for transfer from almost everyone in the scheme. Many of the tenants are untransferable, because of rent arrears among other things. But all seem to want, or go through the motions of signifying that they want, to get out.

A CRIMINAL NETWORK

The idea of a criminal network is useful in any attempt to understand organised crime over a fairly wide industrial region.

Such a network is probably a very loose affair with its various parts, usually dormant, coming into operation as circumstances determine. You can always (one is told) get a man to do a job, either because you know whom you want already, or because you can get someone to put you on to him. Prisons are important centres for the exchange of information of this kind, and for following what is going on in the outside world from a criminal point of view. Although the morning newspapers are not given out in one large prison until afternoon and then only to a few privileged prisoners or to untried prisoners, the speed of the prison grape-vine is such that an item appearing in the newspaper can go all round the prison before any single newspaper can have got into the hands of any prisoner. Moreover the active criminals in prison can interpret the news more accurately than can the ordinary reader. When they read of a safe-blowing or a bank robbery, they have a shrewd idea about the people involved. They will know who would do this kind of thing in this particular way and also which of them is already in prison or outside. Sometimes, even more strikingly, news is passed into a

[1] Anglicé – housing managers or rent collectors.

prison or Borstal before it can be printed: thus the writer was told of a slashing in a cinema in a neighbouring town, on the same evening as it happened, and twelve hours before the episode appeared in the newspaper, the informant being a Borstal resident.

Every prison officer or chaplain, every police detective or crime journalist, is aware of the existence of an intelligence system of this kind, supported by a persisting system of relationships, a common acceptance of a privately enforced code of conduct, and a generally recognised status system. But systematic evidence for its existence, of the kind demanded by sociologists, is uncommonly hard to get. The people who have the practical knowledge, on both sides, generally keep this knowledge to themselves. Valuable work has been done on prison social systems, in U.S.A. and to a lesser extent in this country, and this throws light incidentally on the wider criminal social system of which prisons are a part.[1] Apart from this the main work of delineating the criminal sub-culture, the system of organised criminal relationships which exists in any big industrial region, must so far begin with such information as emerges when the curtain is lifted by a spectacular High Court trial. Evidence of this kind is available for the industrial region centring on Clydeside. Three big trials took place in this region in the five years up to 1960: viz. the Paisley Road bank robbery in July 1955 – trial in January 1956; the Manuel murders 1956–58, trial in May 1958; and the Shettleston Road bank robbery in April 1959, followed by the capture of the chief miscreants in May 1959, the escape of Samuel McKay in July 1959, the trial in September 1959, the recapture of McKay in July 1960, and his trial in November 1960.

The most striking criminal episode in the period was that of the pursuit and capture of the murderer Manuel, as outlined in the court proceedings and in a narrative by the detective[2] who was principally responsible for his conviction. This gives some grounds for holding that a network exists and throws some light in particular on the economic system, the status system and the value system, which are part of it.

The narrative is remarkable for the large number of well-known people (criminally speaking) who come into it.

The first name to come up is that of a notorious gang leader of the inter-war years. This man, as it turned out, had reformed since the war: his intervention in this case was intended to help in the tracing of the gun used in one of Manuel's murders. The next name to be connected with the case is that of Samuel McKay. This is of great interest, for McKay was the

[1] D. Clemmer, *The Prison Community*, New York, 1958; G. M. Sykes, *The Society of Captives*, Princeton, 1958; D. R. Cressey (ed.), *The Prison*, New York, 1961; Terence and Pauline Morris, *Pentonville*, London, 1963.

[2] Detective-Superintendent A. Brown, since deceased. The narrative is in the Scottish *Daily Express*, 19–30 Oct. 1959. See also John Gray Wilson, *The Trial of Peter Manuel*, London, 1959.

leading criminal figure in the region in the period up to 1960. A National
Assistance form found under a vase in Manuel's sitting-room bore the name
'Mr. McKay', and the telephone number of the Gordon Club, a well-known
gambling club with which Samuel McKay was associated. Manuel told
some remarkable stories about this.

The background of one of the stories is that the people connected with the
Gordon Club were determined to discourage the setting up of rival clubs.
Criminal enterprises, like non-criminal, tend towards oligopoly. One rival
was proposing to open a club in a building round the corner. The proprietor of the building received by post a bomb with the explosive left out.
The message this conveyed was that next time the bomb would be live and
would not come by post. This was no empty threat. About this time a
bookmaker's office had been bombed on two occasions and was a few
months later to be put out of action by fire. And this particular threat, the
non-live bomb, was in fact traced back to the Gordon Club. *EE*, co-
proprietor of the club with Samuel McKay, was charged, convicted and
sent for nine months to prison for the crime of sending it. There is reason to
believe that he was not actively concerned in sending the bomb, though he
may have known of it. But he did not talk, and duly served his time.

Manuel's story, which comes into the extraordinary address to the jury
made by himself as his own defending counsel, was that McKay took him
to see *EE*, who was in prison awaiting trial on the bomb charge. During this
visit, Manuel alleged, he was asked to prevent the prospective victim of the
bomb incident, the rival proprietor, from giving evidence against *EE*.
'That', said Manuel, 'was the business I had with McKay, he wanted me to
wait until the night before the trial and get hold of this —— and give him a
right doing so that he would land in hospital and wouldn't be able to go to
the trial. . . .'

It is difficult to judge the accuracy of this story. It is probably nearer the
truth than some other accounts offered by Manuel to explain why McKay
and he came together at this time. But irrespective of the details of the story
it does illustrate rather well the nature of the relationship between the two
men. It throws some light for example on the criminal status-system. Note
the implied high status of McKay. It is quite feasible that he in his role of
criminal tycoon should employ Manuel as a junior executive. Note secondly
the implied low status of Manuel. This also is consistent with the other data
we have. Manuel appears to have been a relatively unimportant figure before
his trial. He was a man of the second rank, a strong-arm man and a relative
outsider to the McKay circle. McKay admitted to knowing him for some
years but only as a minor figure.

Further indications show how status (in the sense of high status) is
acquired in this sub-culture. McKay appears to have achieved his position
in three ways. First by money. Secondly by fear. He is thought to be a violent
man in the sense that he threatens the use of violence to enforce his will on

other criminals and even on non-criminals. (It should be noted that there is little record of personal violence on his part.) Thirdly by skill in outwitting the forces of law and order. McKay's most notable exploit, already noted, was to escape from prison and to remain 'on the run' for a year. This happened in 1959–60, in the last year of his active career to date, but it crowned a reputation already won for agility in avoiding capture.

The *EE* episode shows us something of the value-system accepted by criminals. *EE* was ready to serve the prison sentence imposed on him without complaining. Why? Not because of a feeling of loyalty to his colleagues – there is no loyalty between thieves as such – but because of a common repudiation of the police-enforced code of the wider society. These people have their own sanctions, and prefer to operate them in their own way. They may use betrayal to the police as an occasional method of enforcement but this is rare.

A further episode in the Manuel case illustrates several aspects of the network – its intelligence and economic system and the limited range of the group code. This is the surprising behaviour of *FF*. This episode first came into the light of day at the trial of Manuel in 1958 in the course of evidence concerning the murder of Mrs Watt, her sister, and her daughter in September 1956. At the trial *FF* told how he had helped Manuel to procure the gun which killed these women. The business, which involved two other dealers, both with bad criminal records, was transacted in a series of meetings in Gallowgate public houses.

The surprising behaviour of *FF* consists in the fact that he had told this story a year earlier, and to the police at that. He had gone to Mr Watt, husband and father of two of the murdered women, and had then been persuaded to confide in the police. It is on the face of it unusual that one criminal should inform against another on such a serious charge. All this was before Manuel had become notorious. Why should *FF* break the code? If there is a criminal network throughout the west of Scotland, and if Manuel was part of it, why should *FF* betray him? The answer appears to be that Manuel was not a member of the particular corner of the network to which *FF* belonged. He was an outsider. He didn't 'run with' the Gallowgate crowd. In his own area (he was known to the Lanarkshire police but *not* to the Glasgow police) he did belong. It is also possible that Manuel was distrusted as a deep or queer type. A fellow-prisoner in Peterhead Prison describes him as excessively self-centred and withdrawn. But the main suggestion one gets from all this is that the network, such as it is, is sustained by a common code of not talking to the police, which is strong in local groups or between habitual associates, but does not stretch to casual associates from a distance, and does not stand up well to a major exposure.

Similar considerations may explain the sentences in the Paisley Road bank robbery trial in 1956. Two English and three local men were tried. The Englishmen got eight years and six years respectively. One local minor figure

got three years; the other two were discharged. Scottish criminal opinion
probably approved the system of private information which may have
resulted in these disposals.

We have space here for only a brief reference to the Shettleston Road bank
robbery. This was a very well-planned crime but it led to the final capture
and imprisonment of McKay and the collapse of the Gordon Club group.
In this major engagement one imagines the police came out finally on top.
This may not be a final verdict, since the greater part of the money stolen
was not recovered. But it is probable that all of the stolen money was spent
by McKay in his expensive year on the run. What is certain is that the
network in the shape described here, with its apex in McKay, is now a
matter of history. There are no well-known figures left. But it goes on in a
more anonymous shape. For it has connections with the wider culture in its
more dubious economic aspects.

One main connection is with the gambling world. The Gordon Club has
been succeeded by a number of other gambling clubs some of which harbour
criminals (according to a recent statement by the Chief Constable of
Glasgow). On a lower level there are less conspicuous trades, notably that of
scrap merchant. The nature of this business attracts criminals who wish to
dispose of stolen goods. Some of these concerns are simply fronts for criminal
activities: most have no criminal connections: a number in between have a
criminal corner to their business. There are several well-known resetters of
this kind. They oblige the police from time to time by turning someone in.
This is usually a person from outside the district and who is inexperienced, a
first offender who doesn't know the ropes. One low character, with no place
of business, has a habit of informing on juveniles who refuse to take the
very low prices he offers them for stolen goods. These might be regarded as
society's devices for preventing first offenders and juvenile delinquents from
becoming persistent criminals. It should be added that some resetters,
probably most, will not touch youngsters.

Appendix 12 – for Project 36

Questionnaire for Computer Analysis

Q. 1. Student's code number (between 1 and 10,000).
Q. 2. Is your home in (1) an urban or (2) a rural district? (Take borough or
urban district as 'urban' and rural district as 'rural'.)   Write
number.

Q.3. How many *bedrooms* are there in your home?   Write number.

Q.4. How many *other* rooms are there in your home? (*Exclude* halls, pantries, cloakrooms, bathrooms and other 'non-living' rooms, but *include* kitchen.)   Write number.

Q.5. Give your estimate of the total household income coming in to your family: Give only one of these: annual income.

monthly income
or weekly income.

Q.6. Ring the number:

(1) if you gave annual income *or* (2) if you gave monthly income *or* (3) if you gave weekly income.

Q.7. How many small children (under 5 years old) live in your home? Write number.

Q.8. How many other children (between 5 and 16 years old) live in your home?   Write number.

Q.9. How many adults (aged 17 and over) live in your home? (Include yourself.)   Write number.

Q.10. −2 (This symbol is an end check for the computer.)

(After the last questionnaire has been punched, punch −1 as an end check for the computer.)

Bibliography

Abbott, J. 'Students' Social Class in Three Northern Universities'. *Brit. J. Sociol.* vol. 16, no. 3, 1965.

Abel-Smith, B. and Townsend, P. *The Poor and the Poorest.* London: Bell, 1965.

Abrams, M. 'Social Trends and Electoral Behaviour'. *Brit. J. Sociol.* vol. 13, no. 3, 1962.

Adorno, T. W. *et al. The Authoritarian Personality.* New York: Harper, 1950.

Albig, W. *Modern Public Opinion.* New York: McGraw, 1956.

Alihan, M. A. *Social Ecology: a Critical Analysis.* New York: Columbia, 1938.

Allen, F. A. *The Borderland of Criminal Justice.* Chicago: U. of Chicago, 1964.

Anderson, N. *The Hobo.* Chicago: Council of Social Agencies, 1923.

Argyle, M. *The Scientific Study of Social Behaviour.* London: Methuen, 1957.

— 'Experimental Studies of Small Social Groups' in Welford, A. T. *et al. Society: Problems and Methods of Study.* London: Routledge, 1962.

Bales, R. F. *Interaction Process Analysis.* Cambridge, Mass.: Addison-Wesley, 1950.

— 'Small-Group Theory and Research' in Merton, R. K. *et al. Sociology Today.* New York: Basic Books, 1959.

Banfield, C. *Political Influence,* Glencoe, Ill.: Free Press, 1961.

Banton, M. 'Anthropological Perspectives in Sociology'. *Brit. J. Sociol.,* vol. 15, no. 2, 1964.

Barber, B. *Social Stratification.* New York: Harcourt, 1957.

Barclay, G. W. *Techniques of Population Analysis.* London: Chapman & Hall, 1958.

Barnard, C. I. *The Functions of the Executive.* Cambridge, Mass.: Harvard, 1938.

Bartlett, F. C. *Remembering. A Study in Experimental and Social Psychology.* Cambridge: U.P. 1932.

Bavelas, A. 'Communication Patterns in Task-oriented Groups' in Cartwright, D. and Zander, A. *Group Dynamics.* London: Tavistock, 1954.

B.B.C. Audience Research Department. *Methods and Services.* London: B.B.C., 1962.

Becker, H. S. *Outsiders*. Glencoe, Ill.: Free Press; London: Collier-Macmillan, 1963.

Bell, N. W. and Vogel, E. F. *A Modern Introduction to the Family*. Glencoe, Ill.: Free Press; London: Routledge, 1961.

Benjamin, B. 'The Population Census as a Source of Social Statistics' in Welford, A. T. *et al. Society. Problems and Methods of Study*. London: Routledge, 1962.

Benney, M. *et al. How People Vote*. London: Routledge, 1956.

Berelson, B. *Content Analysis in Communication Research*. Glencoe, Ill.: Free Press, 1952. (Shortened version in Lindzey, G. (ed.), *Handbook of Social Psychology*, 2 vols. Cambridge, Mass.: Addison-Wesley, 1954.)

— and Janowitz, M. *Reader in Public Opinion and Communication*. Glencoe, Ill.: Free Press; London: Collier-Macmillan, 1953, 1966.

Bernstein, B. 'Some Sociological Determinants of Perception: an Enquiry into Subcultural Differences'. *Brit. J. Sociol.*, vol. 9, no. 2, 1958.

— 'Language and Social Class' (Research Note). *Brit. J. Sociol.*, vol. 2, no. 3, 1960a.

— 'Review of Opie, *Lore and Language of Schoolchildren*', *Brit. J. Sociol.*, vol. 2, no. 2, 1960b.

— 'Social Structure, Language and Learning', *Educational Research*, vol. 3, 1961.

— 'A Socio-linguistic Approach to Social Learning' in Gould, J. (ed.), *Penguin Survey of the Social Sciences*. London: Penguin, 1965.

Beveridge, W. I. B. *The Art of Scientific Investigation*, 3rd edn. London: Heinemann, 1957; paperback edn., 1961.

Bierstedt, R. *The Social Order*. New York: McGraw, 1963.

Boggs, S. L. 'Urban crime patterns'. *American Sociological Review*, vol. 30, no. 6, 1965.

Borko, H. (ed.), *Computer Applications in the Behavioral Sciences*. Englewood Cliffs: Prentice-Hall, 1962.

Boskoff, A. and Cahnman, W. J. *Sociology and History*. Glencoe, Ill.: Free Press, 1965; London: Collier-Macmillan, 1964.

Bott, E. *Family and Social Network*. London: Tavistock, 1957.

Bottomore, T. B. *Classes in Modern Society*. London: Allen & Unwin, 1963.

— and Rubel, M. (eds.), *Karl Marx: Selected Writing*. London: Penguin, 1963.

Bronfenbrenner, M. 'Socialisation and Social Class through Time and Space' in Maccoby, E. E. *et al. Readings in Social Psychology*. London: Methuen, 1959.

Broom, L. and Selznick, P. *Sociology*, 3rd edn. New York: Harper, 1963.

Brown, R. G. 'Poverty in Australia – the Evidence', *Brit. J. Sociol.*, vol. 15, no. 2, 1964.

Bruyn, S. T. *The Human Perspective in Sociology*. Englewood Cliffs: Prentice-Hall, 1966.

Buber, M. *Paths in Utopia*. New York: Macmillan, 1950.

Burgess, E. W. and Wallin, P. *Engagement and Marriage*. Philadelphia: Lippincott, 1953.

Butler, D. E. *The British General Election of 1951*. London: Macmillan, 1952.

Campbell, A. A. and Katona, A. 'The Sample Survey' in Festinger, L. and Katz, D. *Research Methods in the Behavioral Sciences*. New York: Dryden, 1953.

Campbell, D. T. 'The Indirect Assessment of Social Attitudes'. *Psychol. Bull.* vol. 47, 1950.

Cantril, H. *Gauging Public Opinion*. New Jersey: Princeton, 1947.

Caplow, T. *The Sociology of Work*. Minneapolis: U. of Minn., 1954. Reprinted as paperback New York: McGraw, 1964.

Carr-Saunders, Sir A. M. *et al. Survey of Social Conditions of England and Wales . . . as illustrated by Statistics*. Oxford: U.P. 1958.

Cartwright, D. and Zander, A. (eds.), *Group Dynamics*, 2nd edn. London: Tavistock, 1961.

Census, 1951, 1961 and following. *General Report*. London: H.M.S.O., 1958 and following years.

Centers, R. *The Psychology of Social Classes*. New Jersey: Princeton, 1949.

Central Statistical Office. *Annual Abstract of Statistics*. London: H.M.S.O., annually.

Chapin, F. S. *Experimental Designs in Sociological Research*. New York: Harper, 1947.

Chapman, D. *The Home and Social Status*. London: Routledge, 1955.

Chein, I. 'Appendix B: An Introduction to Sampling' in Selltiz, C. *et al. Research Methods in Social Relations*. New York: Holt, Rinehart, 1959.

Cicourel, A. V. *Method and Measurement in Sociology*. Glencoe, Ill.: Free Press; London: Collier-Macmillan, 1964.

Classification of Occupations, 1960. (General Register Office.) London: H.M.S.O., 1960.

Clemmer, D. *The Prison Community*. New York: Holt, Rinehart, 1958.

Clinard, M. B. *Sociology of Deviant Behaviour*, 2nd rev. edn. New York: Holt, Rinehart, 1963.

— (ed.), *Anomie and Deviant Behavior*. Glencoe, Ill.: Free Press; London: Collier-Macmillan, 1964.

Cochran, W. G. and Cox, G. M. *Experimental Designs*. New York: Wiley, 1950; London: Chapman & Hall, 1957.

Coleman, J. S. *Introduction to Mathematical Sociology*. Glencoe, Ill.: Free Press, 1964*a*.

— 'Research Chronicle: the Adolescent Society' in Hammond, P. E. (ed.), *Sociologists at Work*. New York: Basic Books, 1964*b*.

— 'The Use of Electronic Computers in the Study of Social Organisation', *European Journal of Sociology*, vol. 6, no. 1, 1965 (this number of the journal is devoted to articles on computer simulation).

Conwell, C. *Professional Thief: By a professional thief.* Annot. and interpreted by E. H. Sutherland. Chicago: U. of Chicago, 1956.

Coontz, S. H. *Population Theories and the Economic Interpretation.* London: Routledge, 1957.

Corlett, T. and Edwards, F. 'Sampling Methods', *The Incorporated Statistician,* Supplement 'Modern Sample Survey Methods', to vol. 5, no. 4, 1955.

Corwin, R. G. *A Sociology of Education.* New York: Appleton, 1955.

Coser, L. A. and Rosenberg, B. M. (eds.), *Sociological Theory,* 2nd edn. New York: Macmillan, 1964.

Cox, P. R. *Demography.* Cambridge: U.P. 1959.

Cressey, D. R. (ed.), *The Prison.* New York: Holt, Rinehart, 1961.

Criswell, J. H. 'Racial cleavages in Negro-White groups'. *Sociometry,* vol. 1, nos. 1 and 2 (July–Oct.), 1937.

— 'Social structure revealed in a sociometric retest.' *Sociometry,* vol. 2, no. 4, 1939.

D'Antonio, W. V. and Erickson, E. C. 'The Reputational Technique as a Measure of Community Power', *Amer. Sociol. Rev.,* vol. 27, no. 3, 1962.

Dahl, R. A. *Who Governs? Democracy and Power in an American City.* New Haven: Yale, 1961.

Dahrendorf, R. 'Out of Utopia: Toward a Reorientation of Sociological Analysis' in Coser, L. A. and Rosenberg, B. M. (eds.), *Sociological Theory,* 2nd edn. New York: Macmillan, 1964.

Davis, K. *Human Society.* New York: Macmillan; London: Collier-Macmillan, 1949.

Douglas, J. W. B. *The Home and the School. A Study of Ability and Attainment in the Primary Schools.* London: MacGibbon, 1964.

Downham, J. S. 'The Function of Coding', *The Incorporated Statistician,* Supplement 'Modern Sample Survey Methods', to vol. 5, no. 4, 1955.

Du Bois, C. *The People of the Alor.* Minneapolis: U. of Minn., 1944.

Dublin, L. I. *Suicide, a Sociological and Statistical Study.* New York: Ronald, 1963.

Duncan, O. D. and Spengler, J. J. *Demographic Analysis.* Glencoe, Ill.: Free Press; London: Collier-Macmillan, 1956a.

— *Population Theory and Policy.* Glencoe, Ill.: Free Press; London: Collier-Macmillan, 1956b.

Dunlop, A. B. and McCabe, S. *Young Men in Detention Centres.* London: Routledge, 1965.

Durkheim, E. *The Division of Labour in Society.* Glencoe, Ill.: Free Press, 1947.

— *The Rules of Sociological Method.* Glencoe, Ill.: Free Press, 1958; London: Collier-Macmillan, 1950.

— *Suicide.* London: Routledge, 1952.

Duverger, M. *Introduction to the Social Sciences.* London: Allen & Unwin, 1964.

Edwards, A. L. 'Experiments: Their Planning and Executive' in Lindzey, G. (ed.), *Handbook of Social Psychology*, vol. 1. Cambridge, Mass.: Addison-Wesley, 1954.

— *Techniques of Attitude Scale Construction*. New York: Appleton, 1957.

Edwards, F. (ed.), *Readings in Market Research*. London: British Market Research Bureau, 1956.

Fearing, F. and Krise, E. M. 'Conforming Behaviour and the *J*-curve Hypothesis', *J. Soc. Psychol.*, vol. 14, part 1 (Aug.), 1941.

Festinger, L. and Katz, D. *Research Methods in the Behavioral Sciences*. New York: Holt, Rinehart, 1954; Dryden, 1963.

— *et al. Social Pressures in Informal Groups*. New York: Harper, 1950; London: Tavistock, 1963.

Fifteen to Eighteen (Crowther Report), 2 vols. Central Advisory Council for Education (England). London: H.M.S.O., 1960.

Firth, R. 'An Anthropologist's View of Mass Observation', *Sociological Rev.*, vol. 31, no. 2, 1939.

— *Two Studies of Kinship in London*. London: Athlone, 1956.

— 'Family and Kinship in Industrial Society', *Sociological Review*. Monograph 8, Keele, 1964.

Fleming, C. M. (ed.), *Studies in the Social Psychology of Adolescence* . . . By J. E. Richardson *et al.* London: Routledge, 1951.

Florence, P. S. *The Logic of British and American Industry*. London: Routledge, 1953.

Floud, J. E. *et al. Social Class and Educational Opportunity*. London: Heinemann, 1956.

Form, W. H. and Miller, D. C. *Industry, Labour and Community*. New York: Harper, 1960.

Frank, L. K. 'Projective Methods for the Study of Personality', *J. Psychol.* vol. 47, 1950.

Frankenberg, R. 'Participant Observers', *New Society*, vol. 1, no. 23, 1963.

French, J. R. P. 'Experiments in Field Settings' in Festinger, L. and Katz, D. *Research Methods in the Behavioral Sciences*. New York: Dryden, 1953.

Friedan, Betty. *The Feminine Mystique*. London: Penguin, 1965.

Fromme, A. 'On the Use of Certain Qualitative Methods of Attitude Research: a study of opinions on the methods of preventing war', *Social Psychology*, vol. 13, 1941.

Gallup, G. *A Guide to Public Opinion Polls*. New Jersey: Princeton, 1948.

Gavron, H. *The Captive Wife*. London: Routledge, 1966.

The Gentle Computer. Series of articles on computers and applications first published in *New Scientist*, 14 Oct.–25 Nov. 1965.

Giallombardo, R. *Society of Women: a Study of a Woman's Prison*. New York: Wiley, 1966.

Gibbs, J. P. *Urban Research Methods*. Princeton: Van Nostrand, 1962.

I

Gibbs, J. P. 'Suicide' in Merton, R. K. and Nisbet, R. A. *Contemporary Social Problems*. New York: Harcourt, Brace, 1961; London: Hart-Davis, 1963.

— and Martin, W. T., *Status Integration and Suicide: A Sociological Study*. Corvallis, Ore.: Oregon State, 1964.

Gibson, Q. *The Logic of Social Enquiry*. London: Routledge, 1960.

Giddens, A. 'The Suicide Problem in French Sociology', *Brit. J. Sociol.*, vol. 16, no. 1, 1965.

Gist, N. P. and Halbert, L. A. *Urban Society*. New York: Crowell, 1948.

Glass, D. V. (ed.), *Social Mobility in Britain*. London: Routledge, 1954.

Goffman, E. *Asylums*. New York: Doubleday Anchor, 1961. (Major essay reprinted in Etzioni, A. *Complex Organisations*. New York: Holt, Rinehart, 1961. Also in full in Cressey, D. R. *The Prison*. New York: Holt, Rinehart, 1961.)

Goodacre, D. M. 'The Use of a Sociometric Test as a Predictor of Combat Unit Effectiveness'. Originally in *Sociometry*, vol. 14, nos. 2–3 (May-Aug.), 1951. Reprinted in Lazarsfeld, P. F. and Rosenberg, M. *The Language of Social Research*. Glencoe, Ill.: Free Press, 1955.

Goode, W. J. *World Revolution and Family Patterns*. Glencoe, Ill.: Free Press; London: Collier-Macmillan, 1963.

— *The Family*. Englewood Cliffs: Prentice-Hall, 1964*a*.

— (ed.). *Readings on the Family and Society*. Englewood Cliffs: Prentice-Hall, 1964*b*.

— and Hatt, P. K. *Methods in Social Research*. New York: McGraw, 1952.

Gordon, M. M. *Social Class in American Sociology*. Durham, N. C.: Duke, 1958.

Gorer, G. *Exploring English Character*. London: Cresset, 1955.

Gould, J. (ed.), *Penguin Survey of the Social Sciences*. London: Penguin, 1965.

Gould, J. E. and Kolb, W. L. (eds.), *A Dictionary of Social Sciences*. London: Tavistock, 1964.

Greenwood, E. *Experimental Sociology*. New York: King's Crown Press, 1965.

Greer, S. A. *Social Organisation*. New York: Random, 1963.

Greve, J. *People and Their Houses*, Bournville: J. S. Fry Ltd. Publication Dept.

Gullahorn, J. T. and Gullahorn, J. E. 'Computers in Behavioral Science', *Behavl. Sci.*, vol. 8, no. 4, 1963.

Gurvich, G. D. and Moore, W. E. (eds.), *Twentieth Century Sociology*. New York: New Philosophical Library, 1945.

Hagood, M. J. and Price, D. O. *Statistics for Sociologists*. New York: Holt, Rinehart, 1952.

Hall, J. and Jones, D. Caradog. 'Social Grading of Occupations', *Brit. J. Sociol.*, vol. 1, no. 1, 1950.

Halloran, J. D. *The Effects of Mass Communication*. Leicester: Leic. U.P., 1964.

Hammond, P. E. (ed.), *Sociologists at Work*. New York: Basic Books, 1964.

Hanson, R. C. *et al.* 'Predicting a Community Decision: A Test of the Miller-Form Theory', *Amer. Sociol. Rev.*, vol. 24, no. 5, 1959.

Hare, A. P. 'Small Group Discussions with Participatory and Supervisory Leadership' in Hare, A. P. *et al. Small Groups.* New York: Knopf, 1955.

— 'Computer Simulation of Interaction in Small Groups', *Behavl. Sci.*, vol. 6, no. 3, 1961.

— *Handbook of Small Group Research.* Glencoe, Ill.: Free Press; London: Collier-Macmillan, 1962.

Harris, A. I. 'The Work of a Coding Section', *The Incorporated Statistician*, vol. 5, no. 4, 1955.

Hatt, P. K. 'Stratification in the Mass Society'. *Amer. Sociol. Rev.*, vol. 15, no. 2, 1950.

— and Reiss, A. J. *Cities and Society*, rev. edn. Glencoe, Ill.: Free Press; London: Collier-Macmillan, 1957.

Hauser, P. M. and Duncan, O. D. (eds.), *The Study of Population.* Chicago: U. of Chicago, 1959.

— and Schnore, L. F. *The Study of Urbanisation.* New York: Wiley, 1965.

Havighurst, R. J. and Davis, A. 'A Comparison of the Harvard and Chicago Studies of Social Class Differences in Child-Rearing', *Amer. J. Sociol.*, vol. 20, no. 4, 1955.

Hawley, A. H. *Human Ecology.* New York: Ronald, 1950.

Henry, A. F. and Short, J. *Suicide and Homicide.* Glencoe, Ill.: Free Press, 1954; new edn. London: Collier-Macmillan, 1964.

Higher Education (Robbins Report). Committee on Higher Education. London: H.M.S.O., 1963.

Himmelweit, H. T. *et al. Television and the Child.* London: Oxford, 1958.

Hoggart, R. *The Uses of Literacy.* London: Penguin, 1958.

Homans, G. C. *The Human Group.* London: Routledge, 1951.

Home Office. *The Sentence of the Court.* London: H.M.S.O., 1964.

Horace Mann-Lincoln Institute of School Experimentation. *How to Construct a Sociogram.* New York: Teachers' College, Columbia University, 1947.

Hubback, J. *Wives Who Went Back to College.* London: Heinemann, 1957.

Huff, D. *How to Lie with Statistics.* New York: Norton; London: Gollancz, 1954.

Hughes, E. C. 'Institutional Office and the Person', *Amer. J. Sociol.*, vol. 43, no. 3, 1937.

— 'The Sociological Study of Work: An Editorial Foreword', *Amer. J. Sociol.*, vol. 57, no. 5, 1952.

— *Men and Their Work.* Glencoe, Ill.: Free Press; London: Collier-Macmillan, 1958.

Hunter, F. *Community Power Structure.* Chapel Hill: U. of N.C., 1953.

Hyman, H. H. *Survey Design and Analysis.* Glencoe, Ill.: Free Press, 1958; London: Collier-Macmillan, 1955.

— *et al. Interviewing in Social Research.* Chicago: U. of Chicago, 1954.

260 Bibliography

Jackson, B. and Marsden, D. *Education and the Working Class*. London: Routledge, 1962.

Jahoda, M. *et al. Research Methods in Social Relations*, 1st edn., 2 vols. New York: Dryden, 1951.

Jennings, H. H. *Sociometry in Group Relations*. Washington, D.C.: American Council on Education, 1948.

— *Leadership and Isolation*, 2nd edn. London: Longmans, 1950.

Jones, D. Caradog. *Social Surveys*. London: Hutchinson, 1949.

Joseph, J. 'Attitudes of 600 Adolescent Girls to Work and Marriage' (Research Note), *Brit. J. Sociol.*, vol. 12, no. 2, 1961.

Kahn, R. L. and Cannell, C. F. *The Dynamics of Interviewing*. New York: Wiley, 1957.

Kardiner, A. *The Psychological Frontiers of Society*. New York: Columbia, 1945.

Katz, D. 'Field Studies' in Festinger, L. and Katz, D. *Research Methods in the Behavioral Sciences*. New York: Dryden, 1953.

Katz, E. and Lazarsfeld, P. F. *Personal Influence*. Glencoe, Ill.: Free Press, 1955.

Kelsall, R. K. *Report on an Enquiry into Applications for Admissions to Universities*. Commissioned by the Committee of Vice-Chancellors and Principals of the Universities of the United Kingdom. London, 1957.

Kelvin, R. P. 'The Non-Conforming Voter', *New Society*, vol. 6, no. 165, 1965.

Kendall, P. L. and Lazarsfeld, P. F. 'Problems of Survey Analysis' in Merton, R. K. (ed.), *Continuities in Social Research*. Glencoe, Ill.: Free Press, 1950.

— and Wolf, K. H. 'The Two Purposes of Deviant Case Analysis' in Lazarsfeld, P. F. and Rosenberg, M. *The Language of Social Research*. Glencoe, Ill.: Free Press, 1955.

Kerr, M. *The People of Ship Street*. London: Routledge, 1958.

Keyes, F. 'The Correlation of Social Phenomena with Community Size', *Social Forces*, vol. 36, no. 4, 1958. (Reprinted in O'Brien, R. W. *et al. Readings in General Sociology*, 3rd edn. Boston: Houghton, 1964.)

Klapper, J. T. *Effects of Mass Communication*. Glencoe, Ill.: Free Press; London: Collier-Macmillan, 1960.

Klein, J. *The Study of Groups*. London: Routledge, 1956.

— *Working with Groups*. London: Hutchinson, 1963.

— *Samples from English Cultures*, 2 vols. London: Routledge, 1965.

Klein, V. *Britain's Married Women Workers*. London: Routledge, 1965.

Kluckhorn, F. R. 'The Participant Observer Technique in Small Communities', *Amer. J. Sociol.*, vol. 46, no. 3, 1940–1.

Komarovsky, M. 'The Technique of "Discerning"' in Lazarsfeld, P. F. and Rosenberg, M. *The Language of Social Research*. Glencoe, Ill.: Free Press, 1955.

— 'Cultural Contradictions and Sex Roles', *Amer. J. Sociol.*, vol. 52, no. 3,

1946. (Reprinted in O'Brien, R. W. *et al. Readings in General Sociology*, 3rd edn. Boston: Houghton, 1964.)

Lapping, A. 'The Unknown Depths of Poverty', *New Society*, vol. 6, no. 167 (Dec.), 1965.

Larson, R. F. and Catton, W. R. 'Can the mail-back bias contribute to a study's validity?' *Amer. Sociol. Rev.*, vol. 24, no. 2, 1959.

Lazarsfeld, P. F. *et al. The People's Choice. How the Voter makes up his mind in a Presidential Campaign.* New York: Columbia, 1948.

— and Barton, A. H. 'Qualitative Measurement in the Social Sciences' in Lerner, D. and Lasswell, H. D. (eds.). *The Policy Sciences.* Stanford, Calif.: Stanford, 1951.

— and Rosenberg, M. (eds.), *The Language of Social Research.* Glencoe, Ill.: Free Press; London: Collier-Macmillan, 1955.

Levens, G. E. '101 white-collar criminals', *New Society*, vol. 3, no. 78 (Mar.), 1964.

Lewin, K. *Field Theory and Social Psychology.* London: Tavistock, 1952.

— 'Group Decision and Social Change' in Maccoby, E. E. *et al. Readings in Social Psychology.* London: Methuen, 1959. (Also earlier edition: Swanson, G. E., Newcomb, T. E. and Hartley (eds.), 1952.)

Liggett, J. and Wakeford, J. 'Sociology as a Laboratory Subject', *Sociological Rev.*, vol. 12, no. 2, 1964.

Lindzey, G. and Borgatta, E. F. 'Sociometric Measurement' in Lindzey, G. *Handbook of Social Psychology.* Cambridge, Mass.: Addison-Wesley, 1954.

Lippitt, R. O. and White, R. K. 'An Experimental Study of Leadership and Group Life' in Maccoby, E. E. *et al. Readings in Social Psychology.* London: Methuen, 1959.

Lipset, S. M. *et al. Union Democracy.* Glencoe, Ill.: Free Press; London: Collier-Macmillan, 1956.

— and Bendix, R. *Social Mobility in Industrial Society.* Berkeley: U. of Calif., 1963.

Little, J. and Westergaard, J. H. 'The Trend of Class Differentials in Educational England and Wales', *Brit. J. Sociol.*, vol. 15, no. 4, 1964.

Llewellyn, E. C. and Hawthorn, A. 'Human Ecology' in Gurvich, G. and Moore (eds.), *Twentieth Century Sociology.* New York: New Philosophical Library, 1945.

Lockwood, D. *The Blackcoated Worker, a Study in Class Consciousness.* London: Allen & Unwin, 1958.

Loveday, R. *A First Course in Statistics.* Cambridge: U.P. 1958.

— *A Second Course of Statistics.* Cambridge: U.P., 1961.

Lundberg, G. A. and Lawsing, M. 'The Sociology of some Community Relations', *Amer. Sociol. Rev.*, vol. 2, no. 3, 1937.

Lupton, T. and Wilson, B. R. *Manchester School*, 1960.

Lynd, R. S. and Lynd, H. M. *Middletown.* New York: Harcourt; London: Constable, 1929.

McClelland, W. D. 'Women's Weeklies', *New Society*, vol. 4, no. 118 (Dec.), 1964.

Maccoby, E. E. and Maccoby, N. 'The Interview' in Lindzey, G. *Handbook of Social Psychology*. Cambridge, Mass.: Addison-Wesley, 1954.

Maccoby, E. E. *et al. Readings in Social Psychology*. London: Methuen, 1959.

McGinnis, R. 'Experiment' in Gould, J. and Kolb, W. L. (eds.), *A Dictionary of the Social Sciences*. London, Tavistock, 1964.

MacIver, R. M. and Page, C. H. *Society*. London: Macmillan, 1957.

Mack, J. 'Full-time Miscreants, Delinquent Neighbourhoods and Criminal Networks', *Brit. J. Sociol.*, vol. 15, no. 1, 1964.

McPhee, W. N. 'Note on a Campaign Simulator', *Public Opinion Quarterly*, vol. 25, no. 2, 1961.

Madge, J. *The Tools of Social Science*. London: Longmans, 1953; New York: Anchor, 1965.

— *The Origins of Scientific Sociology*. London, Tavistock, 1963.

Malinowski, B. *Argonauts of the Western Pacific*. London: Routledge, 1964.

Mann, P. H. *An Approach to Urban Sociology*. London: Routledge, 1965.

Mannheim, H. *Juvenile Delinquency in an English Middletown*. London: Routledge, 1948.

— and Wilkins, L. T. *Prediction Methods in Relation to Borstal Training*. London, H.M.S.O., 1955.

Mannheim, K. *Ideology and Utopia*. New York: Harcourt, 1936; London: Routledge, 1954.

Marriott, R. 'Some problems in attitude survey methodology', *Occup. Psychol.* vol. 27, 1953.

Marris, P. *Widows and their Families*. London: Routledge, 1958.

Marsh, D. C. *The Changing Social Structure of England and Wales 1871–1951*. London: Routledge, 1958.

Mathiesen, T. *The Defences of the Weak*. London: Tavistock, 1965.

Mayer, J. E. *Jewish–Gentile Courtships*. Glencoe, Ill.: Free Press; London: Collier-Macmillan, 1961.

Mead, M. *Sex and Temperament in Three Primitive Societies*. London: Routledge, 1935.

— *Male and Female: A Study of the Sexes in a Changing World*. London: Gollancz, 1950; Penguin, 1964.

Merton, R. K. *Continuities in Social Research*. Glencoe, Ill.: Free Press; London: Collier-Macmillan, 1950.

— *Social Theory and Social Structure*. Glencoe, Ill.: Free Press; London: Collier-Macmillan, 1957.

— *et al. The Focused Interview*. Glencoe, Ill.: Free Press; London: Collier-Macmillan, 1956.

— and Nisbet, R. A. (eds.), *Contemporary Social Problems*. New York: Harcourt, 1961; London: Hart-Davis, 1963.

Michel, A. V. 'Kinship Relations and Relations of Proximity in French

Working-class Households' in Bell, N. W. and Vogel, E. F. *A Modern Introduction to the Family*. Glencoe, Ill.: Free Press, 1960.

Milgram, S. 'Nationality and Conformity' in O'Brien, R. W. *et al. Readings in General Sociology*. Boston: Houghton, 1964.

Miller, D. 'Industry and Community Power Structure: a Comparative Study of an American and English City', *Amer. Sociol. Rev.* vol. 23, no. 1, 1958.

Miller, D. R. and Swanson, G. E. *The Changing American Parent*. New York: Wiley, 1958.

Mills, C. W. *The Power Élite*, New York: Oxford U.P., 1956.

Milner, H. 'The Folk–Urban Continuum' in Hatt, P. K. and Reiss, A. J. *Cities and Society*, rev. edn. Glencoe, Ill.: Free Press, 1957.

Ministry of Labour. *Report of an Enquiry into Household Expenditure in 1953–4*. London: H.M.S.O., 1957.

Ministry of Labour. *Family Expenditure Survey. Report for 1957–9, 1960 and 1961, 1962*. London: H.M.S.O., 1961, 1962, and 1963 respectively.

Ministry of Labour. *Family Expenditure Survey. Report for 1963*. London: H.M.S.O., 1965.

Moreno, J. L. *Sociometry, Experimental Method and the Science of Society*. New York: Beacon House, 1951.

— *Who Shall Survive?* New York: Beacon House, 1953.

— *Facts from Figures*. London: Penguin, 1956; new edn. 1964.

Moroney, M. J. *Facts from Figures*. London: Penguin, 1956.

Morris, R. T. 'A Typology of Norms', *Amer. Sociol. Rev.*, vol. 21, no. 5, 1956.

Morris, T. *The Criminal Area*. London: Routledge, 1957.

— and Morris, P. *Pentonville*. London: Routledge, 1963.

Moser, C. A. *Survey Methods in Social Investigation*. London: Heinemann, 1958.

— and Scott, W. *British Towns*. London; Oliver: 1961.

Mueller, J. H. and Schuessler, L. F. *Statistical Reasoning in Sociology*. Boston: Houghton; London: Constable, 1961.

Mumford, L. *The Story of Utopias*. New York: P. Smith, 1941.

Municipal Year Book. London: Municipal Yearbook Ltd. Published annually.

Musgrove, F. *The Family, Education and Society*. London: Routledge, 1966.

Myrdal, A. and Klein, V. *Women's Two Roles*. London: Routledge, 1956.

Myrdal, Gunnar. *Value in Social Theory*. London: Routledge, 1958.

Naroll, R. *Data Quality Control – a New Research Technique*. Glencoe, Ill.: Free Press; London: Collier-Macmillan, 1962.

Newcomb, T. M. 'The influence of attitude climate upon some determinants of information', *J. Abnorm. Soc. Psychol.*, vol. 41, no. 46, 1946.

Newson, J. and Newson, E. *Infant Care in an Urban Community*. London: Allen & Unwin, 1963.

North, C. C. and Hatt, P. K. 'Occupational Status and Prestige' in O'Brien, R. W. *et al. Readings in General Sociology*, 3rd edn. Boston: Houghton, 1964.

Northway, M. L. and Lindsay, Weld. *Sociometric Testing: A Guide for Teachers*. Toronto: U. of Toronto, 1957.

O'Brien, R. W. *et al. Readings in General Sociology*, 3rd edn. Boston: Houghton, 1964.

Olmstead, M. S. *The Small Group*. New York: Random, 1959.

Opie, I. and P. *The Lore and Language of Schoolchildren*. Oxford: Clarendon Press, 1959.

Orwell, G. 'Boys' Weeklies' in *A Collection of Essays*. New York: (Anchor) Doubleday, 1954; London: Secker, 1961.

Parsons, T. 'Age and Sex in the Social Structure of the United States' in Parsons, T. (ed.), *Essays in Sociological Theory*. Glencoe, Ill.: Free Press, 1954*a*; Collier-Macmillan, new edn., 1964.

— 'The Kinship System of the Contemporary United States' in Parsons, T. (ed.), *Essays in Sociological Theory*. Glencoe, Ill.: Free Press, 1954*b*; Collier-Macmillan, new edn. 1964.

— 'Foreword' to Cumming, E. and Henry, W. E. *Growing Old: the Process of Disengagement*. New York: Basic Books, 1961.

Parten, M. *Surveys, Polls and Samples*. New York: Harper, 1950.

Payne, S. L. *The Art of Asking Questions*. Princeton: Princeton University Press, 1951.

Phillips, B. S. *Social Research*. New York: Collier-Macmillan, 1966.

Phillips, M. *Small Social Groups in England*. London: Methuen, 1964.

Plowman, D. E. G. 'Public opinion and the polls', *Brit. J. Sociol.* vol. 13, no. 4, 1962.

— 'Polls and Might-have-beens', *New Society*, vol. 4, no. 106 (Oct.), 1964.

Political and Economic Planning (P.E.P.). *Population Policy in Great Britain*. London: P.E.P., 1948.

— 'Graduate Wives', *Planning*, no. 361, 1954.

Pool, I. de Sola and Abelson, R. 'The Simultaneous Project', *Public Opinion Quarterly*, vol. 25, no. 2, 1961.

Popper, K. R. *The Open Society and its Enemies*. London: Routledge, 1945; new edn., 1962.

Presthus, R. *Men at the Top*. New York: Oxford U.P., 1964.

Preston, M. 'Is Poverty Increasing?', *New Society*, vol. 6, no. 169 (Dec.), 1965.

Preston, M. G. and Heintz, R. K. 'Effects of Participatory versus Supervisory Leadership on Group Judgement' in Cartwright, D. and Zander, A. *Group Dynamics*. New York: Row–Peterson, 1953.

Proctor, C. H. and Loomis, C. P. 'Analysis of Sociometric Data' in Jahoda, M. *et al. Research Methods in Social Relations*, 1st edn., vol. 2, New York: Dryden, 1951.

The Pub and the People. A Worktown Study. London: Gollancz, 1943.

Quinney, R. 'Is Criminal Behaviour Deviant Behaviour?', *Brit. J. Crim.*, vol. 4, no. 6, 1964.

Radcliffe-Brown, A. R. *Method in Social Anthropology*. Chicago: U.P., 1958.

— 'Introduction to the Analysis of Kinship Systems' in Bell, N. W. and

Vogel, E. F. *A Modern Introduction to the Family*. Glencoe, Ill.: Free Press, 1960.

Radzinowicz, L. and Turner, J. W. C. *Sexual Offences*. London: Macmillan, 1957.

Registrar-General's Statistical Review of England and Wales 1961. London: H.M.S.O., 1964.

Reiss, A. J. *et al. Occupations and Social Status*. Glencoe, Ill.: Free Press, 1961; London: Collier-Macmillan, 1962.

Reissman, L. 'Levels of Aspiration and Social Class', *Amer. Sociol. Rev.*, vol. 18, no. 2, 1949.

— *The Urban Process*. Glencoe, Ill.: Free Press; London: Collier-Macmillan, 1964.

— 'Urbanism and Urbanisation' in Gould, J. (ed.), *Penguin Survey of the Social Sciences*. London: Penguin, 1965.

Rex, J. *Key Problems of Sociological Theory*. London: Routledge, 1961. 2nd edn., 1963,

Richardson, S. A. *et al. Interviewing, its Forms and Functions*. New York: Basic Books, 1965.

Richmond, A. H. 'The United Kingdom' in Rose, A. R. (ed.), *The Institutions of Advanced Societies*. Minneapolis: U. of Minnesota Press, 1958.

Riesman, D. and Glazer, N. *Faces in the Crowd*. New Haven: Yale, 1952, 1956.

— *et al. The Lonely Crowd*. New York: (Anchor) Doubleday, 1953.

Riley, M. W. *Sociological Research*. 2 vols. New York: Harcourt, 1963.

Robb, J. H. *Working-Class Anti-Semite*. London: Tavistock, 1954.

Rose, A. M. 'Sociology and the Study of Values', *Brit. J. Sociol.* vol. 7, no. 1, 1956.

Rose, R. 'Psephology for everyone', *New Society*, vol. 1, no. 8 (Nov.), 1962.

— 'Sampling Variations in Opinion Polls', *The Times*, 28 Aug. 1964. And ensuing correspondence.

— *Politics in England*. London: Faber, 1965.

Rosenberg, B. and White, D. M. *Mass Culture*. Glencoe, Ill.: Free Press; London: Collier-Macmillan, 1957.

Sainsbury, P. *Suicides in London*. Maudsley Monograph No. 1. London: Chapman & Hall, 1955.

Sampson, A. *Anatomy of Britain*. London: Hodder, 1962.

Schachter, S. 'Deviation, Rejection and Communication', *J. Abnorm. Soc. Psychol.*, vol. 46, no. 2, 1951. Reprinted in Cartwright, D. and Zander, A. (eds.), *Group Dynamics*. London: Tavistock, 1955.

Schmid, C. F. 'Scaling Techniques in Sociological Research' in Young, P. V. and Schmid, C. F. *Scientific Social Surveys and Research*, 2nd edn. Englewood Cliffs: Prentice-Hall, 1949.

Schneider, D. M. and Homans, G. C. 'Kinship Terminology and the American Kinship System' in Bell, N. W. and Vogel, E. F. *A Modern Introduction to the Family*. Glencoe, Ill.: Free Press, 1960.

Schnore, L. F. *The Urban Scene*. Glencoe, Ill.: Free Press, 1965.

Schofield, M. *Sociological Aspects of Homosexuality*. London: Longmans, 1965.

Schulze, R. O. and Blumberg, L. U. 'The Determination of Local Power Élites', *Amer. J. Sociol.*, vol. 63, no. 3, 1957.

Schusky, E. L. *Manual for Kinship Analysis*. New York: Holt, Rinehart, 1965.

Schwartz, M. S. and Schwartz, C. G. 'Problems of Participant Observation', *Amer. J. Sociol.*, vol. 60, no. 4, 1955.

Seligmann, B. B. (ed.), *Poverty as a Social Issue*. Glencoe, Ill.: Free Press, 1965.

Sellin, T. *Culture, Conflict and Crime*. New York: Soc. Sci. Res., 1938.

—and Wolfgang, M. E. *The Measurement of Delinquency*. New York: Wiley, 1965.

Selltiz, C. *et al. Research Methods in Social Relations*. New York: Holt, Rinehart, 1959 (rev. edn., 1964); London: Methuen, 1960.

Selvin, H. C. 'A Critique of Tests of Significance in Survey Research', *Amer. Sociol. Rev.*, vols. 22 and 23 (Oct. 1957 and Feb.–Apr. 1958).

— 'Training for Social Research' in Gould, J. (ed.), *Penguin Survey of the Social Sciences*. London: Penguin, 1965.

Shaw, C. H. and McKay, H. D. *Delinquency Areas*. Chicago: U. of Chicago, 1929.

— *Juvenile Delinquency and Urban Areas*. Chicago: U. of Chicago, 1942.

Sheldon, J. H. *The Social Medicine of Old Age*. London: Oxford, 1948.

Sherif, M .*The Psychology of Social Norms*. New York: Harper, 1936.

Shevky, E. and Bell, D. *Social Area Analysis*. Stanford, Calif.: Stanford, 1955.

Shils, E. 'The Primary Group in Current Research' in Coser, L. A. and Rosenberg, B. M. *Sociological Theory*, rev. edn., New York: Macmillan, 1964.

Simey, T. S. 'What is Truth in Sociology?' *New Society*, vol. 4, no. 5 (July), 1964.

Smith, W. D. *Manual of Sociometry for Teachers*. Ann Arbor: U. of Michigan, 1951.

Sorokin, P. A. *Fads and Foibles in Modern Sociology*. Chicago: Regnery, 1956.

Spencer, J. *Stress and Release in Urban Estate*. London: Tavistock, 1964.

Spencer, R. F. *Method and Perspective in Anthropology*. Minneapolis: U. of Minn., 1954.

Spinley, B. M. *The Deprived and the Privileged*. London: Routledge, 1953.

Spiro, M. E. *Kibbutz: venture in Utopia*. New York: Schocken, 1956.

Sprott, W. J. H. *Human Groups*. London: Penguin, 1958.

— *Science and Social Action*. London: C. A. Watts, 1965.

— *et al. The Social Background of Delinquency*. University of Nottingham, 1954. (10 mimeo copies in University of Nottingham.)

Stengel, E. 'Suicide and attempted suicide', *New Society*, vol. 2, no. 45 (Aug.), 1963.

— *Suicide and Attempted Suicide*. London: Penguin, 1965.

— and Cook, N. G. *Attempted Suicide*. Maudsley Monograph. London: Chapman & Hall, 1958.

Stephan, F. J. and McCarthy, P. J. *Sampling Opinions*. New York: Wiley, 1963.

Stouffer, S. A. *et al. The American Soldier.* (Studies in Social Psychology in World War II.) 2 vols. New Jersey: Princeton, 1949.

Sumner, W. G. *Folkways.* Boston: Ginn, 1906; London: Constable.

Sutherland, E. H. and Cressey, D. R. *Principles of Criminology*, 6th edn. Philadelphia: Lippincott, 1960.

Swanson, G. E. 'Some Problems of Laboratory Experiments with Small Populations'. *Amer. Sociol. Rev.* vol. 16, no. 3, 1961.

Swedner, H. *Ecological Differentiation of Habits and Attitudes.* Lund: Gleerup, 1960.

Sykes, G. M. *The Society of Captives: a study of a maximum security prison.* New Jersey: Princeton, 1958. Reprinted as paperback, New York: Atheneum, 1965.

Taba, H. and Elkins, D. *With Focus on Human Relations.* Washington, D.C.: American Council on Education, 1950.

Tate, M. W. *Statistics in Education and Psychology.* London: Collier-Macmillan, 1965.

Taylor, D. W. and Faust, W. L. 'Twenty Questions: Efficiency in Problem-solving as a Function of Size of Group', in Hare, A. P. *et al.* (eds.), *Small Groups.* New York: Knopf, 1955.

Theodorson, G. A. *Studies in Human Ecology.* New York: Row–Peterson, 1961.

Thomas, W. I. and Znaniecki, F. *The Polish Peasant in Europe and America.* Chicago: U. of Chicago, 1918.

Thomlinson, R. *Sociological Concepts and Research.* New York: Random, 1965.

Thornton, A. *et al. Student Views on Morality and the Law.* Oxford: Balliol College, Paul Davies, 1964.

Thrasher, F. M. *The Gang.* Chicago: U. of Chicago, 1927.

Tibbitts, C. and Donahue, W. *Social and Psychological Aspects of Aging.* New York: Columbia, 1962.

Toby, J. *Contemporary Society.* New York: Wiley, 1964.

Townsend, P. *Family Life of Old People.* London: Routledge, 1957; Penguin, A. 634, 1963.

— *The Last Refuge.* London: Routledge, 1962.

— 'Measuring poverty'. *Brit. J. Sociol.* vol. 5, no. 2, 1954.

— 'The meaning of poverty'. *Brit. J. Sociol.* vol. 13, no. 3, 1962.

Tunstall, J. *The Fisherman.* London: MacGibbon, 1962.

— *Old and Alone.* London: Routledge, 1966.

Turner, R. H. *The Social Context of Ambition.* San Francisco: Chandler Pub, 1964.

— in Halsey, A. H. *et al. Education, Economy and Society.* Glencoe, Ill.: Free Press, 1961.

Udy, S. H. 'Cross Cultural Analysis: a Case Study' in Hammond, P. E. (ed.), *Sociologists at Work.* New York: Basic Books, 1964.

Veness, T. *School Leavers, their Aspirations and Expectations.* London: Methuen, 1962.

Vernon, P. E. 'Measurement of Abilities, Attitudes and Personality Traits' in Welford, A. T. *et al.* (eds.). *Society: Problems and Methods of Study.* London: Routledge, 1962.

Wakeford, J. 'Is violence increasing?' *New Society,* vol. 1, no. 33 (May), 1963.

Walker, N. *Crime and Punishment in Britain.* Edinburgh: Edin. U.P., 1965.

— and Argyle, M. 'Does the Law Affect Moral Judgements?' *Brit. J. Crim.,* vol. 4, no. 6, 1964.

Wallach, M. A., Kogan, N. and Bem, D. 'Group Influence on Individual Risk-taking'. *J. Abnorm. Soc. Psychol.,* vol. 65, no. 2, 1962.

Wallis, W. A. and Roberts, H. V. *Statistics, a New Approach.* London: Methuen, 1957.

Walton, J. 'Substance and Artifact: the Current Status of Research on Community Power Structure', *Amer. J. Sociol.,* vol. 71, no. 4, 1966.

War Factory. A Report. London: Gollancz, 1943.

Warner, W. L. *et al. Yankee City Series.* New Haven: Yale, 1946 and following years.

— and Lunt, P. S. *The Social Life of a Modern Community.* New Haven: Yale, 1941.

— *et al. Social Class in America: a Manual for Procedure for the Measurement of Social Status.* Chicago: Science Research Associates, 1949; New York: Harper, 1960.

Weber, M. *On the Methodology of the Social Sciences.* Glencoe, Ill.: Free Press, 1949; London: Collier-Macmillan, 1950.

— *The Theory of Social and Economic Organisation.* Glencoe, Ill.: Free Press, 1947; London: Collier-Macmillan, 1957.

Wedderburn, D. C. 'Poverty in Britain Today – the Evidence', *Sociological Review,* vol. 10, no. 3, 1962.

Welford, A. T. *et al.* (eds.), *Society: Problems and Methods of Study.* London: Routledge, 1962.

West, D. J. *The Habitual Prisoner.* London: Macmillan, 1963.

Whiting, B. B. (ed.), *Six Cultures: Studies of Child-Rearing.* New York: Wiley, 1963.

Whiting, J. W. M. 'The Cross-Cultural Method' in Lindzey, G. *Handbook of Social Psychology,* 2 vols. Cambridge, Mass.: Addison-Wesley, 1954.

Whyte, W. F. *Street Corner Society,* 2nd edn. with appendix. Chicago: U. of Chicago, 1955.

Wilkins, L. T. 'What is Crime?' *New Society,* vol. 2, no. 42 (July), 1963.

— *Social Deviance.* London: Tavistock, 1964.

Willett, T. C. *Criminal on the Road.* London: Tavistock, 1964.

Williams, W. M. *The Sociology of an English Village: Gosforth.* London: Routledge, 1956.

Wilson, B. 'Analytical Studies of Social Institutions' in Welford, A. T. *et al. Society. Problems and Methods of Study.* London: Routledge, 1962.

— 'Review of Zweig, *The Quest for Fellowship*'. *New Society*, vol. 5, no. 142 (June), 1965.

Wirth, L. 'Urbanism as a Way of Life' in Hatt, P. K. and Reiss, A. J. *Cities and Society*, rev. edn. New York: Glencoe Free Press, 1957.

Wolfgang, M. E. *et al.* (eds.), *The Sociology of Crime and Delinquency*. New York: Wiley, 1962.

Woodside, M. 'Eventide Homes', *New Society*, vol. 5, no. 121 (Jan.), 1965.

Wootton, B. *Testament for Social Science*. London: Allen & Unwin, 1950.

— *Social Science and Social Pathology*. London: Allen & Unwin, 1959.

— *Crime and the Criminal Law*. London: Stevens & Sons, 1963*a*.

— 'Sentencing: Art or Science?', *New Society*, vol. 1, no. 24 (March), 1963*b*.

— 'Crime and its Rewards'. *New Society*, vol. 6, no. 156 (July), 1965.

Young, Kimball. 'Culture and Personality' in Young, Kimball. *Handbook of Social Psychology*. London: Routledge, 1957 and subsequent editions.

— *Handbook of Social Psychology*. London: Routledge, 1957 and subsequent editions.

Young, M. 'Distribution of Income within the Family', *Brit. J. Sociol.*, vol. 3, no. 4, 1954.

— and Willmott, P. 'Social Grading by Manual Workers', *Brit. J. Sociol.*, vol. 7, no. 4, 1956.

Young, P. V. and Schmid, C. F. *Scientific Social Surveys and Research*, 2nd and 3rd edns. Englewood Cliffs: Prentice-Hall, 1949 and 1956.

Yule, G. U. and Kendall, M. G. *An Introduction to the Theory of Statistics*, 14th edn. London: Griffin, 1950.

Zetterberg, H. L. *On Theory and Verification in Sociology*, 3rd edn. New Jersey: Bedminster Press, 1965.

Zweig, F. *The Quest for Fellowship*. London: Heinemann, 1965.

Index